The Coming Race War?

The Coming Race War?

And Other Apocalyptic Tales of America after Affirmative Action and Welfare

Richard Delgado

With an Introduction by Andrew Hacker

NEW YORK UNIVERSITY PRESS
New York and London

NEW YORK UNIVERSITY PRESS
New York and London

Library of Congress Cataloging-in-Publication Data
Delgado, Richard.
The coming race war? : and other apocalyptic tales of America
after affirmative action and welfare / Richard Delgado : with an
introduction by Andrew Hacker.
p. cm.
ISBN 0-8147-1877-9 (alk. paper)
1. United States—Race relations.   2. United States—Race
relations—Forecasting.   3. Afro-Americans—Civil rights.
4. Affirmative action programs—United States.   I. Title.
E185.615.D44   1996
305.8'00973—dc20   96-7801
                    CIP

New York University Press books are printed on acid-free
paper, and their binding materials are chosen for strength
and durability.

Manufactured in the United States of America

10 9 8 7 6 5 4 3 2 1

Barbarous acts are rarely committed out of the blue. . . . Step by step, a society becomes accustomed to accept, with less and less moral outrage and with greater and greater indifference to legitimacy, the successive blows. —Daniel Bell, *The Radical Right*

And perhaps you may guess why I love to stay here abroad, and mainly in Italy—it is because people are kind to me, I feel kindness round me, good-will, and love. And I have come to think of my own country as lacking in kindness; at home people are indifferent or absorbed or silent; it is like death, when it is not like killing.

—*Selected Letters of George Edward Woodberry*

Behind the door of every contented, happy man there ought to be someone standing with a little hammer and continually reminding him with a knock that there are unhappy people, that however happy he may be, life will sooner or later show him its claws, and trouble will come to him—illness, poverty, losses, and then no one will see or hear him, just as now he neither sees nor hears others.

—Anton Chekhov, *Gooseberries*

CONTENTS

A C K N O W L E D G M E N T S

I wish to thank Jean Stefancic for continued inspiration and encouragement; and Bonnie Kae Grover, Jennifer Bradfield, and Pamela Compos for invaluable research services. Special thanks go to Derrick Bell, who graciously lent me some of his personae as well as moral support, and to Juan Perea, who contributed suggestions for chapter 6. Marge Brunner, Cynthia Carter, Anne Guthrie, Vanessa Smith, and Kay Wilkie prepared the manuscript with intelligence and precision.

My gratitude goes to Niko Pfund, my editor at NYU Press, and to the Rockefeller Foundation Scholar-in-Residence Program in Bellagio, Italy, where many of the ideas for this book took form.

I am grateful to the following journals for permission to reprint or adapt portions of essays that appeared in their pages: California Law Review, for chapter 1, "Empathy and False Empathy" [84 Cal. L. Rev. ——(1995)]; Pennsylvania Law Review, for chapter 2, "Race, Legal Instrumentalism, and the Rule of Law" [143 U. Pa. L. Rev. 379 (1994)]; and Georgetown Law Journal, for chapter 3, "Merit and Affirmative Action" [83 Geo. L.J. 1711 (1995)].

by Andrew Hacker

Even in his lineage, Rodrigo is telling us a story. His father is of African descent and his mother is Italian. Outside of the United States, he would be known and recognized as an individual of mixed parentage. Latin Americans might call him "mulatto" or "creole," depending on his features and hue. In South Africa, he would be designated as "colored," a group given an identity distinct and separate from the nation's two major races.

The United States, however, remains the only country with no intermediate categories. Where the principal races are concerned, you are either black or white. This may be why Hispanics are eschewing racial labels, preferring to emphasize their national origin and culture. Similarly, persons once grouped in a "yellow" race are now stressing their more specific Chinese or Japanese or Korean heritage. By the same token, Native Americans associate themselves with tribal traditions rather than a common racial affinity.

Not only has Rodrigo a white mother: if his African-American father is in any way typical, he will carry at least some white genes. So Rodrigo must be more than half white. Even so, America has decided that he and others like him must be called "black." This is the case with Lani Guinier, the legal scholar, who had also had a white mother and a black father. It holds for August Wilson, the playwright; Walter Mosley, the creator of the Easy Rawlings detective series; as well as the children of O. J. Simpson and the late Nicole Brown Simpson. Why do we, of all nations, insist on a sharp racial bifurcation with no shadings or blurrings?

The reason is that the gulf was created and then perpetuated by whites, for their own protection. Only blacks could be slaves; an intermediate category would put children with one white parent at risk of the auction block. (Thus plantation owners often freed the offspring they had with enslaved women.) But a historical reason does not explain why whites have had the chasm continue.

The answer is instructive and ironic. Many if not most whites see themselves as belonging to a superior human strain. Needless to say, almost all denounce "master race" theories, and separate themselves from open bigots like Mark Fuhrman. Even so, how many whites have not wondered why other races have not come up with a Shakespeare, a Michelangelo, a Mozart, or a Newton? The creation of intermediate categories would close what is now a chasm. Were persons of mixed parentage placed on a continuum merging into whites, it would diminish the distinctiveness of those who now pride themselves as being the most highly evolved race. This fear means that even Rodrigo, a distinguished legal scholar, must be kept at a distance from his Caucasian colleagues.

At the same time, all who are granted admission to The White Club are deemed to be equal members. Gone are the days when it was common to speak of "white trash" or refer to lesser stocks. Whites now stick together. They have something in common: that all stand far apart from blacks. Note the name that has been given to Rodrigo's amiable antagonist. Perhaps in the past, a Kowalsky might be called a "polack" or made the butt of Polish jokes. And some will be old enough to recall Marlon Brando's portrayal of a crude and brutal Stanley Kowalski in Tennessee Williams's *A Streetcar Named Desire*. However, the Kowalsky on these pages is a fully fledged white, and is indeed portrayed as an esteemed member of his race.

At the same time, the Club looks to its own perpetuation. As Rodrigo himself points out, white parents are not producing enough babies to sustain their race. Thus the Club is willing to co-opt new members, as it did with other marginal groups in the past. Now being considered are persons once called "Orientals," who may be said to be being groomed as probationary whites. This may be why we no longer speak of a "yellow" race. Hispanics are also candidates, so long as they downplay their Latin origins. However, even an intellectual of Rodrigo's stature will not make the list. (Not that he would wish to assimilate, which he calls "identification with the aggressor.") Still, just as Colin Powell will always be the "black general," so Rodrigo will remain the "black professor."

The United States may have styled itself as a melting pot. But from the very outset, one strain of humanity was denied a future of full acceptance and assimilation. Africans were brought here for a purpose, and it was not to become citizens. Despite a war and emancipation, and a century of legislation, the ancestors of slaves are still seen as not quite on a par with other Americans. This may be why every so often Rodrigo throws up his hands, and muses about dissociating himself from mainstream America.

Hence too his continuing critique of American institutions and the assumptions on which they are based. Perhaps the most profound on these pages is his examination of the myth of "merit" and the role it plays in the perpetuation of power. At first encounter, we are all in favor of merit and a system based on that principle. After all, how can anyone oppose choosing persons of superior talent, the highest levels of competence, and who have the best possible qualifications?

But these are vague criteria. The issue Rodrigo addresses is how America defines merit and refines the conception in practice. He begins by saying that "merit is what the victors impose," and has become "basically, white people's affirmative action." He does not hesitate to say that most selection procedures have a racial basis and bias.

This is particularly evident with standardized, machine-graded multiple-choice tests. It is not so much that their questions call for information that white people are more likely to have, although that is frequently the case. Rather, the very format of the tests reflects a culture that is essentially European in its antecedents and character. (Even allowing for successive waves of immigrants, the system remains mainly "Anglo-American," a phrase created by Alexis de Tocqueville and still relevant today.) The tests, used as selection mechanisms on employment and education, were initially cast as neutral arbiters. The few who achieved high scores would be given preference regardless of their origins. This is why Jews in the past, and Asians today, regard the tests as an equitable innovation.

However, as Rodrigo points out, the Scholastic Assessment Test and those used for graduate school admissions and civil service promotions, all "emphasize linear, rationalistic thought." By this he means that they require the candidate to display a certain mental mode. Just to start, one must be prepared to sift reality through the matrix of the multiple-choice framework. Not least, the test taker must accept the premise that there is one correct answer, which the test makers have chosen and you must respect. In addition, the questions must be answered at a one-a-minute rate, which hardly allows time for pondering meanings and exploring implications.

But what, it may be asked, is "racial" about linking synonyms, interpreting short paragraphs, or solving algebraic equations? Class may be involved. As we know, scores are strongly related to income. Not surprisingly, persons from better-off homes tend to be better prepared for the tests. So let's take a look at a sample of students who took the SAT in a recent year. To neutralize the economic factor, all the students who were examined came from middle-class families, with incomes between $50,000 and $60,000. So we may presume that they attended decent schools and escaped the pitfalls associated with being raised in poorer neighborhoods. Here were the average scores, broken down by four major groups: Asians, 999; Whites, 942; Latins, 875; Blacks, 798.

Since the Asians outscore Caucasians, it could be argued that the SAT is not a "white" test. But really? One could as easily suggest that the current generation of Asians has learned how to do things the white way, and are indeed beating whites at the game that whites themselves created. This has happened with technology along the Pacific Rim, and is coming to roost in our own backyard. While Asians obviously wish to preserve their own cultures, they have shown that they are avid to enter the modern world, and have been doing just that. And insofar as tests like the SAT decide "merit" in that world, they can be seen as another technology that has to be mastered. Due to Asians' success, whites are frequently finding they are falling to second place. In the freshman classes at Berkeley and UCLA, Asians are outnumbering Caucasians.

Which leads to the question of why middle-class black students do less well on the tests. In their case, one cannot blame inner-city schools and lack of money for coaching courses. The reason lies largely in the "linear, rationalistic" expectations that Rodrigo cited. Black Americans, including those with middle-class careers, are still apt to spend most of their lives in segregated surroundings. Those settings are more likely to encourage mental styles other than the linear structure of the multiple-choice mode. Black culture tends to be at home with what might be called a discursive style, which takes a more forthright approach to intellectual inquiry. Rodrigo elaborates on this when he proposes that courts admit testimony based on storytelling. Instead of being bound by rigid rules, the search for truth should encourage a more relaxed ambiance.

Given the hegemony of the tests, society's dominant positions go to those with the highest numerical scores. But in allowing this, we are not getting a meritocracy so much as a testocracy. Hence Rodrigo's conclusion that "our traditional merit criteria are ensuring mediocrity." Several examples will suffice. Our automobile industry is filled with MBA graduates, who presumably did well on the tests. Yet a dozen other countries are selling their cars in Argentina and Egypt and Indonesia, and each passing year leaves the United States with a smaller share of the world market. At home, our police departments make multiple-choice tests their first hurdle. As a result, many if not most forces end up with commuters from the suburbs, who know little about the people and places they are supposed to protect and serve. Similarly, our medical care has been in the hands of high-scoring physicians, who have made us first in the world in high-tech instrumentation and not far from the bottom in the state of our health.

Our society has no shortage of men and women who would make excellent executives and physicians as well as inspiring police officers. However, they are unlikely to be found so long as irrelevant tests remain as barriers and we allow talent to be defined by printed-out numbers.

In his opening chapter, Rodrigo has some harsh things to say about white liberals. All too often, he remarks, they walk away "when the going gets tough." Hence their retreat on affirmative action, along with a readiness to disapprove of leaders that black people choose. Whites who style themselves as friends are also prone to display "false empathy," in which they claim affinity with people they hardly know and then only in a superficial way.

Rodrigo has apparently concluded that little is to be gained from alliances with whites. Even liberals "support and tolerate group gains for blacks only when these also benefit them." So he proposes that well-meaning whites should work with—and on—their own people. Some good may come of this, since white people are generally unwilling to listen to blacks, apart from those who pitch messages that whites want to hear.

Calls are increasingly heard for a system that makes the best of separation. Integration has not worked, largely because whites never believed in it, except on the most token of levels. It also requires that blacks abandon much of their culture, whether in embracing white

mental styles, including diction and demeanor. Such disparate figures as Clarence Thomas and Louis Farrakhan have counseled that
blacks do themselves a disservice if they feel they can only advance
in the company of whites.

Even while it has extolled the melting pot, America has often
respected groups that wish to remain separate. The Amish, for example, are not compelled to send their teenagers to high school. Ortho-
dox and Hasidic Jews can create enclaves having only minimal contacts with the secular world. The same holds for adherents of the
Nation of Islam. But if these communities are to prosper, they must
do more than buy and sell to their own members. They must also
have something to offer the larger economy. In the case of the Amish,
their high-quality crops readily find buyers in the national market.
In New York City, if not elsewhere, observant Jews dominate the
diamond trade and retail outlets for electronic equipment. If African
Americans wish to move toward a more formal separation, they will
need to bring money into their communities. The options—which
are not mutually exclusive—are to build daytime careers in the
white world, or to establish enterprises that appeal to a spectrum of
clients and customers. Moves in these directions will be a central
challenge in the decades ahead.

Similar strictures hold for education. Much has been said and
written about the growth of a black middle class. And, as Rodrigo
points out, talk of this kind is especially common among white
conservatives, who hold "that the race problem has been solved."
(Witness the title of Dinesh D'Souza's book, *The End of Racism*.) As
has been noted, whether by their own choice or lack of options, most
middle-class black Americans continue to live in segregated settings.
These areas are well tended and have a affluent air, as can be seen in
Baldwin Hills in Los Angeles, University Heights in Atlanta, and
throughout much of Prince Georges County adjacent to the District
of Columbia. But what is lacking in these suburbs are truly elite high
schools, like those readily found in their white counterparts. There
should be a strong enough tax base and a large enough catchment of
students to create high schools which are essentially black and compete well by national standards. Of course, there remains the issue
that Rodrigo raised: whether black Americans wish to conform to
the modes of thought that the white world expects. As has been

noted, there are alternative styles, and they promise an excellence in principle and performance. This is a complementary challenge: new intellectual heights to match investments in the economic sphere.

A sad fact of public life is how infrequently white Americans have been willing to elect black office holders to represent them. Although exceptions can be cited, most whites prefer to have laws and policies made by persons of their own race. This is why many blacks have concluded that their best chance for sharing political power lies in creating districts where they comprised a majority. Due to these designs, the number of black members in the House of Representatives has almost doubled during the past several years. But as we all know, these constituencies are under constitutional attack. If they are redrawn, black voices will have less of a hearing in the halls where laws are made, which is obviously the aim of those challenging the districts.

Still, another situation needs to be addressed. It is not yet clear that members from majority-black seats have achieved a balance of power in the assemblies where they sit. This became evident in the Congress, when black members sought to alter the federal law that punishes selling cocaine as crack much more heavily than the traffic in its powdered form. These lawmakers were not exonerating the drug trade: on the contrary, they knew at first hand how it has debased neighborhoods they represent. But they were alarmed at the long prison terms being given to so many sons and nephews within their constituencies. Yet the House as a whole gave them short shrift. In a vote in October of 1995, the Black Caucus's amendment was rejected by a margin of 332 to 83. This meant that not even 50 white members out of 400 were willing to support a measure that meant much to their black colleagues. And it also shows that success in the legislative sphere requires building coalitions with white policymakers.

Rodrigo's conclusion is somber. He sees a strategy forming to "increase minority misery . . . to the point where violence breaks out." However, he continues, "the rebellion will be put down . . . with whites wielding power over a large but powerless black and brown population of laborers and domestics." Yet even here he may too sanguine. Yes, minority women may be forced into domestic service, since aid to single mothers is being whittled away. But it is not clear that even jobs as laborers will be available for the men. At this point, white society is more willing to fill prisons than create gainful occupations for men whose people built so much of this country. Hardly an upbeat ending. Yet recall the title of this volume: *The Coming Race War?* The only question is whether to keep the question mark.

Introduction: *In Which the Author Explains Who Rodrigo and the Professor Are, and What They Have Been Doing So Far*

In *The Rodrigo Chronicles*, published in 1995, the reader meets my brash, talented young friend and graduate lawyer, Rodrigo. When we first encounter him, Rodrigo has flown back to the States from Italy, at his sister's suggestion, to meet "the Professor" and discuss the young man's future. Rodrigo is thinking of obtaining an LL.M. (advanced law) degree from an American institution in hopes of a career as a law teacher. The son of an African-American serviceman and half-brother of famed U.S. civil rights scholar and activist Geneva Crenshaw, Rodrigo had grown up in Italy where his father had been assigned to a U.S. outpost. Rodrigo finished high school at the base school, then attended an Italian university ("the oldest one in the world, Professor") and law school on government scholarships, graduating second in his class.

Despite their age difference, the two become close friends, discussing affirmative action, racial politics, black crime, relations between black men and women, and many other subjects over the course of the volume. The reader learns how two intellectuals of color talk and think, what they worry about, like to eat, and how they deal with the many challenges of life, including the ubiquitous hate stare. The reader gets to follow Rodrigo through his adventures with the INS (which tries to deport him), his settling in the same city as his professor-mentor, and his year of graduate study at a famous U.S. law school. The reader also meets Giannina, his roommate and life companion, a published poet and playwright with her own interest in the law.

In this book, Rodrigo enters the adult world. When it opens, he is a young law professor in his first year of teaching. He and the professor meet in airports, on committees, and at conferences, maintaining their relationship and extending their range of subjects. Now on a more equal plane, the two discuss empathy and false empathy, and why people of color find they often cannot rely on white liberals when the going gets tough. The reader listens in while the two discuss black despair, the assault on affirmative action, and the current debate over genetics and "merit." Rodrigo, a highly cosmopolitan person who speaks several languages, nevertheless considers himself a racial activist and adherent of identity politics. Are these not inconsistent? The professor pins him down; the reader learns the answer.

And in the most chilling chapter of all, Rodrigo's young colleague and friend, Lazlo Kowalsky, a brilliant young conservative who is nevertheless sympathetic to blacks, spins out a dark tale of why his fellow conservatives are trying to kill the goose that laid their golden egg—affirmative action. Kowalsky observes that eliminating affirmative action does not make sense for the political Right, since it reliably delivers votes, outrages blue-collar whites, and allows conservatives to appear principled in opposing it—in contrast to the fuzzy liberals who have trouble defending it. So, why are conservatives in think tanks, a dozen states, and in Congress trying to abolish it entirely? As Kowalsky implacably makes his case, the reader learns what America's future may hold.

The six chapters, or Chronicles, in this book tell a story, with characters, adventures, and an unfolding plot. Thus, the best way to read it is consecutively. But readers with limited time or a more specific focus may wish to read chapters 1 and 2 if they have an interest in the critique of liberalism and mainstream law and politics. If they are interested in learning what is wrong with conservatism and the new Right, chapters 3 and 4 are the ones they may wish to read first. Readers interested in international law and human rights should not miss chapter 5. The middle-aged reader who has been just as interested in the professor as in the youthful Rodrigo, and who wants to know his fate as he approaches the golden part of his career, will want to read chapter 6.

This book, like its predecessor, is an example of legal storytelling or narrative jurisprudence, a trademark of Critical Race Theory. The reader who enjoys learning and thinking about law and social theory through dialogues, reflections, and the give and take of different voices and points of view will have no difficulty finding much more in the burgeoning literature and in NYU Press's own Critical America series.

Empathy and False Empathy: The Problem with Liberalism

Rodrigo Returns and Accounts for His Recent Activities

I was sitting in my darkened office one afternoon, thinking about life. To tell the truth, I was missing my young friend and protégé, Rodrigo. Not long ago, I had consigned him to the Great Beyond. But now, I was flooded with regret and sadness. I missed his brashness, his insouciant originality. Odd, I had not thought of myself as senti-mental. How could I have allowed him to succumb to the critique of narrativity in "Rodrigo's Final Chronicle?"[1] Now a young law profes-sor at a well-known university in the Midwest, Rodrigo had sought me out for career advice, nearly three years ago, during a return trip to the States. The son of an African-American serviceman and an Italian mother, the brilliant and audacious young scholar saw the United States with new eyes.

Despite our age difference—he was then just embarking on an LL.M. (graduate law) program at a major law school in the same city where I teach—we had become good friends, discussing civil rights, law and economics, relations between the sexes, and many other subjects over the course of the next two years. I had gotten a great series of articles out of our meetings. He had pushed my thinking, challenged me to explore new realms of thought, helped dispel some of the loneliness of this godawful job. And now, he was gone.

I was just getting ready to drag myself out of my funk, turn on the light, and resume reading the pile of seminar papers that had awaited me since my return from the American Association of Law Schools (AALS) annual meeting, when I heard a shuffling sound outside my door. A brown envelope materialized on my carpet, pushed through the crack by someone whose footsteps I now heard disappearing down the hall. "I'm here," I shouted.

"Oh, I didn't see your light," a familiar voice said.

I turned on the switch and opened the door. "Rodrigo!" I exclaimed. "I was just thinking about you. What are you doing here?"

"I brought you a note explaining how I got back after that incident at the AALS. I didn't want it to be too much of a shock. I also brought you a book—a magazine, actually."[2]

"Come on in. What on earth happened to you? I was afraid I would never see you again."

Rodrigo picked up the envelope from the floor, laid it on the corner of my desk, then glanced at my couch. "Do you have a minute?" He gestured toward the pile of neatly typed student papers in the center of my desk. "It looks like you're busy."

"Quite the contrary," I assured him. "These grades aren't due for another week. What happened to you? And, before you begin, can I offer you some coffee?"

Rodrigo nodded enthusiastically, and as I busied myself measuring the water and grounds for my office espresso maker, he began.

"Do you remember, Professor, where we were when the lights went out?"

"Yes, we had been talking, rather late at night as I remember, in that basement dive in the giant AALS hotel. We were discussing the critique of narrativity and legal storytelling, and in particular that section meeting where several of our colleagues attacked the new forms of scholarship as nonlegal, unfair, even exclusionary.[3] Others questioned the role of student-run law reviews. You had just said something about how we are all creatures of our own narratives, which immediately filled me with alarm. Then, the lights went out."

"I figured it was the kids playing at the video arcade next to our booth, and that the lights would be back on again in a matter of minutes.[4] I saw you put your head down, assumed you were tired, so got up to stretch my legs and walk outside. I thought of leaving you a note, but didn't."

"When I woke up, you were nowhere to be seen. Cream and sugar, right?"

Rodrigo nodded. "Yes, please."

"I was afraid you had deconstructed yourself, allowed yourself to become a casualty of Farber, Sherry, Tushnet, and the critique of narrativity."[5]

"Nothing so fancy, Professor, although I think you'll enjoy the story. In fact, what took place prompted me to come see you. Aside from reassuring you that I haven't expired, I wanted to discuss something. If you're up for it, that is." Rodrigo looked up solicitously. "It's late."

"I'm going strong," I demurred. "Besides, I'd love to know what happened. The coffee's ready."

I handed Rodrigo a steaming mug of espresso, he stirred in creamer and his trademark four teaspoons of sugar, and continued.

"You won't believe this, but I was kidnapped."

"Kidnapped? Are you serious?"

"I am. Do you remember those kids who were playing at the video games along the wall?"

"Sure. They borrowed change from us once. I remember that they looked at you closely, but thought nothing of it at the time. So what happened?"

"It turns out they were not kids at all, but members of an anti-British terrorist group. This I only found out later. I had just stood up when, quick as a flash, there was a cloth bag over my head, my hands and feet were being tied, and I was carried outside and into a car. The whole thing took maybe thirty seconds."

"My God!" I exclaimed. "What happened then? And why were they after you?"

"This requires some memory on your part, Professor. Do you recall how I got back to the U.S. that first time?"[6]

"I do," I said. "It was a neat little two-step maneuver. After being deported back to Italy, you resettled in Ireland, using your law degree and taking advantage of the liberalized guest worker provisions in the European Community. You got a job as a paralegal in Dublin, hung around coffeehouses for a while, then got back to the United States by means of a private bill."[7]

"With a little help from the Irish Immigration Society and a certain famous U.S. senator who sponsors these bills routinely. But do you remember what I did first, Professor?"

"I'm not sure."

"I think I mentioned this to you before. I bought a title of nobility from a down-at-the-heels member of the British aristocracy.[8] I really wanted to get back and start my LL.M. studies, and didn't want to take any chances. It turned out my investment was probably unnecessary—my U.S. forebears and Italian law degree were probably enough—but that small act led to my adventure."

"You mean your kidnappers thought you really were the third duke of Crenshaw?"

"They did. It turned out that the group was a collection of exiles just chafing for something to do. And when they heard from headquarters that someone on their list was apparently right here in the U.S., they decided to pick me up and give me a going-over."

"But of course their grievance was not with you, but with the real duke of Crenshaw, the one who sold you the title."

"Apparently he was a royalist and something of a bad actor, from the liberationists' perspective, at least. The whole thing didn't become clear until they got me to their hideaway."

"Did you have to do some fast talking?"

"The team that commandeered me did. You should have seen their faces when they took the bag off my head and saw a black man instead of a light-skinned English aristocrat! Their leader was furious. They tried to explain that the restaurant had been dimly lit. They got out the photos. I actually do look slightly like the duke, except for skin color. I met him briefly when I paid for the title— we're about the same height, weight, and age. So, their mistake was understandable."

"What happened when they got through blaming each other?"

"That's when *I* had to talk fast. One of them wanted to give me a hard time for having bought the title of nobility in the first place. 'A little would-be Englisher' he called me. I could see trouble coming, so I explained to them how I was a leftist and a race reformer. I think I even mentioned I was a disciple of yours. I told them I had wanted to get back to the States because it was my homeland and I had a mission here. They looked dubious at first, then finally gave in when I compared critical race theory to their own antiroyalist movement. We ended up drinking Irish whiskey and singing songs. After a while, they swore me to secrecy for seventy-two hours and drove me back to the hotel. I tried to look you up, but you had already checked out and headed back to the airport."

"It's quite a story," I said. "Reminds me of a certain professor's adventure in 'Small World.' "[9]

"The parallel did strike me," Rodrigo acknowledged. "Although at the time I wasn't sure it would turn out so well."

"Well, I'm very happy you're back and in one piece."

While Rodrigo took a swig of his coffee, I took the opportunity to ask: "But you said you had something you wanted to talk to me about. Did it have to do with your kidnapping?"

"It did, in a way. And also with that magazine I brought you. The whole thing got me to thinking of the role of empathy. The republicans who snatched me, even though they were at first taken aback, came around quickly when they learned I was a fellow reformer. At first, I was afraid they'd just push me off a bridge somewhere. But we ended up comparing notes. It turned out we had a surprising amount in common."

"They identified with your struggle, and you with theirs, in other words." I was silent for a moment. "So, the critique of narrativity caused you to disappear, but empathy brought you back. Kind of pat, and, I must say, a little upbeat for a young crit like you. Or am I reading you correctly?"

"You and I did talk about the role of empathy once before, Professor. We agreed it is getting in shorter and shorter supply, particularly with respect to minorities of color.[10] Yet I was able to connect quickly with my captors, once they got over their shock of finding a black man under the bag when they expected a blueblood English aristocrat."

"Maybe there's some level on which marginalized people of all sorts can understand each other,"[11] I suggested. "And so, do you think this is something our people can tap in these troubled times, when society seems to be devoting less and less attention to our needs, the Republican right is in full cry, affirmative action is under attack, and welfare programs are being cut left and right?"

"No," Rodrigo said quickly. "I believe the opposite is the case. May I start with a thought experiment that occurred to me as the terrorists were driving me back to the hotel?"

"I'd love to hear it."

Rodrigo's Inquispro Example and What It Shows about the Possibility of Reliance on Empathy as a Source of Succor for Outsider Groups

Rodrigo drained his coffee cup, and looked up. "Imagine, Professor, that some scientific genius develops a computer called Inquispro, which is aimed at making things easier for our overworked court system. Inquispro is able to scan any segment of space and time and tell us what happened."

"So, we wouldn't have to rely on witnesses and fading memories," I said. "That sounds like a big help."

"Not only that, but Inquispro knows all the substantive law. We would program it so that it knows the elements of every cause of action or crime."

"So, if Smith accuses Jones of negligence, for example, in failing to clear his sidewalks of snow, we could simply ask the computer to apply the elements of a negligence cause of action to what happened when Smith slipped in front of Jones's house the day of the accident."

"Exactly," Rodrigo replied. "And so with all the other causes of action in the law books. Inquispro could methodically go through all the cases filed, solving them in a fraction of a second each."

"This would obviously be a great boon to our overworked judiciary," I said. "Not to mention witnesses and jurors, none of whom would be necessary. There wouldn't be much need for lawyers or law professors, either, although I suppose someone would have to program the computer so it would know what substantive law to apply."

"What else would you have to program the computer with, Professor?" Rodrigo looked at me quizzically.

I hesitated a moment. "It wouldn't need much civil procedure." I was silent while Rodrigo looked at me expectantly.

"Do you remember our recent conversation, Professor, in which we talked about white-collar and black crime? [12] We discussed the role of discretion and leniency for the sorts of crimes that are committed by corporate executives, suburban youth, and governmental figures."

"Of course," I said. "Everyone knows what happens—the inner city black youth guilty of stealing hubcaps or selling a small amount of drugs is sent away for a long period while the well-regarded white figure receives probation or a light sentence—even though the latter's crimes may be more serious, in both a monetary and a physical-safety sense.[13] And so this is the type of thing your computer could not take into account."

"I'm afraid not," Rodrigo replied. "And so, after a while, society would rebel. We would insist on programming sentencing discretion and plea bargaining laxity into the computer. Otherwise automobile executives would receive long sentences when one of their badly designed cars killed someone. Savings and loan executives would receive fifty-year sentences. And so on."

The impact of what Rodrigo was saying sank in on me. "So, Rodrigo, you are saying that society would never tolerate Inquispro. A genuinely fair judiciary that provided equal justice for whites and blacks would be intolerable. We would insist on reprogramming Inquispro so that it was, basically, racist—had a bias in favor of clean, neat, well-educated white defendants and against black ones—and in favor of upper-class people of all colors and against poor ones."

"We would. Otherwise, society wouldn't accept it."

"And the moral you draw from this fiendish experiment, Rodrigo, is . . . ?"

"As a society we don't really want empathy, or anything that favors folks of another kind.[14] Quite the contrary, we prefer preferential treatment—would never accept anything less than that, in fact."

"Which is what your Inquispro example shows," I replied glumly. "Would you like another cup?"

Rodrigo, who had been eyeing my espresso machine, nodded enthusiastically and held out his cup. As he was stirring in his condiments, I asked: "And I gather you think this lack of empathy is somehow responsible for our current predicament?"

"Thanks, Professor. This is a good blend—a little milder than last time. French roast?"

I nodded yes, and my young friend continued: "It is, in large part. You see it as clearly in our profession, law, as elsewhere. A colleague of mine, Kowalsky, and I were talking about this the other day. Even in those aspects of law, like clinical scholarship, that you would think would be most empathic. Even some of the young stars admit they sometimes make the mistake of thinking they know what the client wants, and imagine that they are able to tell the client's stories as he or she would want them told. Real empathy, in the sense of putting the client first and getting fully inside the client's mind and experience, is rare."

"It sounds as if you've been thinking about this a good deal," I said. "I suppose you have a theory for it all?"

"Not so much a theory as a way of seeing what is wrong. I'll be glad to tell you about it, if you have the time."

"I do, although I don't want to make you late for dinner. Is Giannina expecting you?"[15]

"She's attending a workshop uptown. My schedule's my own, although I may want to borrow your phone later, if it's okay, and give her a call. We usually talk around dinnertime when one of us is away doing something."

"Of course," I replied, pointing at the phone. "Anytime you want. I'll punch in the code, and give you privacy."

"Thanks, Professor. Maybe a little later. And no, I won't be needing privacy. Giannina considers you almost one of the family."

"I'm honored. But tell me more about your theory of empathy. And incidentally, if you get hungry, let me know. I have snack food in the refrigerator . . ." (I indicated my small office fridge, which I had recently purchased and of which I was proud.) "Or we could go out for a bite."

"I appreciate the empathy," Rodrigo said, smiling. "Maybe a little later. I had a snack with some friends just before coming here. But, back to our subject. Empathy is highly limited. Not only that, it tends to become rarer over time. Yet we think we—and others—have much more empathy for the downtrodden than we, in fact, do. I even have a name for this. You've heard of Gramsci's concept of false consciousness?"[16]

"Of course," I said, a little sharply. (These impudent young pups sometimes think us old-timers haven't read anything!) "Gramsci coined the term to mean the kind of identification with the aggressor that a subjugated people can easily develop. They internalize the perspectives, values, and points of view of the very people who conquered and are oppressing them, thus becoming unconscious agents in their own oppression."[17]

"And so false consciousness is a danger for blacks, at least if we aren't careful. But have you ever wondered, Professor, if there is anything comparable for whites?"

"Comparable to false consciousness, you mean?" I wasn't sure what Rodrigo was driving at.

"I think there is, and it's empathy. Or rather, what I call false empathy, in which a white believes he or she is identifying with a person of color, but in fact is doing so only in a slight, superficial way."

"It *is* a kind of parallel," I said. "But I think I could use an example."

"Sure," Rodrigo replied. "Consider the early Settlement House movement.[18] The upper-class ladies who worked there professed to be highly concerned over the plight of the immigrants who lived in the houses. But their sympathies did not extend to learning their languages or ways. Instead, they taught them personal hygiene, housekeeping, English—how to be American.[19] Lawyers make this mistake, too, even public interest ones. Maybe especially public interest ones."

"I assume you are referring to Derrick Bell's famous article," I asked. "The one about serving two masters?"[20]

"That and others. Bell points out that lawyers working on behalf of black groups would often pursue a strategy favored by the litigation team—say, desegregated schools—when what the client really wanted was better schools, ones with more resources.[21] And, as we were discussing before, even the best clinicians make similar mistakes."

"So, you are saying," I summarized, "that when a white empathizes with a black, it's always a white-black that he or she has in mind—someone he would be like if he were black, but with his same wants, needs, perspectives and history, all white, of course."[22]

"Right. False empathy, a sentimental, breast-beating kind, is common among white liberals, and is the mirror opposite of false consciousness, Gramsci's notion."

"Nice and neat," I said. "Like the periodic table."

"It's not just elegant," Rodrigo replied. "It has real consequences for civil rights strategy. With false consciousness, a person of color identifies with and adopts the consciousness of the oppressor, in this case a white. With false empathy, a white pretends to understand and sympathize with a black. Each is counterfeit. The first type—the upward climber—is readily recognized and unmasked. These are the Great Gatsbys, and tend to be objects of ridicule by both whites and blacks. The second, false empathy, is likewise despised—but by blacks. We see through it, know by a kind of instinct that these people won't be with us when trouble comes down. Derrick Bell got it right in his *Serving Two Masters* article. Gerald Lopez, in *Rebellious Lawyering*,[23] did, too. But some of the top clinical theorists are getting it wrong, being satisfied with too little. A recent article shows how empathy is limited by cognitive and narrative-theory barriers, including what the authors call the 'empathic fallacy.' "[24]

"You make it sound as though the problem lies mostly on the white folks' side. Don't our people sometimes commit the same mistakes?"[25]

"They do, sometimes." Rodrigo conceded. "Although I think less frequently. Most whites lack double consciousness.[26] They have little practice in seeing things two ways at once. We have a great deal."

"Someone who is in the grip of false empathy has a shallow identification with the other," I said. "He or she walks on the surface, uses the wrong metaphors and comparisons. It's a little bit like false piety, like those folks who go to church on Sunday but don't allow themselves to be seized by real religion."

"The most unsympathetic thing you can do is think you have empathized with those of a radically different background. You can easily end up hurting them."

"By doing the wrong thing—by not supplying what they need?" I asked.

"Even worse than that," Rodrigo replied. "Are you familiar with the story of La Malinche?"[27]

I was silent for a moment, straining to remember. "You mean Hernan Cortes's translator?"

"Yes," Rodrigo replied. "I was talking with one of my Latino students the other day about her. La Malinche was an Indian woman who served as Cortes's translator. She ended up helping him destroy her own people."[28]

"I think our Mexican friends have a phrase for it."

"They do," Rodrigo replied. "*La traducción es traición.* Translation is treason. One who moves too easily back and forth between different communities can end up betraying the one with the least power, simply by making its secrets accessible to the other. Clinical theorists, some with the most impeccably liberal credentials, have been accused of something similar when they spill a client's stories out on the pages of a law review for all to read."[29]

I stood up to turn off the coffee pot, which had come perilously close to boiling itself empty. "We can come back to this later if you like," Rodrigo interjected. "Can I interest you in a bite of dinner? I think I'm hungry, after all."

"You certainly can," I replied, looking at my watch. "And if we hurry, we can get to some good places before they fill up."

In Which Rodrigo Explains How Empathy, Like Knowledge, Reproduces Hierarchy and Why Genuine Sympathy Is in Short Supply

We walked briskly down the sidewalk in front of my law school. "Vietnamese okay?" I asked. "This new place opened a couple of months ago. I haven't been there yet, but everyone tells me the food is great and the service good."

"Fine with me," Rodrigo replied, and a few minutes later we were seated in a comfortable booth in the clean, light restaurant. While waiting for the waiter to take our orders, I asked my young friend, "Rodrigo—let me see if I understand you. Are you saying that empathy is bad, per se, or that it is good, but that there is too little of the real article to go around?"

"In a way, both," Rodrigo replied, looking up at the waiter who had just brought our menus. We ordered appetizers and beverages (yet another cup of coffee for my irrepressible friend, herbal tea for me) and continued our conversation:

"Empathy is dangerous if not genuine, as it often is not. Like knowledge, it has a power dimension.[30] Empathy reproduces hierarchy. And the real kind, true empathy, is in extremely rare supply."

"Tell me about how the false, or superficial, kind reproduces hierarchy," I asked. I had just been reading about the sociology of knowledge, and was intrigued by Rodrigo's notion that emotions might reinforce the status quo just as knowledge does.

"We mentioned the case of La Malinche a minute ago. A member of the oppressed group tells the oppressor what it wants to know. The more powerful group then uses the information to destroy the translator's group."

"The translator is a dupe, in other words," I said.

"It works the other way, as well," Rodrigo went on. "Some liberals write about horrible conditions in the community, believing that others will want to remedy them. Their readers draw the opposite conclusion, however—that minorities are lazy, slothful, like to live that way, and so on.[31] And there is a third way, in which the liberal does not actively harm the member of the weaker group, but merely does him no good. The Good Samaritan offers the wrong sort of rescue."

"Like the Settlement House ladies who taught Italian immigrants how to cook and eat American food, when they had perfectly satisfactory recipes and cuisines, or taught immigrant mothers to use bottles and infant formula instead of breast feeding, which they considered un-American, and not modern."

"It's what you were saying earlier," I interjected. "When we visualize helping another person, we end up helping ourselves in the form of the other. A white helps a black who is, in effect white—a postulated recipient who will like and appreciate what the white would have wanted had the white been in exactly that situation."

"I'm sure you've noticed, Professor, that people almost always give presents that they would like to receive themselves?"

I remembered with a pang a time or two when my late wife had scolded me for doing something similar. "It's something of a joke with married folks," I said. "The husband gives the wife a lug wrench. She gives him two tickets to the opera, and so on."

"So you see what I mean about the way empathy reproduces power relations," Rodrigo said. "And also how it sometimes can amount to outright betrayal."

We fell silent while the waiter set down our appetizers, some sort of skewered chicken for my rail-thin friend, a hot and sour soup for me.

"You were also going to explain why it is in such short supply," I said, ladling myself a spoonful of the steaming concoction. "The real kind, I mean. And I believe you were also going to explain why the other kind is not merely harmless, but can kill."

Rodrigo removed his chicken morsels from the skewer, neatly speared one with his fork, and began.

Rodrigo Explains Why Empathy (The Cross-Race Variety) Is in Short Supply

"Empathy ought to benefit the possessor," Rodrigo began, "because it enables him or her to make beneficial trades. If one has the ability to perceive what others want, one can offer them that and get what one wants in return. Our law and economics friends would say it promotes marketplace efficiency.[32] Empathic people ought to get ahead. The capacity ought to confer an evolutionary advantage, enabling its possessors not merely to be good parents, friends, and lovers, but good traders, politicians, and marketers."

"But you believe things are not working out that way?' I asked.

"No. For some reason, the evolutionary momentum seems to have stopped, even reversed itself, with respect to people of color. I've been trying to figure out why this is so."

"No one can doubt that it is. Civil rights, affirmative action, Head Start, and dozens of other programs necessary to our people are under attack.[33] Politicians and writers no longer even have to speak in code when casting aspersions on us.[34] Black parents believe that things are now the worst they have been in twenty years, that their children will be denied jobs or educational opportunities because of discrimination, and that their sons are at risk of harassment, or worse, at the hands of the police every time they leave the house.[35] And I gather you think this is not just an aberration or part of an ordinary political cycle."

"I wish it were," Rodrigo replied. "But the downturn in our fortunes is more serious than that. I think the increasing bureaucratization of modern life may account for part of the decrease in fellow-feeling.[36] Modern social relations are apt to be distant and perfunctory. We run across fewer and fewer people of radically different class or race. A new branch of social psychology called norm theory[37] may supply part of the answer as well."

I strained my memory. "Norm theory?" I asked.

"Yes. Norm theory holds that our reaction to another person in distress varies according to the normalcy or abnormalcy of his or her plight, in our eyes. If you see an upper-class white family being evicted from their nice suburban home, you feel alarmed because you know that sort of situation is abnormal for them. You realize they must be experiencing real distress. But if you see starving Biafrans on TV, you feel less empathy because you know that is their ordinary situation. Famines are common in that part of the world, so your heart does not go out to them as it would if your neighbor materialized on your doorstep not having eaten in eight days."

"I've read of experiments dealing with helping behavior that appear to bear that out," I said. "A black woman drops a bag of groceries and no one stops to help. A white woman confederate does the same, and everyone stops.[38] I had thought these experiments manifested simple racism, but maybe they illustrate your phenomenon as well. Everyone assumes the black person has a rough road in life, so hardly anyone stops to help."

"Experiments with stranded motorists show the same thing,"[39] Rodrigo added. "Norm theory explains why empathy decreases over time, even though it would seem to benefit the possessor. The poorer and more wretched blacks become, the less white people will empathize with them. They will dismiss our cries of pain, thinking to themselves that's our normal condition."

"And the poorer and more wretched we become, the less we will have to offer in trade. Empathy with us will be useless. Who wants to trade with a slave, who has nothing to offer? There is no reason for empathy with one who is permanently destitute."

"My point exactly," Rodrigo continued. "Empathy is least useful where we need it most. When inequality is deep and structural, empathy declines. It's a downward spiral. Empathy *would* work in a just world, one in which everyone's experience or access to resources were roughly the same. But we don't live in a world like that."

"Is there any solution, any hope?" I asked.

"The only one I see is to show that our people have something to offer whites. We were talking about this the first time we met.[40] If one can convince elite whites that blacks have something to offer, our treatment will shift overnight, as it did in wartime.[41] The prevailing narratives and myths will change magically to facilitate trades and exchanges, services, and so on that the dominant group need. None of this will take place on a conscious level."

"The trouble is that many of them seem ready to write us off. The Republicans now realize they don't need our votes. They can count on backlash voters, angry white males,[42] while the Democrats seem not to want us, either.[43] And if I understand your argument, our few remaining liberal friends can't be counted on because their empathy is shallow. They think they know what we need, but don't. They visualize themselves in our places and ask what they, themselves, would want."

"False empathy is worse than indifference, Professor. It encourages the possessor to believe he is beyond reproach. It's like a certain type of religiosity. If you believe you are saved, you can easily come to believe that you can do no wrong. Because you believe in God, you will believe you *are* God, or at least that you are chummy with Him. He's on your side—you understand each other. Once you reach this point, you can do no evil, as you *are* God—or at least His messenger."

"You will then think you are being extremely empathic—as the Spanish conquistadores did—because you are acting on behalf of God in the other person.[44] Not what that other person is, but what he or she might be. The other person may not believe he or she has *that* God in him or her. But you will know better. Is that your general idea?" I asked.

"Yes," Rodrigo said. "In fact, I'm reminded that the helping experiments we were talking about showed that religious people helped out even less than nonbelievers.[45] This was particularly true if the experiment was staged just as they were coming from church."[46]

"So ideology of all sorts decreases empathy," I summarized. "The more politically fractured our nation becomes, the less important will seem its commitment to racial justice and help for the poor. Religiosity also decreases empathy, all things being equal, as does bureaucracy. And the conditions of modern life add a fourth element: as the gap in earnings and family wealth between blacks and whites grows wider, there is less to trade.[47] With the decreased need to understand and empathize with the other, empathy naturally decreases. And the poorer those others get, the more norm theory clicks in. Their misery seems normal, so why get excited when we see they are hurting?"

"And don't forget the decreasing pie. The slowing of growth in the U.S. economy and the greater competition we are facing from foreign markets mean that there is less empathy to go around," Rodrigo added. "Socioeconomic competition increases racism.[48] But it also decreases empathy. As one's own well-being and security decrease, one looks to oneself and one's friends. Expanding markets give a reason for increased empathy: one is in a position to make trades, so understanding other people confers an advantage. Bad times cause you to hunker down. During human evolution, the main function of empathy was to facilitate bonding and solidarity, so that collectivities could form.[49] But with racism—a relatively new phenomenon— the attitude promotes white bonding, white solidarity. This benefits elite whites, since it assures that struggling workers won't turn against them.[50] And it consoles workers. Even though their share of the pie gets smaller and smaller, they can say to themselves that they're at least better off than the blacks."[51]

"Six factors that augur little good for our people," I said. "A pretty gloomy scenario, coming from someone as young and upbeat as you. I hope you have a solution. Does it include law?"

"Oh, here's our waiter," Rodrigo interjected. "Can I tell you in a minute?" We both examined the menu in silence, while the waiter waited patiently.

"I'll have number twenty-seven," Rodrigo said.

"And I'll take thirteen. It doesn't have MSG, does it?" "Doctor's orders," I added to Rodrigo, who shot back a sympathetic look.

The waiter shook his head no, departed with our orders, and we continued as follows.

Rodrigo Explains Why Law Is Not the Solution, and Why We Need a Due Process of Legal Storytelling

"I do have a solution," Rodrigo replied, "but unfortunately it does not include law. At first, I thought it might. After all, one does not need empathy to file a lawsuit. A judge does not need it to rule on technical motions, or see whether a complaint satisfies the elements of a statutory cause of action. Many of these acts are mechanical, requiring no large amount of judgment. In fact, some race-crits have advocated the formality of the court setting as a positive advantage over nonformal dispute resolution, such as mediation, for cases presenting an imbalance of power—as most civil rights cases do.[52] Unfortunately, I think litigation is not a very promising avenue of relief for society's most wretched, most disadvantaged classes."

"We talked in a general way about some of these things before," I recalled. "I think it was when we were discussing that problem you had over the LL.M. skit when you were a graduate student."[53]

"Your memory is good, Professor. We are not the only ones to question faith in law as an instrument of social reform. There are many others, both on the left and on the right.[54] But some think things would be better if we only had more empathic judges, or ones with wider experience.[55] Or if lawyers learned to tell better, more vivid, stories in their pleadings, for example."[56]

"But you think this would not help at all?" I said, a little dubiously.

"Less than we might hope," Rodrigo replied. "Law is structurally biased against any display of empathy."

"Is that because of what your Inquispro example shows?" I asked. "Namely, that we do not really want law to be uniform and nonracist, treating everyone alike. We *want* it to promote class advantage. If it didn't we would change it back."

"That's part of it," Rodrigo replied. "But there's more. Even perfectly nonracist judges, ones like Inquispro, who treat blacks and whites absolutely alike, would end up doing very little good. Incidentally, I think this is even more true for lawyers, but we'll come back to that later. Let's focus on law at the more systemic level."

"Go ahead. I'm all ears," I said. "Why can't law redress the injuries of society's most needy and oppressed? What about times like the sixties? Then, courts were in the forefront of the social revolution, handing down decrees protecting civil rights protesters, desegregating schools and lunch counters, requiring due process in school disciplinary cases, and so on."

"True," Rodrigo conceded. "But that was, unfortunately, an aberration. Most of the time courts are no more kindly disposed to us and our causes than is any other group, say grocers or accountants—even less, in fact."

"And I assume you have a theory for why this is so?"

"I do—actually a group of explanations, corresponding to the different roles of judges, lawyers, and litigation as a whole."

"I'd love to hear them," I said, sitting back expectantly.

Rodrigo Explains Why Litigants Cannot Command the Empathy Their Situations Ordinarily Would—There Is No Due Process of Storytelling

The Litigants Themselves

"Let's take the litigants first. Say you are a plaintiff who has suffered a civil rights injury, maybe a black undergraduate or member of a family who has been injured by hate speech. You file suit, but soon find out that it is very hard to tell your story in court. The legal system requires that you tell a different narrative from the one that happened. Law slices up your narrative into little bits, into unfamiliar pieces. The pleading requires a short and plain statement, divided into paragraphs. It turns out that the law does contain master narratives that correspond fairly closely to commercial grievances, to what industrialists want to say about each other in antitrust cases and so on. But it contains few narratives that seem written for us, no pleading form for 'You were unfair.' Thus, when the plaintiff starts to tell her story, for example that her husband beat her for ten years, we interrupt and say, 'Don't tell us that story, tell us about imminent threats of death or violent injury. What was your husband about to do to you when you killed him?'[57] If it turns out the woman has nothing to tell of this kind of story, we tell her to keep quiet. She had no story after all."

"So the law requires her to tell a stylized story that might or might not correspond to the injury she sustained."

"Sometimes it's even worse than that," Rodrigo continued. "Sometimes the law requires you to tell the other person's story—the perpetrator's, not your own. For example, in a civil rights complaint, you will end up having to tell the judge and court that the other side acted intentionally, had a certain type of motivation."

"That's *Washington v. Davis*,"[58] I interjected. "Which holds that in many civil rights cases the plaintiff has to prove that the defendant's conduct was intentionally discriminatory, not merely that it had a differential impact on persons like oneself."

"Exactly. And not only that. The plaintiff has to prove tight chains of causation between what the defendant did and his or her injury."[59]

"And probably that the defendant had no legitimate business reason for denying the plaintiff a job or promotion,"[60] I added. "Half the plaintiff's case does seem to concern the defendant, not the plaintiff, who, after all, is the one who suffered the injury."

"Exactly. Consider the hate-speech case we mentioned a minute ago. The defendant, let's say, has burned a cross on the family's lawn.[61] Or a group of fraternity kids shouts, 'Nigger, go back to Africa; you don't belong on this campus,' to an eighteen-year-old black undergraduate.[62] If you take this case to court, you'll find that the defendant immediately turns it into a First Amendment issue. The issue now will be whether he or she had a right to burn the cross or yell the epithet. You, who were merely trying to sleep in your room at home, or walking home from the library late at night, will find yourself on the defensive, depicted as someone who was trying to take away the precious free-speech rights of the skinhead or bigot."[63]

"Hmm," I said, "I see what you mean by the narratives all being against you. In fact, I was just re-reading Justice Scalia's opinion in the Minneapolis cross-burning case the other day. He hardly mentions the family at all. They were an abstraction, almost entirely missing from the opinion, which is all about speech categories and the dangers of censorship—of what he calls viewpoint discrimination."[64]

"A more perfect irony could not be imagined," Rodrigo continued. "The Jones family, who awoke to find a cross burning on their lawn, and the city which intervened on their behalf—considered guilty of discrimination!"

I paused for a moment while the waiter set down our food, a vegetarian stir fry for me and some sort of chicken in curry sauce for Rodrigo. "Looks good," Rodrigo said. "Thanks." The waiter departed.

"So," I summarized, "the plaintiff often does not get to tell her story. And even when she does, it's rarely the story she would like to tell and thinks of most naturally as what happened. She cannot 'go back to the beginning.' She often finds that things she thought vital to the claim are irrelevant and cannot be told. The court interrupts, makes her tell her story in little slices, in response to direct examination. The other side gets to object every thirty seconds. Most of the 'material elements' concern the defendant and what he or she did. It's only when you get to the end—damages—that you really get to tell about yourself and what happened to you. The law makes you take what Alan Freeman calls the perpetrator perspective."

"Sounds dire," I said. "But maybe the solution is to litigate more, not less—to get the law to recognize new causes of action. Then, new narratives will be capable of being told, as happened with the tort of intentional infliction of emotional distress, for example. Or, in our time, sexual harassment of women in the workplace. Before Catharine MacKinnon's path-breaking work, women could not tell those stories in court. Today they can. Maybe our people can do the same."

"I doubt it," Rodrigo replied with uncharacteristic gloominess. "The courts' and the country's mood is all in the other direction. American society is impatient with what they call activist judges. We believe the rights revolution has gone too far. Affirmative action is under attack. All the dominant narratives have shifted. In the sixties African Americans were long-suffering victims or righteous warriors. Then, the images changed to those of terrifying gangsters and Black Power advocates. In the last decade, we've seen the Willie Hortons and Cadillac-owning lazy welfare cheat, the affirmative action office worker who won't work, 'knows her rights,' and blocks a spot that should go to a more deserving white."

"So," I said, returning to Rodrigo's previous example, "in the hate-speech debate, the narrative of harm is given short shrift—even though quite provable.[65] Courts and commentators quickly substitute the wholly unproven narrative of censorship, as though every campus that enacts a mild hate-speech rule will immediately turn into an Orwellian nightmare with Big Brother looking over everyone's shoulder.[66] This is quite speculative, and in my opinion extremely unlikely. Or take another narrative, the chilling effect that speakers are said to suffer if any speech-limiting code is put into place. Set that alongside the terror, demoralization, and high dropout rate that are demonstrably associated with campus hate speech, according to dozens of studies. Which one is more certain to occur? One finds that all the prevailing narratives have to do with enabling elite and not-so-elite whites to do what they are accustomed to doing, and then defending it in court. They have all these narratives going for them—Big Brother, the state as censor, the terrified speaker just waiting to be chilled, and the thin-skinned hypersensitive black just waiting to run to the authorities instead of shrugging it off."

Our Treatment of Witnesses

"That's not all," Rodrigo added. "Not only do we give plaintiffs a hard time, make it difficult for them to tell their story. Consider how we treat witnesses."

"You're going to say rudely, I bet. I've just been reading about a famous criminal trial where every witness got raked over the coals, left the courtroom feeling impugned and maligned, even though they were just trying to do their job—namely tell what they saw."

"Exactly," Rodrigo replied. "Let's say the plaintiff tries to bring in some friends to help him tell his or her story. These are people who know something about the event that gave rise to the lawsuit. The witness soon learns that in our legal culture it is okay to treat witnesses with suspicion and contempt. The other side gets to badger them, imply they might be lying, insinuate all sorts of unsavory motives." [67]

"Yet we insist that everyone treat the lawyers and judge with the greatest respect. Anyone who stood up in court and said that the prosecutor or judge might be lying or biased would be treated as having done something scandalous. Yet we do this sort of thing with witnesses routinely."

"And with women who bring charges of rape," Rodrigo added.

"In the courtroom, certain types of emotional display will get you a contempt citation; others not. Judges can shout, interrupt, show exasperation or disbelief. So can a defense lawyer questioning a witness. But the plaintiff and his or her attorney are expected to be models of decorum."

"Emotional rules are the underside of power and ideology," Rodrigo said. "It's okay for an empowered actor, say, your boss, to be angry at you. But you may not show anger at your boss. [68] It's the same way in court. The interaction you see there always has a power imbalance visible in who speaks first, who interrupts, who gets to initiate and terminate interaction, who gets to paraphrase and sum up at the end."

"It's true," I said, "that plaintiffs and witnesses find their roles limited in court by rules of evidence, relevancy, cross-examination, and so on. But that's the way things are in an adversary system — there have to be some rules, or else it would be a free-for-all and things would be even worse for what you call disempowered litigants. Aren't you forgetting that every plaintiff has the perfect counterbalance to all this power and cumbersome machinery that is deployed against him in court, namely an attorney, a gladiator who is trained to negotiate the maze of court rules and who is professionally and ethically bound to represent the client to the best of his ability? Doesn't the lawyer cancel all or most of that power imbalance out?"

The Lawyer

"I wish it were that way," Rodrigo said with a sigh. "But a lawyer's training and culture discourage him or her from challenging the narrative structures we just mentioned. Lawyers who spoke up, or mimicked the emotional tone of the judge, would be sanctioned or disbarred.[69] Lawyers cannot depart much from the stylized, desiccated stories spelled out in the rules of pleading. Gabel and Harris proposed different standards for lawyers representing political clients. But few followed their suggestions. The clinical literature shows that even famous radical lawyers miss opportunities to tell their clients' stories, instead settling for the dry, cautious tone set out in the pleading books and encouraged by the prevailing ethos, the bland decorousness of the courtroom."[70]

"Even public interest lawyers are prone to put the client's story second to the lawyer's own. I'm reminded of the article you mentioned by Derrick Bell, in which he points out how civil rights attorneys end up litigating one thing when their clients really want another."[71]

"It's not necessarily that the lawyer has a superficial understanding of the poor, black client. Rather, it's that he believes he knows best. He believes he has to collaborate with the court in retelling the client's story so that it comes out in the sanitized, approved version. And since most lawyers are white, male, and middle-class, this can be a serious problem. No lawyer, of course — white, black, male, or female — likes to be demurred out or have an evidentiary objection sustained against him or her. But if the lawyer's experience, background, and history are radically different from those of the client, the lawyer can easily dismiss the client's real objective and substitute his own. Lawyers may know the client's misery, understand full well the story he or she wants and needs to tell, but still end up putting the law story, the familiar one, the one he was trained to tell, first."[72]

I remembered something I had just read. "Rodrigo, you have some empirical evidence on your side. I was just reading Paul Finkelman's review of a history of black lawyers in America.[73] Finkelman commented how few lawyers, black or white, were in the forefront of the civil rights movement. All the great leaders were nonlawyers— Martin Luther King, W. E. B. DuBois, Frederick Douglass, Malcolm X, Jesse Jackson. They are historians, or teachers, or ministers—very few lawyers. Do you think that is because a people in trouble know instinctively that a lawyer is not the one to tell its story? Or is it that lawyers shy away from leadership roles, preferring to remain in the background, conducting backroom negotiations, filing for injunctions, doing the nitty-gritty work that allows the real leaders to be effective, to stay out of jail, and so on?"

"It may be both," Rodrigo replied. "Some lawyers do propose useful things. Thurgood Marshall and the other lawyers in the NAACP Legal Defense Fund certainly did, which Finkelman of course acknowledges.[74] But the further removed a lawyer is by experience and background from the group represented, the less effective he or she seems to be. No white male middle-class lawyer advocated attention to racial slurs and hate speech until a minority lawyer did.[75] No middle-class white male proposed to eliminate sexual-history testimony in rape cases or proposed a new cause of action for sexual harassment in the workplace until Catharine MacKinnon did.[76] No white male—except that genius, Alan Freeman—proposed that civil rights law, that jewel in the crown of our jurisprudence, systematically disadvantages its very beneficiaries, minorities.[77] No straight white male—except Joshua Dressler—championed gay rights and opposed slurs and gay-bashing until very recently.[78] The Supreme Court saw no serious problem with capital punishment that falls disproportionately on minorities.[79] And so on. The basic problem is the legal narrative: One simply cannot tell stories of many kinds of injustice through the law. And if one's training is in the law, one has virtually de-trained oneself to represent society's outcasts. It takes a superhuman effort to be an empathic human being. To be both a lawyer and an empathic human is practically an impossibility. Our review of civil rights history shows that the legal narrative is less effective than that of practically any other profession, such as teaching, the ministry—or a grocer, for that matter."

"And, as we mentioned earlier, the rules of courtroom etiquette require that one not use emotional discourse, that one speak within the legal paradigm, adhere to rules of evidence that carve one's narrative into little pieces, destroying its momentum and integrity. Lawyers are trained to observe these rules until they become second nature. We are trained not to empathize but to be technocrats, concentrating on the small, not the big, picture. We focus on motions and pleadings, not stories, much less things like injustice, love, and compassion.

"We do allow victim-impact statements,"[80] Rodrigo interjected. "That's one kind of new story we do like."

"We find it easy to empathize with the victims of crime," I said. "Particularly if they are middle-class people like us."

"Even better, they are not required to testify through a lawyer. They can speak for themselves. When we want someone to speak really effectively—that is, to help society condemn the criminal even more fully—we let them speak uninterrupted. We could do the same for civil rights plaintiffs, but don't."

"But, Rodrigo," I interjected, "there is a whole new literature on effective lawyering.[81] It is being written by clinical faculty, some at the best schools. Writers like Menkel-Meadow,[82] Lopez,[83] Cunningham,[84] and Alfieri[85]—others as well—are writing about client narratives. They are writing about the need to listen more carefully, to translate better, to get inside our clients' heads.[86] They are warning about the dangers Derrick Bell first raised, of putting the law and the lawyer's objective first. Do you not think things are changing for the better?"

"I would like to think so," Rodrigo replied. "But I'm skeptical. A lawyer cannot easily escape the confines of his or her background, culture, and professional discipline. Herb Eastman shows that even top lawyers, like William Kunstler, tell dull, lifeless, stereotyped stories, at least at times.[87] And Anthony Alfieri, one of the best of the young clinicians, confesses that he often falls short in empowering his clients and letting their voices and personalities shine through.[88] He goes on at great length about how he erased the pain and identity of one of his clients, a certain Mrs. Fields."[89]

"I read that article," I replied. "And even though his *mea culpa* is drawn out over several pages, I kept wondering: Did he ever really understand Mrs. Fields? He recounts how his client, a Social Security applicant who sought relief because she lost her job due to an inability to read, finally broke down and wept. The woman was undoubtedly frustrated—the judge was refusing to believe she could not read enough to hold a job—and Alfieri was forced to demonstrate graphically to the court, by holding up various signs and charts, that she could not. But Alfieri read more into it than that; he believed the woman was frustrated at being unable to tell her story of segregated classrooms and growing up in a house without many books."[90]

"I see what you mean," Rodrigo said. "Alfieri, although a fine lawyer and progressive scholar, was reacting to her life experience as though he had lived through it; in his imagination he was a black-white. And for him, an educated, sensitive person, growing up in an environment without books and relegated to inferior schools would have been intolerable. Mrs. Fields, though, might have been quite happy with her all-black schools, as Bell reminds us.[91] And whether she experienced the lack of books in her parents' house as a deprivation, even we have no way of knowing. She did experience the cutoff of Social Security benefits as a harsh deprivation—that we know. The author seems almost as concerned with where *he* fit in as with his client's own expressed desires—namely for Social Security benefits."

"Progressive lawyers may go on and on about their consciences[92] not because they want empathy for the clients, but for themselves. They lose all their cases. Their clients sometimes lie to them. The judges are rude. Often their clients want X when they (the lawyers) want Y—the grand declaration of principle—as we mentioned before.[93] Liberal empathy is often of just this misdirected or solipsistic sort."

"The sort that is the opposite of Gramsci's false consciousness, you mean?"

"Exactly."

"Would you gentlemen like some dessert?" The waiter had materialized at our table side while we were talking. I looked at Rodrigo, who shrugged back, I thought a little eagerly.

"Could we see your dessert tray?" I asked. The waiter disappeared, taking our empty dinner plates with him. "But you mentioned that there is another way in which litigation prevents people from telling their stories."

The Court System

"Oh, yes," Rodrigo replied. "Law disaggregates and atomizes, even though many grievances have a group dimension. This leaves the litigant lonely and without allies. It encourages him or her to think about his own grievance, not those of the group."

"I can think of a few ways it does this," I chimed in. "Doctrines of standing and real party in interest limit who can sue or be sued.[94] While joinder is possible to a degree, and class actions are possible in some situations . . ."

"Although we both know the many ways the federal courts have been cutting back on the class action vehicle in recent years," Rodrigo interjected, "by insisting on satisfaction of the minimum amount in controversy for every plaintiff,[95] for example, and by requiring notice to all class members who are identifiable through reasonable effort."[96]

"True. But there are other features that render courts unattractive to social reformers. Courts are bound by precedent, which may contain bad stories. If the only narrative the law recognizes is a bad one—one that requires that you demean yourself or tell your story in a strange and contorted way, or jump through very high hoops even to be heard at all—you will not choose to tell your story there very often. Judges' experiences and life perspectives are those of a certain class. There are very few African American, lesbian, or disabled judges or ones from a working-class background. Since their experience is limited, judges may be ill-equipped to understand your plea. Rules relating to ripeness, mootness, and standing mean that the court can only consider the case before it, not the broad story of dashed hopes and centuries-long mistreatment that afflicts an entire people and forms the historical and cultural background of your complaint. And the decree, even if favorable, will fix only your story, not that of others—and especially so after recent cutbacks in res judicata law and the class action vehicle.[97] In short, courts are ill-equipped to hear and act on the stories they need most urgently to hear."

"Another way of putting it," Rodrigo said, summing up, "is what I'm thinking of calling the *reconstructive paradox*. It's an aspect of what you said just now. It begins by observing that the greater the evil—say, black or female subjugation—the more entrenched it will be. The more entrenched any evil, the more massive the social effort that will be required to dislodge it. An entrenched social evil will be invisible to many—maybe most—in the culture, simply because it is embedded, entrenched, and ordinary-seeming. The massive social effort will inevitably collide with other social values, settled expectations, the way things are, and so on. It will entail dislocations, new priorities, and spending shifts. These *latter* efforts, by contrast, will be highly visible, will spark resistance and opposition. One is apt to be characterized as 'Big Brother,' a fascist, a reverse racist, and so on. Resistance then will feel principled to the resister—because the other side will appear to be sacrificing real liberty, real money for a nebulous and dubious social goal, like helping blacks."

"Reconstruction and reform, then," I said gloomily, "will always seem unprincipled, premature, wrong, and will spark resistance—until one hundred years later when consciousness changes, at which time we will look back and wonder how we possibly could have resisted *that*."

"Oh," Rodrigo exclaimed. "Here's the dessert tray!"

In Which Rodrigo Offers a Solution to the False-Empathy Dilemma, and Suggests Two Roles for White Reformers and Fellow Travelers

We picked out our desserts, which the waiter quickly brought. After a few moments in which we tacitly agreed to eat in silence while enjoying our confections—a creamy French Vietnamese pastry of some sort for Rodrigo, sherbet for me—I looked up. "I hope that my real dessert will be that you tell me what your solution is to the predicament we find ourselves in. Reformers get little if any real empathy in courts, or indeed anywhere, and can count on no one but themselves to climb out of poverty and despair. If we can't look to our liberal friends, to whom can we turn?"

"Empathy would work in a just world, one in which everyone's experience and social histories were roughly the same—that is, not marked by radical inequality. In such a world, we would have things to trade. There would be reasons for needing to get to know others, for understanding what they feel and need. But, as we mentioned earlier, we don't live in such a world."

"And since we don't," I said, "what should we do? We can't give up, can't just sit around bemoaning our plight or plotting revolution. There must be a strategy, a set of procedures for operating in an imperfect world."

"I do have a plan," Rodrigo said, drawing a deep breath. "It contains three provisions. It's all based on the idea that false empathy is worse than none at all, worse than indifference. It makes you overconfident, so that you can easily harm the intended beneficiary. You are apt to be paternalistic, thinking you know what the other really wants or needs. You can easily substitute your own goal for his. You visualize what you would want if you were he, when your experiences and needs are radically different. You can end up thinking that race is no different from class—that blacks are just whites who happen not to have any money right now. You can think that middle-class blacks or ones with professional degrees have it made, need no further attention, when their situation is in some respects worse than that of the black who lives in an all-black, working-class neighborhood."[98]

"Your solution, Rodrigo, your solution," I urged.

"Oh—I think the solution lies in three parts. The first is essentially to give up on, to foreswear the very idea of, empathy as any sort of primary tool for our advancement. We must realize that persons of radically different background and race cannot be made vicariously to identify with us to any significant extent. Their help, if any, is likely to be misguided, paternalistic, mistaken, and unhelpful. This is especially so if they are lawyers and other court officers. Legal empathy is even rarer and less reliable than other kinds. Law carves up your story, serves it up to an uncomprehending judge, atomizes your claim, and sparks real resistance when it tries to do something—as it does every century or so. We should give up on the entire route."

"And then what?"

"The next step—after abandoning hope in liberal empathy and

cross-race, cross-class identification—is to urge one of two strategies that I think *will* work. Would you like to hear them?

"Yes, yes," I said impatiently.

Rodrigo's First Plan for Whites: The Race Traitor Idea

"The first role for white folks who would like to be helpful is what Noel Ignatiev and John Garvey call the race traitor.[99] Have you heard of the idea?"

I strained to remember. "I think I have. Don't they have a magazine by that title?"

"Yes," Rodrigo replied. "I brought you a copy. It's in that envelope back in your office. But I see you know about it already. Just when I think I have an idea or approach that will surprise you, it turns out you know about it already. It's kind of discouraging talking with you, Professor."

"Stop the flattery. You're miles ahead of me in most things. I just have a little more experience. Tell me how you see the race traitor idea applying to our empathy dilemma."

"White people who want to help can become traitors to the white race. As Ignatiev and Garvey put it, 'Treason to whiteness is loyalty to humanity.'[100] For example, if a white person is in a group of whites and one of them tells a racist joke or story, the white can look up in surprise and say: 'Oh, you must have told that story in front of me because you assumed I am white. I am not. I'm black. I just look white, but my ancestry is black. And let me tell you why I found that story offensive.'"[101]

"In other words," I said, "they identify with blacks—and even identify themselves as blacks."

"Yes," Rodrigo continued. "And that includes rejecting white privilege, so far as a white-looking person is capable of doing that. In dozens of encounters in life, one takes on the role of being, acting, and speaking out as though one were a black—that is, one of us."[102]

"I'm not sure how that is possible," I said. "Could you give me an example?"

"Ignatiev and Garvey themselves give many. Whiteness is a social construct, basically a readiness to accept many privileges that come to you if you look a certain way.[103] If you refuse to be white you begin the process of destabilizing that construction, which society relies on to preserve the current system of racial subordination. So, suppose a neatly dressed white person, who happens to be a race traitor, is pulled over by a police officer and then let go with a warning. The person ought to question the officer, 'Would you have done this if I had been black?' " [104]

"So whites ought to reject racial privilege and challenge manifestations of racism that they observe."

"Yes. And if enough people do this, the system will collapse, because whites will never be sure which other whites are disloyal to the white race in the sense of refusing unearned privilege and declining to cooperate in the myriad ways society keeps blacks down. The race traitor not only opposes racism but seeks to disrupt its normal functioning, and does so from within. Therein lies its power. The color line is not the work of a few racist individuals but of a system of institutions and practices. Race traitors challenge these at every turn: tracking in public schools; location of public housing on the other side of the tracks; so-called meritocratic criteria that firms and institutions rely on unthinkingly even though they exclude blacks and women." [105]

"So the idea is to show total solidarity with us and our causes."

"Yes, even though this means putting one's job and friendships with whites on the line. If the police and courts could not be sure that every person who looks white is loyal to it, the system will fall.[106] For then, what would be the point of extending privileges based on race? Whites would reject loyalty to their own race, rejoin the human race, and the idea of the white race would fall of its own weight."

"A radical proposal, Rodrigo," I said. "I'm not sure many of our white friends would adopt it."

"It does entail a radical commitment," Rodrigo conceded. "But, as I mentioned, if only a small proportion of whites did, it would seriously jeopardize the system of white-over-black hegemony that has reigned in this country for over four hundred years. And the form of identification it would generate would be real. As we were discussing earlier, empathy is not particularly reliable. One learns only from his own experience, not that of others. The race traitor role allows people to begin to acquire that experience."

"And it would certainly get us past the kind of halfhearted, generally misguided empathy that you were describing earlier and that does so little good for us and our people. But I think you said you had a second plan."

Rodrigo's Second Plan for Whites: Subversion from Within

"My second plan sounds almost like the opposite of the first, but as you'll see it's not."

"Please go on. But, by the way, do you need to call Giannina?"

Rodrigo looked at his watch. "Her workshop won't be letting out for another forty-five minutes. Why don't we go on?" (I nodded.) "My second plan would envision whites working with whites to lift the yokes of oppression that burden both them and us. I wonder, Professor, if you heard the keynote speech by the famous white radical at the recent critical legal studies conference."[107]

"I did. It was spellbinding—delivered with great panache. He held the entire room, even without a microphone."

"And I'm sure you recall what he said. He described his own upbringing as a member of the ruling class, as he put it—prep school, Harvard, antiwar rebellions, SDS. He was a creature of the sixties, and when he grew up turned to Critical Legal Studies for inspiration and support."

"He not only turned to cls, he helped develop it," I interjected. "He was a founding father, helping the new movement carve out such notions as indeterminacy and the theory that law is essentially politics."

"And do you remember what he said, Professor, about his own engagement with racial identity groups?"

"I do. He said he had sided with Black Power and the Panthers, although as a more or less distant cheerleader and fellow traveler. He said quite candidly that he thought he had little role beyond that, and that as a member of the white privileged class he could not do much more, that there is a sort of built-in limitation. Consequently he turned to institutional politics, the politics of daily life, teaching elite law students how to survive in the corporate world and subvert their own offices and institutions. That and deconstructing legal doctrine."

"What's wrong with that?" I asked. "I was there when he said it, and thought at the time that he was being commendably honest. What else could someone like him have done in life?"

"I don't want to seem harsh," Rodrigo said, falling quiet. "He's a famous figure, from whose work all of us have learned much."

"But you feel there is more he could have done?"

"Yes. I keep thinking that someone with his charisma and prodigious talent could have done more. All it would have taken would have been a slight shift—a few degrees this way, rather than that."

"And that shift is . . ." I cajoled.

"I think our famous friend should have devoted himself, at least in part, to working with his own race, that is, with disaffected working-class whites. He could have supplied them with the analyses and leadership that they needed, and at a crucial time. Working-class, blue-collar whites, ethnic whites, and poor Southern whites today are arrayed against minorities. They have turned against us with a vengeance. They are the 'angry white men' who helped bring about the Republican revolution that is setting back the cause of social and racial justice, challenging affirmative action, and demanding the end of welfare to the poor and desperate."

"You are saying that if the famous white radical, and people like him, had stopped flirting with radical chic social movements like the Panthers back in the sixties and gone to preach to their own blue-collar brothers and sisters, we would not be in the fix we are in today?"

"Yes. They might have listened to him. Lower-class whites are not our natural enemies. Quite the contrary. But they think they are. Elite whites neatly use them to deflect attention from their own crass materialism, manipulation, and profits—from the way they maintain unsafe workplaces for the workers, pay bare subsistence wages, phase out factories at the drop of a hat creating real destitution, and send jobs overseas if it suits their interest, all at the expense of workers."[108]

"So you are saying fancy crits in elite positions at the top schools are responsible for the Republican revolution and the terrible turn things have taken for our people and for the poor?"

"I am," Rodrigo replied with conviction. "They took the easy way out. Instead of taking their campaign to the factories and lower-class tenement districts, they listened to the Panthers, shivered a little, and went and wrote elegant law review articles about the structure of Western legal thought—mostly for each other's benefit. They abandoned their own people. Empathy—the shallow, chic kind—is always more attractive than *responsibility*, which is hard work." [109]

"Is it too late?" I asked.

"It's never too late. Look at what Ralph Nader is doing. He writes for workers in dangerous factories, consumers who buy unsafe products. [110] He has a fancy law degree, yet he addresses his message to those who unfortunately have been led to think *we* are the cause of their economic pain. He's trying to redirect their attention upward, to the corporate elite that is oppressing us all, much as Martin Luther King was preparing to do toward the end of his life, just before he was assassinated. [111] Robert Kennedy, too. [112] There's no reason Nader should be working at this alone."

"Nader also spoke at the conference you mentioned. He scolded the crits for devoting their lives to figuring out how many angels can dance on the head of a pin." [113]

"I missed that session," Rodrigo said. "I'm hoping it's on tape. I'd like to see it sometime."

"I think they were taping it," I said. "Maybe your library can get it."

"I'll see when I get home," Rodrigo said. "But, speaking of getting home, Professor, I think I'd better be moving along soon. Thanks for the company. As usual, you're a great sounding board."

"You've helped me as well. I'd often wondered why empathy for our people, our causes, and for the poor seems to be sharply declining. You've helped me figure out why, and what we might do about it."

"Speaking about doing things—Giannina's workshop ends tomorrow at noon. We were thinking of taking in that new show of early Industrial-era art down at the cross-town museum. Want to join us? We've got a few free hours before we have to go to the airport."

"I'd love to," I said. "Maybe I'll pick up a postcard at the gift shop and send it to my radical friend you were mentioning. We know each other. Maybe I'll suggest the three of us get together sometime for a small summit conference. What do you think?"

Rodrigo smiled, fished a few bills out of his wallet for his share of the tab, and gave me a quick squeeze on the shoulder. "I'm game," he said. "I kind of like the guy, too. Want to share a cab?"

"You bet. I don't want you self-deconstructing on me again. Ready?"

2

Legal Instrumentalism and the Rule of Law: A Blueprint for Reformers in Hard Times

I was sitting dejectedly in the airport waiting lounge, cursing myself for having taken a winter flight that changed planes in a northern city, when I heard a familiar voice from behind me.

"Professor, is it you?"

I turned. "Rodrigo, for goodness' sake! What are you doing here?"

"I'm just getting back from a speaking tour. I think I told you I'm workshopping my first article. I gave three talks in six days!"

"You must be exhausted," I commiserated.

"Oh, it wasn't so bad," my irrepressible protégé replied, "although it went by in something of a blur. I'm afraid I'll get a telephone call from Professor Jones and not remember what school he's from."

"Tell him you enjoyed meeting his colleagues. He may mention a name and that'll ring a bell. The older I get the more trouble I have remembering students' names. But I don't have your excuse—I have them all term long."

"Your students like you, Professor. If you forget an occasional name it doesn't matter. They know you care about them, just as I know you care about me."

"Enough of that," I said. "Tell me about your trip. My flight was canceled. I've got nearly three hours before the next one.[1] I was just sitting here trying to build up courage to open my briefcase, but I'd much rather talk with you."

"I've got plenty of time. I'm early, having caught a standby flight in the nick of time from Chicago. Giannina's not expecting me till this evening.[2] Can I buy you a drink or cup of coffee?"

"Maybe in a minute. Sit down," I said, indicating the empty seat next to me. "Tell me about your trip."

"Well, as I said, I spoke at three law schools, all in the Midwest. Something happened at the one I left just this morning. If you have a minute, I'd love to tell you about it."

"Go ahead. As I've told you more than once, I get at least as much out of our conversations as you do. What happened?"

"I was having one of those informal sessions. Four professors and I were meeting in the office of one of them. It was my last one before going to meet the dean and off to the airport. It really got me going— I've done nothing but think about it the whole flight. It's providential that I met you here. I would have called you in a day or two."

"Was it something that came up during your talk?"

"Only tangentially. I spoke about the relation of laissez-faire economics and the plight of the black poor, an aspect of my dissertation.[3] One professor apparently got the idea that I'm interested in Critical Race Theory, which of course I am, even though my talk didn't touch on that at all. So he had this question ready for me when we met later in the office."

"What was it? The usual one about affirmative action?"

"No, not at all. It was about racial realism, [4] but with a pedagogical twist. You're familiar with the critique of Derrick Bell's work as being too despairing?"

"I am. A number of authors have taken Bell to task for that, notably Alan Freeman, an otherwise friendly writer, in a review of Bell's first casebook.[5] He and others have questioned whether preaching gloom and doom is wise, particularly if it ends up discouraging students from going into civil rights or public interest practice.[6] How did you answer the question?"

"I pointed out that Bell might well be right, and if so, there's little to be gained by holding on to false hopes. But it turned out the professor was making a much more subtle 'as if' argument, questioning whether, even if we thought the condition of blacks and other minorities of color is unlikely to improve, enjoying only periodic peaks of progress followed by regression,[7] we ought to act as though we believed the opposite. Otherwise we'd be paralyzed. There would be no reason to struggle."

"That is a different version," I agreed. "It reminds me of recent writing about myths and the way society organizes itself around certain beliefs and credos.[8] Even if not literally true, the myths help society run more smoothly."

"I conceded as much, but nevertheless stuck to my position. We had a spirited discussion."

"I wish I had been there. Tell me, how did you defend Bell's thesis?"

"I began by laying it out, beginning with the interest-convergence idea—that whites will support and tolerate gains for blacks only when these also benefit them[9]—then traced it through Bell's analysis of *Brown v. Board of Education*,[10] and finally into its modern form, *racial realism*."[11]

Just then, the public address system announced the arrival of a flight from Dallas, and I realized we would soon have a planeload of passengers streaming past us. "This area is filling up, Rodrigo. I'd love to hear how you answered the professor's question, which incidentally strikes me as both intelligent and admirable. It lets you show how you would deal with a recurring pedagogical issue. And at the same time it allows you to strut your stuff on an important point of legal theory. That professor had obviously done his homework. Why don't we continue this conversation somewhere else? There's a little noodle shop just down the concourse. It smelled good when I passed by. Could you use a bite?"

"Always," Rodrigo replied. "They didn't feed us much on the flight home—just a tiny, dry sandwich."

I made a sympathetic face and stood up. As we walked in the direction of the restaurant, Rodrigo continued: "The myth question wasn't too hard, at least until I started thinking more about it later. I told the group in the office that minorities and members of the majority group need different myths because they are differently situated. With respect to race, what white people need is hope. They need to believe in black progress, because otherwise they would be consumed by guilt. Most of them have a higher standard of living than ours, longer life expectancy, lower rates of incarceration and infant death, and so on[12]— all directly traceable to slavery and social neglect. Consequently, they fasten onto any indicator of progress for blacks or other minorities, even during times when our despair, our misery index, is higher than ever. They read somewhere that there are more left-handed Hispanic plumber's apprentices in Ohio than twenty years ago and seize upon that as proof that things are getting better."

"The conservatives aren't consumed by guilt," I pointed out. "They think that if our progress is stalled, it's our fault. We have dysfunctional families or allow ourselves to succumb to a culture of poverty."[13]

"You have a point," Rodrigo acknowledged. "Yet they do hold to a myth of progress—namely, that the race problem has been solved. The playing field is now level, as a result of the 1960s-era reforms, so that any black or Latino who is not progressing today has only himself or herself to blame."[14]

"So white folks subscribe to and place great stock in the myth of black progress. I agree with you on that. A recent poll showed that black parents believe things are now as bad for black children as at any time since slavery.[15] The same study showed that homicide is the leading cause of death for black youths between fifteen and twenty-four years of age. Nearly half of all black children live under the poverty level, and 34 percent of all teenagers looking for work could not find it, a rate twice that of their white counterparts. Nearly half of all black babies are not adequately immunized, and fully 65 percent of black adults believe that their kids will be denied jobs because of racial prejudice. Nevertheless, most of our white friends cannot be made to see that things are getting worse, not better for us. But you mentioned that there is a counterpart myth on our side of the equation."

"Oh, yes. Whites need the myth of civil rights progress to be able to function. We, by contrast, need a stone-cold sober assessment of our chances, even if they are not very good. For just as whites need guilt-avoidance, we need to avoid self-blame. For us, the paralyzing mental process is internalization of the terrible images society has disseminated about us through the ages—unintelligent, lazy, sexually lascivious, and so on.[16] We also need to avoid connecting our low estate—our poverty, high crime rate, high degree of social pathology, and so on—with ourselves and our own efforts. We need to keep in mind that our current condition is the direct result of our subordination. For us, this bleak realization is healing, is psychically necessary, just as the more sanguine, upbeat interpretation is what whites need." [17]

The hostess at the restaurant, where we had been waiting briefly, beckoned us to come in. We followed her to a booth, sat down, and picked up the menus. Before we started scanning them in earnest, I asked Rodrigo, "And did that answer satisfy them?"

"It seemed to. At least, we soon moved on to something else. But it didn't fully satisfy me. On the flight back I realized there's more to it than that. I'd love to run some ideas past you, if you've got the time."

I nodded enthusiastically. "Should we order first?"

In Which Rodrigo Reconciles Mainstream Civil Rights Law and the More Pessimistic Racial-Realist (Critical Race Theory) Version

A few minutes later the waitress took our orders, first patiently explaining to my ebullient young friend how a certain Korean dish differed from one he had learned to like in his favorite restaurant in Chinatown. After she had gone, Rodrigo continued:

"Nice woman. Where were we? Oh, yes—the optimism-pessimism gap. What I realized on the flight home is that it's not enough simply to explain *why* our folks are on the whole less upbeat than whites. We need a theory of what folks like us should do. Should we sit around in despair? Try harder? The principal purveyor of the Realist view, Derrick Bell, says that the situation is grim, but one must struggle anyway. Even though one knows in advance that the gains will be very slight, the effort must nevertheless be made. [18] Yet he doesn't explain why, exactly."

"It seems to be an article of faith, a kind of existential commitment, something that gives life meaning, enabling us to carry on in an otherwise bleak and desolate world," I suggested.

"That's the interpretation I drew too, but then I began thinking we can go further. The theory I propose is not so much a replacement as a modification of Bell's. Under it, subordinated people would acknowledge that in many eras and in many courts, success is really not possible. At these times, it is best to look elsewhere for relief."

"To what Gerry Spann calls 'pure politics,' "[19] I ventured, "mass marches, picketing, lobbying, the legislative arena—forums other than courts?"

"Exactly. And when these avenues seem foreclosed, when society as a whole seems to close its face to us, we can turn to our own sources, our own communities."

"That's self-help, cultural nationalism, building our own communities, looking to black colleges," I said in excitement. I could see the outlines of the long-awaited theory of social change forming, something that had eluded some of our finest minds. I longed to hear more. "And so, Rodrigo, you think that what's needed is an overarching theory to tell us which approach to use at any given moment in our quest for racial justice. The interest-convergence theory tells us there will be times when courts will be hostile or indifferent, but if I understand you correctly, that need not be a counsel of despair. Rather, it simply means that we should then look to other means for progress and succor."

"Exactly," Rodrigo replied. "We should look upon law as we would any other social institution, a tool that is useful for certain purposes and at certain times, but less so for other purposes or at different times. We need not succumb to the totalizing despair of some of our most eminent theorists, one that actually can prove enervating, despite my rather flip answer to the group this morning. Nor need we embrace the saccharine optimism of conventional civil rights theories grounded in liberalism and faith in progress. That's dangerous too, because it leads to disillusionment and burnout. We need a more sustaining approach, which my more pragmatic view provides. What do you think, Professor?" Rodrigo looked up cheerfully.

"I'd love to hear more details. But my first impression is that the idea has much promise. It has ties with a new legal movement, pragmatism.[20] And it offers an approach to our condition that promises to be liberating—to avoid the Scylla and Charybdis of overoptimism on the one hand, and despair on the other. Do you have a name for your brain child?"

Rodrigo looked up and smiled, whether because of my question or because of the arrival of the waitress with a trayful of steaming, savory-smelling bowls, I could not tell. "Legal instrumentalism," he said, moving aside his water glass and making way for the bowls and plates full of tempting soups and crepe-type dishes.

Rodrigo Explains and Defends Legal Instrumentalism as a Civil Rights Strategy

"What are you having?" I asked.

"A noodle dish. I can't remember what it's called. It's a lot like something Giannina and I have at a Chinese restaurant near where we live. But it's different—it has more ginger. Want a bite?"

We traded morsels, and Rodrigo commented, "Mmmmm. Your stir fry is really good. So you think my theory has promise?"

"Emphatically so. I like its synthetic, umbrella quality, the way it allows for differentiation of strategy depending on the times and circumstances. And I especially like—how shall I call it?—the mental health overtones. It promises a much more liberating way of looking at civil rights progress, one that avoids both false optimism and undue despair. But I'd love to know two things. First, how you thought of it. And second, how you would defend it against the charge of cynicism. You've already explained more or less how it would work—we'd choose whatever tool seemed most promising at a given period in history. And I'd also like to know how you would respond to the accusation, one you are certain to hear leveled against you, that it goes against the rather noble ideal of the rule of law.[21] If not frankly 'antilegal,' your theory verges on demystification of law and litigation, for it seems to say, follow the law when that will work for you, and avoid or break it when it won't. There are precursors of your theory, and they are not in particularly good favor today."[22]

Legal Instrumentalism

Rodrigo paused to spear a last noodle stuck in the bottom of his cup, then continued. "I know about Thrasymachus[23] and that other dialogue,[24] as well as some of their latter-day versions including 'By any means necessary.'[25] But Socrates was not vindicating a system of laws that systematically oppressed a minority of its citizens, and so the tribunal that sentenced him to death was much more legitimate than ours, at least vis-à-vis him. Our Constitution excluded blacks, women, and those without property from the very beginning.[26] It provided for the institution of slavery in no fewer than ten passages.[27] And even when we abolished that institution a hundred years later, a system of Jim Crow laws kept our people in circumstances little better than those they had just escaped. It was not until yet another hundred years passed that separate but equal—legal apartheid—began to be repealed.[28] We were not the first nation to repeal slavery—not even among the first ten."

"But surely, Rodrigo," I interjected, "things have changed. And even if our system of civil rights laws is not perfect, does it not provide at least a degree of protection? What do we have that is any better? Anarchy?"

"Good points," Rodrigo replied mildly. "I don't want to exaggerate. Sometimes the courts are our staunchest allies. But sometimes they are not. During these times we should look to other avenues. Otherwise one is just beating one's head against a stone wall."

"What you called perseveration before."

"Actually, your two questions turn out to be related. Legal instrumentalism occurred to me in reflecting on the idea of legitimacy and the way in which recent revolutionary leaders have viewed law. Few of the great ones held to any sort of romantic ideal. Gandhi, of course, considered the British system of laws and civil service entirely illegitimate and had little hesitation about ordering strikes and boycotts, even though they were technically illegal. Martin Luther King believed one had no obligation to obey unjust laws."

"Although King did believe that one should be prepared to suffer punishment as a consequence," I interjected.

"To be sure. And in more recent times, the Black Panthers took a position very much like the one I am suggesting.[29] Their leaders understood that the forces of law would often be arrayed against them, but that sometimes one could employ litigation, injunctions, and other legal strategies to make very real progress for the black community. Cesar Chavez and the farmworkers seem to have had a similar attitude. There is a long history of outsider groups seeing law in pragmatic terms, as sometimes legitimate and helpful, and at other times not."

"In more recent times, Critical Race theorists have been calling attention to the way this happens, not just in enforcement, police abuses, and the like, but also overtly in legal doctrine. They have been pointing out that wherever legal principles and rules conflict with the interests of the mighty, the law simply coins an 'exception.' In time, the loophole comes to be regarded as ordinary and usual, not even looked upon as an exception at all. Look at all the special doctrines the law has carved out in the free speech area.[30] These days, minorities, gays, and women are calling for hate-speech rules that would punish vicious name-calling and slurs. But our friends over at the ACLU consider this heresy and sue every university that enacts such a code. They argue that the First Amendment should be a seamless web, ignoring that we have literally dozens of exceptions that come into play in the case of speech that threatens powerful groups."

"I can think of several," Rodrigo said. "The wealthy and powerful are considered to have a kind of property interest in their reputation, so speech that damages them is compensable even though words are the sole means of causing the harm. And the same is true for words that violate a copyright, communicate a threat, form a monopoly, or constitute misleading advertising. Disrespectful words uttered to a judge, teacher, police officer, or other authority figure are also punishable, as are untruthful words uttered under oath or words that disseminate an official secret. Each of these exceptions or special doctrines exists to promote the interests of a powerful group such as the military or consumers."

"So, you are saying that the rule of law in all its majesty never holds for us, but always for our adversaries or for empowered groups?"

"In general, yes," Rodrigo said. "Business necessity is a valid excuse for discrimination. The police can search or arrest you without a warrant if they can show good faith, which sometimes takes the form of simply pointing out that you were a black man walking or standing in the wrong neighborhood. Discrimination is permissible if it cannot be proved intentional. And the tax code, as everyone knows, contains so many exceptions that many who earn over one million dollars a year are able to escape paying taxes altogether."[31]

"Your point, then, is that people of color should straightforwardly recognize that the law will often not protect them because it is designed to promote the interests of others, and that they should make the best of the situation."

"You and I were discussing normativity and the intensely civic-minded turn legal theory has taken recently.[32] While on the plane, it occurred to me that one of the main uses of normative discourse is to keep people like you and me from criticizing the rule of law. If everyone, including outsiders, can be made to revere the law, even when it is doing obvious and demonstrable harm, we will reason: 'Oh, well, it's a great institution, so we shouldn't criticize.' We'll agree to remain silent, fixating on the few times that legal institutions have really helped us . . ."

"Like the sixties," I said.

"Right," Rodrigo agreed. "And ignore that the rest of the time the law is either indifferent or positively injurious to our well-being. In no other area of human endeavor, with the possible exception of religion, do we succumb to such totalistic, all-or-nothing thinking. Imagine, for example, a butcher who sold rotted meat defending his action by saying, 'But I followed the procedure.' Or imagine a teacher, all of whose students failed standardized tests, insisting 'I taught them that.' In all these other areas we insist on results. Imagine the butcher defending his practice by saying that the institution of butchery does more good than harm. We'd call this the nonsense it is!"

"I see what you mean," I agreed. "Many have pointed out that procedure is something that bad men love and follow most assiduously. Kafka and other novelists wrote about that."

"So, minorities should invoke and follow the law when it benefits them and break or ignore it otherwise—when it gets in the way, is unresponsive, or is adverse to their interests. We should treat it like any other social institution, the highway department, for example. No one hesitates to call the highway department to task, to criticize it if it is always fixing the potholes on the other side of town and ignoring the ones in their neighborhood. No one speaks of the majesty of the rule of highway procedure or the grandeur of pothole fixing. If the department is doing its job, we leave it alone or give it a pat on the back. If it's not, we call it to account, or else work out some other way of getting the potholes fixed."

"Rodrigo, you are saying that social reformers should subsume law under their agenda, which is to achieve progress for minorities. Law-types approach things in just the opposite way, insisting on subsuming racial reform under law. Law people place law at the center, and then ask where racial justice should fit in. Should Martin Luther King be allowed to march in the face of an injunction? Should civil disobedience be countenanced? Should a white charged with discrimination be able to escape by showing a business necessity, or a lack of intent or causation?"

"I agree. We should demand the opposite—that race reform be placed in the center, following which we should ask where law fits in. That's the model I'm proposing, and does it not make just as much sense as the other approach?"

"It seems to me," I said, "that it all depends on what is uppermost in your mind, on what your objective is. The law-lover will subscribe to mythic, heroic views about the rule of law and insist that everything else be addressed within that framework. We, by contrast, will take a more utilitarian view of law, as the Panthers did. We'll ask: 'What can law do for us at this time and place?' "

"And that's the view I suggest under the rubric of 'legal instrumentalism.' We should demystify law, see it as the social institution it is: good for some things, less so for others. As we observed before, theory-fitting is everything. It makes no sense to use Gramsci[33] to help you prepare a budget, nor law and economics to try to make this a fairer world for excluded groups. We should avoid counsels of despair. But, by the same token, we should disavow failed liberal programs that achieve too little because they promise too much. Hence, legal instrumentalism: try everything until you find what works."

Rodrigo Defends Instrumentalism against the Charge That It Is Unprincipled

The waitress appeared at our table: "Would you gentlemen like some dessert?" Despite my doctor's orders to cut down, I looked up at Rodrigo inquiringly, as I very much wanted to prolong our session. His enthusiastic nod did much to allay my guilt. "You've been through a lot," I said. "Besides, I don't think they're serving supper on this make-up flight I'm taking in two hours." We both scrutinized the dessert menu, gave the waitress our orders (a sweet steamed bun for my high-energy young friend, an abstemious plate of mandarin orange slices for me), and returned to our conversation.

"Rodrigo, I love your theory. It's exactly what we need, both tactically and psychologically. As you pointed out, it has much honorable historical precedent. And, it squares with my sense of how law works to preserve the advantage of the powerful, accepts and takes account of that, and enables us to go on nevertheless. But perhaps your theory is something that we should not speak of too openly. Perhaps we should keep it in-group. Perhaps it should remain on the level of myth, as you spoke of before, and not be put out for public consumption."

"Why would we do that?" Rodrigo looked concerned.

"I meant no criticism of your theory as a way to interpret and organize experience. On that level, it's a fine insight. But won't mainstream scholars accuse you of cynicism, of weakening the social fabric? And won't they have a point? You do seem to be saying that obeying the law is not important, at least for minorities."

"I believe deeply in the social fabric," Rodrigo replied, suddenly solemn. "But I don't equate that with the law any more than I think we should equate society with the highway department, or with the institution of conscription. Each of these is a means to an end. Anyone who argued that we should venerate the highway department or the military draft would be seen as a little strange. I'm suggesting that we think of the law in the same way, and that for minorities, at least, there are even stronger reasons for doing so. None of us was at the Constitutional Convention, only three of us have been elected to the Senate, none to the presidency or vice-presidency, and there is not a single black CEO of a Fortune 500 company. Not to mention the way in which legal doctrine, the law on the books, as well as the law in action, are almost always arrayed against us."

I was silent as Rodrigo stole a look at the items on the tray of the waitress as she passed by our table. "Those look good. Too bad they're not for us," he continued. "Notice that large institutions never subscribe to the rule of law, at least never venerate it the way everyone tells minorities they are supposed to. A corporation that calculates that it is cheaper to market a product with a design defect the corporation knows will cause X injuries or Y deaths will often do so if it figures it can get away with it or that the cost of compensating the victims is cheaper than that of retooling its assembly line."[34]

"Or they reason that some members of the public won't sue. The victims may know they have been injured but not by whom.[35] They may not want to make trouble. Or they may fear that filing a lawsuit will take too long and cost too much money.[36] So a corporation that causes ten injuries may only be sued five times. The cost of repairs may be great enough that they simply decide to internalize the deaths, broken bones, and cases of cancer as costs of doing business," I added.

"Corporations are not the only ones who behave this way. Nations do as well. If a large power needs to take action to promote its interest, it will often do so even if this violates international law or a treaty to which it is a signatory.[37] In doing so, it realizes this will have a cost—that other nations will be resentful and not trust it so much in the future. It knows its action will weaken the tenuous compact among nations to be law-abiding, even when there is no superpower to enforce the rules. It knows these things, but factors them in as just another cost of its course of action, like the lives and airplanes that will be lost in the invasion or coup."

"Great political theorists, old and new, have recognized this: nations act in their own self-interest."[38]

"I'm sure we're thinking of the same people," Rodrigo added. "It only makes sense to approach civil rights law nonideologically. We should be zero-based and as dispassionate as possible, choosing legality when doing so will benefit us, and straightforwardly pursuing other means when it does not. Ideology, which includes the slavish devotion to law, always has costs. It prevents you from making alliances, from pursuing an avenue that might bring you benefit. Nietzsche thought that was its whole purpose.[39] He may have had a point."

"There's been some writing on a similar notion, namely that minorities ought to rethink their historic, and now near-reflexive, embrace of the Democratic Party,[40] one that has been yielding fewer and fewer gains. Some suggest that blacks should consider switching allegiance to the Republicans, at least to the moderate wing of that party. If the Democrats are allowed to think they can count on our vote no matter how diffidently they treat us, why should they not begin withdrawing from us and begin courting conservative whites?"

"Something like this seems actually to have happened," Rodrigo observed. "I wasn't here for most of the period you are describing, but I read of it in the Italian newspapers, which take a lively interest in U.S. affairs. And I read that article you are referring to."

"The zero-based one?"

"Yes. Oh, those look great!" The waitress had brought our desserts.

As she placed them in front of us I asked Rodrigo: "I hope we can get through at least two more matters before I have to head off. First, I'd like to know what thoughts you have on whether legal instrumentalism—which, by the way, I think is bound to draw fire from centrists and even from some of our friends—will not turn out to be just a phase, or moment, in civil rights history. As things improve for us, as society becomes more multicultural and demography shifts, will we not join the majority and then have a stake in proclaiming the rule of law as loudly as anybody else?" Rodrigo looked up dubiously. "And second, are there not risks in adopting such a calculating view of law? If one makes trades and compromises, is there not a danger that these things may come back to haunt one? Perhaps it's better to stick to principle, after all."

Rodrigo held up one finger as he chewed his bun.

"I know it's kind of a big order, all for dessert." Rodrigo snorted at the double entendre. "But maybe we could make a start. Actually, I've got"—I looked at my watch—"almost an hour. So, if you have the energy, why don't we start."

Rodrigo put down his fork and began.

Rodrigo Explains Why Self-Interest, Not Idealism, Is the Best Course for Minorities, and Why One Should Rarely Put Too Much Faith in Interest-Convergence with the Dominant Group

Why Self-Interest Is the Safest Course for Disempowered People

"We can only look to our own self-interest, Professor, and rarely to the altruism of the majority group because our social construction—the images and pictures of us that the majority culture disseminates and consumes—limits the amount of good will that comes our way. We discussed some of this before—the way in which the dominant society finds it convenient to depict us as lazy, criminal, lascivious, not very smart, and so on. Over time these pictures begin to seem like the truth, begin to seem real."

"Some whites escape those forces," I replied quietly. "Some of them are humane, generous, treat us as equals. You mentioned your thesis adviser, for one."

"True," Rodrigo conceded. "But I'm talking about politics, about large numbers. And when you look at that level—by which I mean the level of polls, attitudes, the ways the American people as a group look at race—you find something that I call 'guilt by definition.' "

"The term is new to me, but I think I know what you mean. We're a group whose very social construction inclines members of the majority race to fear us, to regard us as potential troublemakers, to cross the street when we approach them on the sidewalk at night, that sort of thing?"

"That is indeed part of it. We discussed this earlier when we talked about black and white crime.[41] But now I think that some of those earlier observations can be generalized into an argument for legal instrumentalism as the only sane approach to civil rights—for blacks and people of color, at any rate."

"Let me guess how that generalization might go," I said. "You are going to say that incessant characterization of blacks in demeaning terms means that the average member of society virtually equates any one of us with trouble. We come to be seen as absent fathers, welfare mothers, lazy office worker 'quota queens,' and so on. Once this sets in, we have little chance of appealing to the better natures of persons who hold this unconscious image of us. The image renders us 'Other.' It means people simply don't think of us as individuals to whom love, respect, generosity, and friendliness are due. We are 'beyond love,' as you and I discussed before.[42] The psychological experiments of helping behavior show this conclusively. A black female confederate spills a bag of groceries and only blacks will help her. A blond, blue-eyed woman does and everyone rushes to her aid. And the same with stranded motorists and other people in distress.[43] Is this the general mechanism you were thinking of?"

"Yes. And to anticipate your question, I do believe one can extrapolate from the personal to the political level—what is true of individuals is also true of groups. So that any theory of race must take into account this lack of good will or fellow-feeling. Do you have a garden, Professor?"

The question took me by surprise. "Yes, I have a small one. Not that I have been tending to it as much as I should. We had a much larger one before we moved here. What connection are you trying to make between gardening and civil rights?" I half winced, knowing of Rodrigo's penchant for colorful metaphors and extrapolations. It turned out that my fears were unfounded.

"If you've gardened, Professor, you know about the concept of weeds. A weed is any plant that a society deems undesirable, such as dandelions. Yet, in my home country, there are regions where dandelions grow wild, populate entire hillsides, and are regarded as rather beautiful."

"I remember," I said. "I was in your country not long ago. As you know, I spent last summer at a conference study center in northern Italy. While there, I drove through the Dolomite mountains in the late spring. The fields of bright yellow dandelions were very beautiful."

"Racial features are like weeds and dandelions. There is no DNA divide that separates common weeds, like thistles, dandelions, and clover on the one hand, from fine grasses and flowers on the other. The category is constructed and varies from society to society. The same is true of race. Our facial features, skin color, and hair do not set us apart in any important way from white people, who according to scientists share virtually all of their genetic makeup with us.[44] We are the same species. It is only because society chooses to regard the small physical differences between blacks and whites as marking out different races that we even construct such categories instead of some other ones, such as heavily eyebrowed persons versus thinly eyebrowed persons or something similar."[45]

"But we do, and the categories come loaded. We place value judgments on them—they are not neutral," I said, building on Rodrigo's observation. "We notice color not just as a curiosity, as a minor difference of no great importance, but in order to organize society, to assign people to statuses. You and I are the weeds, they the flowers."

"Our very category implies that we are one-down, the sort of people whom majority society can afford to give disparate, and usually worse, treatment, all with impunity and while feeling perfectly ethical about it.[46] Therefore, we need to tend our own gardens. My approach—legal instrumentalism—is simply radical individualism applied to the racial predicament. If our construction were different, this approach might not be necessary. But because of our history and culture, because of how we were brought here, the institutions of slavery, conquest, Bracero programs, racist immigration quotas, and so on that kept minority populations suppressed for years, it is. In a way, it's like the bootstrapping and self-help approaches that neoconservatives like Sowell and Loury have been urging, but for different reasons." [47]

"The negative images may change, may even now be changing," I said, determined to play the devil's advocate as long as possible. "In every era, some mainstream writers or moviemakers take our side, depict us sympathetically. The image may in time be supplanted by a more nuanced, humane one."

"I know," Rodrigo conceded. "The trouble is that our defenders tend to have no audience. Their work is seen as political, as 'message' pieces.[48] It is only later, after consciousness changes, that we see that they were right after all. Harriet Beecher Stowe's abolitionist novel sold well only after decades of activism had sensitized the American public to the possibility that slavery might be wrong.[49] Nadine Gordimer won the Nobel Prize only when her country was on the verge of repudiating apartheid. And have you heard of the role of 'attestors,' Professor?"

I strained, trying to remember where I had recently read about such a thing. "Does it have to do with authentication of the slave narratives?" I asked.

"It may arise there," Rodrigo said. "But I was reading about it in connection with the work of some early African-American poets."

"Oh yes, now I remember," I said. "Phillis Wheatley was one. Didn't the American publishing world refuse to believe that she, a onetime slave, actually wrote certain collections of poems?"[50]

"Exactly. Several Bostonians, including the governor of Massachusetts and John Hancock, had to step in. They knew Ms. Wheatley and testified that she indeed had written the poems in question. Most others in American letters did not believe an African-American woman was capable of such a thing. But the odd thing is that the attestors themselves were not poets at all, whereas Wheatley had gained recognition in Boston and in England for her poetry. It's like going to the local mayor for confirmation that Alexander the Great was really a major political figure."

"And you think the presence of attestors shows something about our social quandary?"

"It does. Attestors wouldn't be necessary if we had an equal chance to be recognized on our own merits. And when society today hears from, say, Frank Michelman or Gary Peller that minority work is good, it comes as a surprise, like hearing a scientist say that a certain kind of common weed in your garden might be good."

"I believe you had said earlier that the situation today is even worse than it's been, that we are more ensconced as weeds now than in recent years."

Rodrigo smiled at my use of his metaphor. "I did. Not only are we one-down, we are on the defensive when we merely want to rise, want to change our position. Affirmative action, under which a paltry few of us get hired, has come under attack as unprincipled and an affront to innocent whites.[51] Our poverty is seen as a choice, as something we enjoy or wallow in, as evidence of the pathological nature of our culture, values, or family structure. Our demands for justice are seen as requests for entitlements, for things we don't deserve."[52]

"Consider the whole 'political correctness' movement," I suggested.

"A prime case. Our detractors apply the term to those who are merely asking for a slight modification in the canon, the list of books that are taught at universities. It's applied to those who ask for ethnic studies courses or departments in universities that offer hundreds of other courses of study, to those who ask for controls on vicious slurs like 'nigger,' 'kike,' 'spic,' and 'fag.' The conservatives who wield the term put us on the defensive, as though we were nags pursuing petty concerns."

"Yet their label has certainly caught on," I conceded ruefully.

"Despite its disreputable history. I wonder why nobody has pointed this out. Political correctness is little more than a modern, sanitized, prettified version of an old term. It means one who sympathizes with the blacks, who takes their point of view."

"I'm sure we both know what word you mean," I said.

"Nigger lover," Rodrigo replied with distaste. "That's what it comes down to. Although it's naturally a sanitized version, that's what it means. Those who use it ought to be ashamed of themselves. Yet they are not, which proves my point about our current estate. Most of our defenders, most liberals, do not identify the term for what it is, but rather back away from the accusation. 'Oh, no,' they say. 'I'm not being politically correct, I just . . .' "

"Just like in the old days," I observed wryly.

Just then the waiter arrived to ask if we wanted anything else. Rodrigo moved to get out his credit card, but I said, "Please let me. The airline said they'd pay. I have this voucher because of the canceled flight. Would you like some coffee?"

"Do we have time?" Rodrigo asked.

"I do. And I'm looking forward to hearing about that last point you promised to address. Two coffees, please—one decaf, the other . . . ?"

"Do you have espresso?" Rodrigo asked. The waitress nodded. "A double please."

Rodrigo Explains Why His Plan Is Better than Interest-
Convergence, Which Can Easily Lead Reformers to Take the
Short View and Make Sacrifices That Turn Out to Be Unwise

"I forgot to say regular," Rodrigo said with a slightly worried look on his face. "I've noticed that more and more places are selling decaffeinated espresso, which I consider practically a contradiction in terms, like a nice weed."

I looked at my animated, rail-thin young friend with his exuberant manner and said, "Don't worry, I have a feeling she'll bring you the high-octane kind. If not, we can send it back. I did order decaf, but that's no reason she should assume you'd want the same."

Rodrigo was silent for a moment, then looked up. "Oh yes, I remember the last point. It has to do with a serious disadvantage of the interest-convergence approach. I don't want to be too critical. My approach is intended to reconcile the best of interest-convergence and the excessive and unwarranted optimism of liberal civil rights theory. So, in a way, legal instrumentalism includes interest-convergence as a special case and doesn't really contradict it."

"Never mind," I said. "Criticizing their elders is what young people do. Everyone expects it. People like Bell and me have come in for much worse criticism than what I imagine you are likely to deliver. So, get on with it. Do you mean that interest-convergence sends you looking for the rare miracle—the one moment in a decade or century when white and black interests coincide—and leaves you without direction the rest of the time?"

"It does have that drawback," Rodrigo said. "But I think there's a more serious one that Bell, for all his brilliance, did not see." Rodrigo paused.

"I do want to hear it. I never thought I would accuse you of being too respectful, and here you are holding back. Besides, I've got to catch a plane in"—I glanced at my watch—"less than forty minutes. They could announce my flight any time now."

The waiter arrived with our coffees. "Decaf for you, Professor," she said. "And the real thing for you," she added, smiling. I wondered idly how she knew I was a professor.

"Mmmmm. This is good," Rodrigo said, slurping his espresso. "I'm glad you suggested this." Then, after allowing me to take a sip of my own brew, he continued as follows.

"You know how the few great ringing victories—the sort of thing that happens once a decade or so, like *Brown v. Board of Education*[53]—have a way of slipping away, cut back by narrow interpretation, obstruction, or delay?"[54]

"Of course. Bell and others have pointed out that more black schoolchildren attend predominantly black schools now than was the case forty years ago, when the Supreme Court decided *Brown*.[55] The South mounted real resistance; in the North many white families simply moved away. Courts eventually decided that segregation that results from housing patterns is irreparable.[56] Education is not a fundamental interest,[57] nor poverty a suspect class,[58] so that property-rich school districts may offer first-rate educations while poor ones have much less to offer. Our youth suffer suspension, dropout, and assignment to special-education tracks and classes at rates that ought to be a national embarrassment."[59]

Rodrigo agreed. "We seem destined, as Bell puts it, for periodic peaks of progress followed by valleys of regression. Once every blue moon the stars line up, and the system grants us a seeming victory for reasons of its own . . ."

"Such as Cold War politics, as Mary Duziak and Bell have noted," I interjected.[60]

"And other reasons, too," Rodrigo continued. "And in a way this points out a deficiency with the interest-convergence theory for understanding racial politics. It can deceive you into thinking the convergence will last longer and prove more stable than it will, when in fact the stars have only found themselves lined up for a moment, like in an eclipse. But a more serious problem," Rodrigo continued, "is that one can easily take the short-term view and get so caught up with capturing and exploiting the approaching convergence that one gives away a long-term asset of inestimable value."

"Do you mean that we can become so hungry for a victory, so anxious for some sign of progress that we leap to the bait regardless of whether we should?" I didn't quite get Rodrigo's drift and hoped he would explain.

"Let me give an example from recent history," he said. "Recall the period just before *Brown v. Board of Education*. Everyone knows that we were then in the early stages of the Cold War. Russia had emerged as a world power. We were engaged in a worldwide struggle for the loyalties of the uncommitted Third World."

"Most of which was black, brown, or Asian," I added.

"Indeed, Bell's thesis holds that is the reason why the U.S. establishment intervened on behalf of civil rights. It would hardly do for us to be maintaining that our system was better than godless communism when the front pages of newspapers around the world carried stories and pictures of lynchings, cross burnings, whites-only drinking fountains, and the Emmett Till murder."[61]

"So, according to Bell, the American establishment pushed for civil rights breakthroughs, not to advance black interests, but their own. Mary Dudziak recently confirmed Bell's hypothesis through an analysis of State Department and other government documents, which showed that the U.S. Attorney General finally decided to throw its weight behind the NAACP Legal Defense Fund only when the State Department sent it various urgent messages requesting that it do so."[62]

"And so we got *Brown*," I added.

"And singing and dancing in the streets followed by disappointment a few years later when we learned the decision was scarcely going to restructure American society or even benefit that many black school kids."

"And you think that instrumentalism avoids this mistake?" I asked.

"I think excessive optimism is always a risk with a group that has been excluded, that has been down so long. But instrumentalism at least points us in the right direction, gets us to ask the right questions: Will this strategy work? What will happen to this breakthrough a few months or years later? If we put X dollars into litigation this year, will the Supreme Court reward us, with what, and for how long? Interest-convergence just tells you that this may (or may not) be the time to strike. One should always look further down the line and ask what the practical effect of anything will be."

"That seems to me quite useful," I observed. "But does it amount to anything more than reminding ourselves that 'interest' ought to be seen longitudinally, as a long-term thing? Smart revolutionaries do that now."

Rodrigo winced. "Touché. But let me go on a bit. Perhaps instrumentalism—the theory that one ought to resort to law in the way one would resort to any tool, like the yellow pages, only when it promises concrete benefits—does indeed offer a more fruitful approach than either of the principal alternatives."

"Just a minute," I said, indicating that I had heard something. We were silent a moment while I absorbed a message coming through on the loudspeaker. "Oh, no," I groaned. "Another twenty-minute delay. Well, at least my flight seems to be coming in, even if it's late. Take your time, then. My gate is only two or three down the concourse, and I'm already checked in."

"My point is cautionary only. The idea is that you must always be careful about pursuing interest convergence with the dominant group, because in your eagerness you can easily give away the store, sacrifice something of too great value. The dominant group gives you what you wanted, but the value of what you've gained quickly erodes, so that you have little left in the long run, and in the meantime you have forfeited something even more precious."

"I assume you are thinking of more than the thousands of hours of gallant lawyering and tens of thousands of dollars in legal costs that went into bringing about the *Brown* victory?"

"Those as well as human costs of a different sort. They have to do with self-definition. If a community begins to think of itself in terms of its relation to a different community, it may start to lose its sense of itself, who it is. If we and our folks are constantly placing ourselves in the mind-set of powerful white folks, trying to see what they will want, how they will factor us in, trying to stage-manage interest convergence, we can easily start to change not just what we want, but who we are. Human beings are coterminous with their social surroundings. Our identities largely derive from whom we identify with, whom we try to please, whom we empathize with imaginatively. In some respects, the black community is safeguarded from overidentification with the majority of society because of the way the majority regards us."

"As we discussed earlier," I commented.

"Right. But some of us do have a tendency to try to identify with them. They have all the power, can dispense rewards, control who is seen as beautiful, smart, acceptable, and so on."

"It's a trap all subordinated people can fall into," I said. "Psychologists call it identification with the aggressor.[63] A milder term is assimilation."

"And so this can easily happen. But a more serious problem arises from another means by which groups define themselves and change their contours: expulsion. At any given time, a subordinated group has leaders, theorists who rail against the group's mistreatment and are able to articulate it. These may be writers, playwrights, or Marxists—persons with an acute understanding of the group's condition and a fervent commitment to changing it."

"And you're saying that a minority group bent on pursuing the interest-convergence strategy may too easily jettison, too easily ostracize geniuses such as these?"

"There have been many examples. In our day, there could soon be more."

"Could you give me an example?" I asked.

"Two recent leaders who come to mind are Paul Robeson[64] and W. E. B. Du Bois.[65] Both were major figures, extremely serious losses. Both died in bitterness and sorrow, effectively cut off from their communities—purged, really.[66] All this happened because black leaders decided, in the late 1940s and early 1950s, that they were too radical, had too many ties with the Soviet Union.[67] Du Bois, in particular, was a giant figure, yet he was expelled from the NAACP, an organization he had helped found decades earlier, only to be later reinstated, but relegated to a minor role.[68] Both men were casualties of the Cold War, pure and simple. Our community expelled them, traded them in hopes of presenting a purified, sanitized, non-Communist front. The strategy worked—it brought about *Brown v. Board of Education*. But in one way of looking at it, it was not worth the price. *Brown* quickly faded, while the penetrating critiques these two figures had to offer were muffled and lost. It was not until the advent of the Black Panthers and of Malcolm X decades later that anything approaching a radical critique of American institutions and racism sprang up again. We sold our birthright for a mess of pottage."

"And you think this is inherent in interest-convergence philosophy?"

"No, not inherent. But it is an ever-present and very real risk. If you place momentary interest and alignment with the major power players as your first priority, what is to stop you from sacrificing your leaders, your young, or anything else that stands in the way, for that matter?"

"I see what you are saying. Instrumentalism at least makes you stop and ask whether the action you are taking has long-term costs. It also prompts you to think whether the more powerful interest group you are trying to get to act in certain ways may not at the same time be seeing you in instrumental terms. The approach's radical individualism reminds you that others may not have your interests at heart, a useful thing for subordinated groups to keep in mind. You are less inclined to tell a towering figure like W. E. B. Du Bois he or she is not needed anymore. By the way, you seem to have been reading up on this period in history. Was Du Bois's banishment merely a coup within the NAACP, or broader than that?"

"Much broader," Rodrigo replied soberly. "The entire black community was turning to the right, just as America was jumping aboard the anti-Communist bandwagon, McCarthy was holding hearings, and people were seeing Communists under every bed. Before that time, the African-American community had been quite receptive to radicalism. Marxists and labor unionists had been given places of honor. Paul Robeson even traveled to the Soviet Union. Then the tide changed. African-American newspapers, ministers, and other leaders began speaking out against communism, began urging black people to rekindle their patriotism, join the army, and so on, in hopes of securing better treatment as a race. If successful, it was only marginally so. The fifties were not a good period for us, and the sixties, although a time of breakthroughs, established little in the way of a lasting foundation. Yet we lost the beginnings of radicalism, and, as a result, today we are flailing about trying to find out where to start, how to see our condition anew."

My reverie was disturbed by an urgent message: my flight was boarding right now. With a start, I realized I must have missed the boarding announcement in my fascination with Rodrigo's story.

"Is that your flight?" Rodrigo asked.

"Unfortunately, yes," I replied, scrambling to pick up my things. "Will you give the cashier this voucher? It should take care of everything. It's been stimulating as always, Rodrigo. I'll call you when I get back, okay?"

We shook hands quickly, wished each other well, and three minutes later I was fastening my safety belt in preparation for takeoff.

As the plane banked steeply and gained altitude I wondered why, after forty years of civil rights scholarship, it was left to Rodrigo, a mere youth of twenty-five years or so, to hit upon such an obvious solution as legal instrumentalism. Did it have something to do with Dewey, whom Rodrigo recently had described to me as a much-neglected, and very brilliant, philosopher? I realized that Dewey had written that experience and problem situations were what called upon and enabled people to develop intelligence. In that sense, all the brilliant constitutional scholars I had read would be unlikely to have come up with Rodrigo's insight. Not experiencing racial injustice as immediately or acutely as a black such as Rodrigo, they might not think as probingly, as clear-headedly, or as urgently as one who has suffered such bigotry. I wondered if this solved the problem of "racial voice" and justified resisting imperial scholarship, the domination of civil rights theory deplored by some minority-race writers. Did it validate the unique insights of scholars of color, or were we just as likely to succumb to the intellectual and moral sins of sloth, lazy thinking, cowardice, and co-optation as anyone else?

Once again, I realized what good fortune I had to be a teacher, exposed to minds such as Rodrigo's. I pulled down the tray table from the seat in front of me and prepared to work on the speech I was to deliver the next day, taking pleasure in the thought that Rodrigo was not unique—many African-American students and junior faculty had the same talent, the same insight of my friend and protégé—that there were many Rodrigos, all of them growing up, waiting to take their places in the world.

Merit and Affirmative Action

In Which Rodrigo and I Meet by Chance at the New Professors' Conference and I Learn of a Recent Event at His School

I had just put down my papers from the talk that, as one of three graybeards, I had just given to a roomful of eager new professors when a familiar face materialized in front of me.

"Rodrigo! I didn't see you in the room. Where were you sitting?"

"Over there," my young friend and protégé replied, "behind Henry Abercrombie. He's a giant—I'm not surprised you didn't see me. That was a great talk."

"Thanks," I said. "They called me up at the last minute. I didn't have much time to prepare. Have you been here for the entire conference?"

"I have. I missed it last year. But my dean is good about paying for this sort of thing. She sent both of us new professors—Barney, over there, and me."

"It's a lot different than when I was starting out," I said. "We were sent straight into the classroom with the casebook and our notes. It was sink or swim—no teachers' manuals, no conferences like this one, and often no older hands to give us advice. Most of us were the only professors of color at our schools. Do you have any company in that respect at your school?"

"Barney is Asian," Rodrigo said. "We get along great, even though he teaches tax. And there's Elaine, the assistant dean. She's black and teaches professional responsibility."

"Not bad," I replied. "But this session looks like it's breaking up." I pointed to the crowd starting to straggle out of the auditorium. The conference staff was already busy changing the name tags on the speakers' table in preparation for the next session. "Do you want to go somewhere for a drink or a bite to eat?"

"I'd love to," Rodrigo replied with alacrity. "I got up early for the constitutional law session and missed breakfast. I was going to go to the one on networking, but I'd much rather talk with you."

As we filed out of the conference room, I asked Rodrigo how he liked his new job.

"It's great," he said. "I love the students. I'm teaching two new preps, but I have this terrific research assistant. It looks as if we may actually get some writing done. Maybe you and I can talk about that later. But something curious happened just last week that I'd like your opinion on. Perhaps we could discuss it over dinner."

"I'm famished," I said. "Public speaking always does that to me. Have you found a good place to eat around here?"

"There's a decent sandwich shop up on the mezzanine. But yesterday Barney and a few of us went to this little Middle Eastern restaurant a couple of blocks away. The food is good and the prices reasonable. I think they start serving dinner at five."

"Middle Eastern sounds good to me," I said. "So, what happened at your school?"

Rodrigo fell silent for a moment as we rode down in the elevator in the company of a few strangers and one of my acquaintances. When we got out, he continued. "It concerns the way I got appointed. I'm not worried or upset. But I thought it was curious and made a note to ask you about it sometime. By the way, did you know you were not listed on the program?"

"I spoke last year," I explained, "but this year they had a last-minute cancelation. I agreed to help them out, and now I'm glad I did. I'll get to do two of my favorite things—eat Middle Eastern food and talk with you!"

We set out down the crowded city sidewalk. "I can vouch for the food," Rodrigo said, "but I don't know how much you'll get out of the conversation because it'll be mostly about me. The incident did get me thinking, though, about the whole issue of merit. We've talked about this a little before,[1] but my thoughts have gone further, thanks to the incident I'm about to recount."

"I'm sure you'll notice this, Rodrigo, if you haven't found it out already. We older hands get just as much from our younger colleagues as they do from us. Our conversations over this last year have stimulated many thoughts in my mind, and not a few publications. Sometimes I think *you're* the mentor and I'm the pupil."

Rodrigo waved aside the compliment. "What happened concerns a colleague of mine named Kowalsky—an interesting guy from a poor background. He's got a brilliant law school record and terrific publications despite being in only his third year of teaching. Kowalsky came to my office the other day. It's no secret that he's conservative—the sponsor of the Federalist Society at my school, in fact. But he's a nice guy. When I started teaching, he offered me his teaching notes and tried to be really helpful."

"So, what did you learn from your conservative and presumably Polish friend?"

"That my appointment was part of the school's affirmative action policy. They call it a special opportunity appointment. Nobody had bothered to mention this to me, not even the dean, during the discussions leading up to my appointment. Kowalsky dropped this bombshell in the course of a discussion we were having on affirmative action and then was taken aback and apologetic when he discovered that I hadn't known about it already. He had offered my appointment as an example of the way affirmative action works. He pointed out that he himself had not been eligible for a special appointment even though his own parents emigrated to this country when he was two, were poor, and lived in a rough neighborhood. Meanwhile, I, as an African American, was eligible for preferential treatment."

"Sounds like the two of you must have had a—how shall I say?—tense conversation. I hope it came out that your own credentials are also quite impressive."

"He already knew that. And it was tense for a minute. Then I told him that I saw no problem with my being hired that way if the school used the special funds that the president's office was making available to hire an additional professor that they otherwise would not have been able to hire."

"In other words, you didn't displace anyone, not even the prover-bial more highly qualified white," I said. "And did that get you off the hook with Kowalsky?"

"More or less. At any rate, we went on to have a good talk about affirmative action and merit. He kept insisting that, present com-pany excepted, affirmative action is unprincipled because it gives the edge to someone on the basis of a morally irrelevant factor, namely race. He also worried that it would end up stigmatizing even profes-sors of color like myself because everyone would assume we had inferior credentials and did not really deserve our professorships. It also could cause tensions between whites and blacks because the former would assume that whenever they lost out on an appoint-ment, job, or other opportunity, it must have been because a black or other minority person won out."[2]

"These are the standard arguments," I observed. "And as you know, they all have answers.[3] Oh, here we are." We were both silent as we entered the small, homey restaurant. The maitre d' ushered us to a booth decorated with Persian bric-a-brac.

We seated ourselves, and Rodrigo continued as follows:

"I know, and I gave them. But then the conversation took a differ-ent turn. He cited an argument I had heard mentioned, in D'Souza and elsewhere, that the multiculturalism movement, not racism, is driving the recent wave of racist incidents, graffiti, and name calling on campuses.[4] According to this view, minority groups who are call-ing for theme houses, special dormitories, and antihate-speech rules are misdiagnosing the situation. They have only themselves to blame—or, more precisely, affirmative action—and the cure is less, not more, of what they demand.[5] This, in turn, led to a discussion of the whole idea of merit, but we were cut off when we both had to go to a faculty meeting."

I made a face. "Now *there's* an institution whose merit really ought to come under scrutiny. And I gather you've had some further thoughts on the whole question—merit, I mean?"

"I have. Do you have time to listen? Oh, here comes our waiter."

We immersed ourselves in the menu while the waiter stood pa-tiently. We gave our orders—kabob for Rodrigo, vegetarian couscous for me—and then continued as follows.

In Which Rodrigo and I Explore the Connection between Markets and Merit

"Professor, have you ever noticed how conservatives seem to love the First Amendment?"

"I have. But not only them. Lots of old-line constitutionalists, including some who consider themselves liberal, do too. We talked a little about this once before. You see this strange alliance form over hate-speech codes. Conservatives like Dinesh D'Souza hate them, of course.[6] But they have allies in moderately leftist, progressive organizations like the ACLU.[7] Every time a college thinks of enacting such a code to protect minorities and gays against the tide of vicious insults and name calling that has been welling up these days, the conservatives say that Western civilization is ending, and the ACLU files suit. It's an odd alliance, somewhat like the way the religious right and radical feminists often find themselves on the same side fighting pornography, but, of course, in reverse."

"Politics makes strange bedfellows," Rodrigo added. "Is that how the expression goes?"

Rodrigo, who had spent the last half of his life growing up in Italy, sometimes misused an expression or idiom.[8] But this time I nodded. "Exactly right. And what moral do you draw from this, Rodrigo?"

After a moment of thought, Rodrigo replied, "I wonder if you saw the recent *New Republic* cover story that asked, 'Is the First Amendment Racist?' "[9] I indicated that I had. "The author's answer, of course, was no and that minorities and others clamoring for hate-speech regulations are deeply misguided."

"And I gather that you think that it is—racist, I mean?"

"Not inherently," Rodrigo responded. "But I do find intriguing the way in which conservatives and traditionalists, people who basically don't want blacks changing their position too rapidly (at least as a group), are enamored of the First Amendment. Consider that throughout history, top satirists and commentators have scrupulously reserved their sharpest slings and arrows for the high and mighty, for kings and other public officials who abused their power, and so on. Never, or rarely, did they use their wit to put down the halt, the lame, and the poor."[10]

(Ah, he knows that idiom, I thought. He catches on fast.)

"A root word of humor is humus," I interjected. "Like earth.

Humor brings the powerful down to earth. That's a principal function of satire. The Roman emperors employed slaves to follow them during victory parades and celebrations, whispering, 'Thou art but a man.' Nobility of all ages employed jesters to mock their mannerisms and prevent them from becoming too enamored of themselves. But I gather you think all this has something to do with the First Amendment."

"It does. The First Amendment is a marketplace mechanism, like many others. One of its functions is to assure that life's victors continue winning—in this case, speaking more effectively than others and thereby convincing themselves that their positions are right, the best. The top satirists, Molière, Swift, Twain, and in more modern times, columnists like Russell Baker, have carefully avoided making fun of the poor, minorities, and those of lower station and power than themselves. These individuals are already lowly, like humus, down to earth. But the First Amendment can't capture this simple moral intuition. Indeed, I believe one of its functions is to blind us to this asymmetry, to the way in which vituperative speech aimed at the poor, gays, or minorities stands on a very different moral footing from criticism of government or the powerful."

"The First Amendment treats all speech alike. You have just as much right to criticize the Italian or U.S. government as a campus bully has to tell you to go back to Africa."

"An example of decontextualized, neutrality-based jurisprudence, as we discussed before," I added. "And deeply mistaken."

"One could argue," Rodrigo added, "that this type of perverse application of First Amendment principles violates the equality principle. It makes us dumb, deprives us of the ability to see differences that matter, like the one I just mentioned. Treating unequals as though they were equal is just as much a violation of equality as treating equals unequally. It also enables life's winners to think they won fair and square. When the campus bully notices that next year there are fewer blacks on campus because they have dropped out or transferred to a less racist institution . . ."

"Like Morehouse," I ventured.

"Exactly," Rodrigo continued. "Resegregation is a real problem. Black colleges are increasing enrollment just as the numbers of black students in large, white-dominated colleges are declining.[11] Parents of color are opting to send their sons and daughters to historically black colleges where the climate will be less racist. And one of the reasons is the reign of terror and catcalls that our First Amendment purist friends insist continue unabated."

"A friend of mine is doing that very thing," I mused. "Sending his kid to Morehouse, that is. Yet our ACLU friends insist that hate speech remain unregulated. The First Amendment must be a seamless web.[12] But we were talking about merit. I assume you think there is a connection."

"Oh yes," Rodrigo resumed, furrowing his brow slightly. "Let me bring myself back on track. I was going to make the point that all formalist devices, like merit, free speech, and the economic free market of trades and exchanges, serve a similar purpose. They decontextualize the transaction and so enable the powerful to exclude from consideration past actions, like slavery and female subjugation, that have effects even today which prevent some from entering the competition on equal terms.[13] In fact, the First Amendment is a special case of merit. The guarantee is designed to winnow out meritorious from nonmeritorious speech and ideas. Supposedly, through a clash of ideas, the truth, the most robust idea of all, will emerge.[14] Thus, if one culture is dominant, it must deserve to be that way. Our ideas competed against those other, more easygoing, ones and won. It was a fair fight. Merit serves the same function in slightly different spheres."

"It does this by consolidating advantage. Any society's elite class will deem what they do well as constitutive of merit, thus assuring that their own positions become even more secure. Merit is a resource attractor. Those who have it make more money and gain more power. They use that money and power to purchase more increments of merit for themselves and their children."[15]

"The rich get richer."

"Not always," I interjected. "They send their children to the best schools, where some flunk out. But others go on to be rich. The gap between the haves and the have-nots gets greater every generation, one reason being this host of seemingly neutral market-type mechanisms that assure that everyone has exactly the same chance—all the while ignoring that it takes a microphone to speak effectively, a college education to become a neurosurgeon, and so on."

"Merit supplies a defense to an equal protection challenge," Rodrigo added. "If society decides to distribute a good to A and not to B, courts will sustain this decision if the government can show that A had more merit than B, that A was more deserving. But what you are saying is that the preexisting level of merit may be skewed, and that supposedly neutral mechanisms prevent us from seeing this."

"Not only seeing, but even looking for it," I replied. "There is no reason to. If A is more deserving of the job than B, why should we even inquire into how he or she came to deserve it? He may have had greater opportunities than B, may have had more solicitous parents or teachers. Better-known people may have written him letters of recommendation. When he was a teenager, perhaps he got a summer job or internship through a family connection. A friendly teacher may have proposed an extra credit assignment that enabled him to change a B plus into an A minus, or helped him get into an honors section of a class that an equally talented black or working class kid might not have gotten into."

"Yet white people do not see it that way," Rodrigo replied. "Anytime a black gets into a special program or a law school by means of an affirmative action program, they are certain that *this* is an affront to principle, that it is unfair to innocent whites. Even our liberal defenders consider affirmative action a perilous program, designed to work for a short time only. They regard it as fraught with many risks, such as the stigmatization of able blacks."

"So Rodrigo," I summarized, "you think there are two kinds of racism. The old kind is overt and takes the form of laws and social practices that expressly treat blacks and others of color worse than whites. This type of racism might be typified by whites-only drinking fountains, or university admissions practices at many schools that excluded all but a handful of blacks until about 1965. But there is another kind evident in facially neutral laws and practices that require the decision maker to ignore history, context, and things that everybody knows are important. And you think that merit is a prominent example of such a mechanism, along with others that take the form of market-type, hands-off fairness."

I paused to see what Rodrigo would say. He nodded, but quickly added: "I know what you're going to say, Professor. I've made only a start. And you're right. Kowalsky pointed that out—my argument is merely formal. I must go on and give affirmative reasons why merit often serves dishonorable ends. He kept saying that merit *could* deflect us from seeing important things, including those that lie in the past. But he said that he didn't think there were many such things today, and that, on balance, a merit-based scheme is apt to be fairer to minorities than one that relies on discretion, like affirmative action. He said my categories were not exclusive, and that he personally knew people without a racist bone in their bodies who nevertheless believed in merit. He also pointed out how his father and mother rose from abject poverty. He kept saying he meant no offense to me, but affirmative action could only produce lazy, unmotivated beneficiaries—and sullen, resentful whites convinced that minorities are responsible for every setback and defeat they suffer in life.[16] He also inquired whether I felt stigmatized on account of the way I was hired and seemed surprised when I said no."

"Of course, you did graduate near the top of your class at the oldest law school in the world, have an LL.M. degree from a top U.S. institution, and are the winner of two competitions for student writing.[17] Still, Kowalsky sounds like a great foil."

Rodrigo waved aside my attempt at praise. "Laz keeps me on my toes, makes me think—just as you do, Professor. Oh, and did I mention that he's not opposed to speech codes? He says racist speech is disgusting and has nothing to do with the First Amendment—like many conservatives, he also supports regulating pornography. All this even though he opposes affirmative action and thinks it lies at the root of all our current troubles. If you've got the time, I could run past you some things I've been thinking about in the wake of our discussion."

I nodded enthusiastically, reminding my brilliant young protégé, once again, how much I got out of our conversations. I sat back expectantly.

Rodrigo's Three Reasons Why Merit Often Serves Dishonorable Ends, Advances Racism, and Deepens Minorities' Predicament

"My thoughts mainly have to do with the connection Kowalsky persuaded me to make between merit and discrimination. Why don't we take them up one by one. Oh, here's our food!" We were silent while the waiter served our sumptuous-looking dinners.

"This looks great," Rodrigo said. "Usually I like trying different restaurants, but this one was so good last time I'm glad I came back."

When I beamed my own approval, he continued: "As I mentioned, my arguments fall into three groups. One set of considerations is analytical and has to do with the way merit operates, on a discursive and conceptual level, to strengthen the hand of the powerful at the expense of the disempowered. A second has to do with the after-the-fact quality of neutral, marketplace-type mechanisms, that is, the way they enable life's winners to justify the status quo. They are almost impossible to apply evenhandedly. And a final critique is historical, consisting of showing connections between today's merit-ocrats and those of former, more racist times. How's your couscous?"

Rodrigo's First Argument: Merit's Invisible Nonformality and the Way This Guarantees the Continued Ascendancy of Elite Groups

"Great, for vegetarian fare," I replied. "You probably know my doctor told me to cut down on meat. It's hard, especially when you're traveling. So I'm glad you brought me here. Even in my old meat-eating days I loved Middle Eastern food."

Rodrigo gave me a sympathetic look. "Giannina is mostly vegetarian, too. So, I have some idea of what you're going through. Want to hear the first argument?"

"Whenever you're ready," I said, taking a forkful of my steaming hot concoction.

"The first problem I have with the idea of merit has to do with its majoritarian quality. Writers contributing to the critique of normativity in legal thought, among others, have pointed this out.[18] Merit is what the victors impose.[19] No conquering people ever took a close look at the conquered, their culture, ways, and appearance, and pronounced them superior to their own versions. Those in power always make that which they do best the standard of merit. This is true at all times in history, including our own. The SAT, for example, has test items about toboggans, lacrosse, polo, and other activities prominent in white, middle-, and upper-class culture.[20] Graduate programs often emphasize linear, rationalistic thought over other kinds, and so on."

"There's the famous chitlins test,"[21] I mused, half-seriously, wondering if Rodrigo, who grew up in Italy but was half African American, had heard of such a thing.

He smiled appreciatively and went on. "Not only does this aspect of merit disadvantage the poor, minorities, and anyone else whose upbringing and experience differ from the norm, it also can disadvantage women, many of whom have strengths and approaches that differ from those of their equally talented and successful male counterparts. A man might choose to sit down with a calculator and a legal pad while a woman might start by thinking and talking about a decision with others. The man might believe that the logic stemming from his own reasoning skills can solve the problem without consultation with others. He might also believe that he and the others around him will be similarly affected by the decision he makes. A woman, on the other hand, may tend to believe that a collective decision is the most likely to succeed and to be accepted by others, who may or may not be touched by the decision in the same way that she is. But because men tend to be in charge of most things in this world, including hiring and admissions decisions, they will look for the logical and analytical skills that have worked for them. Not surprisingly, they will find these skills predominantly in other men. When a woman has those skills that men deem important, she will, of course, be hired, but only because she has this male-defined set of skills. Frequently the woman's skills will include the ability to read and understand the people she has to work with and to motivate coworkers and subordinates. These abilities are necessary for the smooth operation of the workplace and the campus, but it is often left to chance that they will reside in the same people who possess the level of logical and analytical skills demanded by the evaluative committees. Therefore, imposition of the male standard not only discriminates against women, it also robs the group or institution of the diversity that makes it effective."

"I think you and I discussed something similar before," I said, straining to remember.[22] "Did we not agree that two candidates, one white and one black—or one male, one female, for that matter—will often compete for the same position? Both are equally capable of doing a stellar job. But the interview, or job test, rewards the candidate who has the greatest store of cultural capital, the one who soaked it up so easily at his father's or mother's knee. The household had the right kind of music and books. The dinner table conversation taught precisely the mannerisms, conversational patterns, and small talk skills that the employer finds comforting, familiar, and reassuring. The more conventional candidate gets the job, even though the other one could have done just as well, maybe better. This is an aspect of your majoritarian critique, is it not?"

"It is," Rodrigo replied. "And it never ceases to amaze me how tenaciously elite groups resist a realignment of merit that you would think would benefit them as well. Racism—any form of irrationality, really—is economically inefficient and bad for a society. So is a merit scheme that excludes and discourages the contributions of a major sector. Which leads me to the second observation, that merit is, basically, white people's affirmative action, as we once put it.[23] Oh, but before I forget, I told Kowalsky all this, and do you know what his answer was?"

"No, what?"

"He said that all this may be true, but that *formal* racism ended in 1964.[24] Now, the only kind lies in attitudes, unconscious predispositions, that sort of thing. Formally the playing field is level, and if the merit criteria are biased, the solution is to change them, not advocate dangerously inegalitarian measures like affirmative action—which, by the way, he insisted on calling 'reverse discrimination.' "

I winced. "And how did you deal with this objection?"

Rodrigo's Second Argument: Merit's after-the-Fact, Apologetic Function

"Historically. I pointed out that the emphasis on merit began in earnest in 1964. He got the connection quickly. Formal racism was phased out, veiled or nonformal racism came in—racism under the guise of excellence, fairness, equal opportunity, all the things that make up the constellation of attitudes and standards we call 'merit.' "

"That's good," I acknowledged. "And if memory serves me correctly"—I was much older than Rodrigo—"that is more or less what happened. Before 1964 white males benefited from old-fashioned laws that cut down the competition by eliminating blacks and women. They also benefited from old-boy networks by which they helped each other. The events of 1964 changed just the first part—

the other remained intact. In fact, merit today is a principal means by which empowered people, ones who have been to the best colleges, taken the same tests together, know each other, and talk the same way, ensure that they and their class remain in charge. It's especially important today because the population is changing. Whites are no longer going to be a numerical majority. In some parts of the country, they are already in the minority. Thus, it's even more important than before to have the mechanisms to ensure that their class replicates itself in circles of power."

"Not only that," Rodrigo added. "Today, conditions are different. The era of economic growth is over. There is a shrinking pie. Thus, merit, which is a principal measure of distributive justice, assumes even greater prominence."

"I'm not sure I follow you," I said. "With a shrinking pie, isn't it even more important to have clear-cut rules and standards to determine how that pie is to be distributed? Perhaps your problem with merit is not with the concept itself, but with the way it is applied. Merit is a kind of formalization.[25] Many of us have written of the connection between fairness and formality, the way in which courtroom rules—related to the presentation of evidence, allowing both sides a prescribed time to speak, and so on—promote fairness and reduce prejudice. They confine discretion, which could easily be used against the minority, the woman, or other disempowered litigant."

"Good point," Rodrigo conceded. "The trouble is that merit illustrates the wrong kind of formality. Its standards exclude morally relevant data, particularly events that happened in the past. They prevent us from considering another principle of distributive justice, namely reparations or making amends. Blacks, Chicanos, and Native Americans were formally oppressed throughout our history by the many mechanisms with which you and I are familiar. The merit advocate says, 'Let's ignore all that and start being perfectly fair right now. How high did you score on the SAT?' "

"An examination that, as we said, tests only a narrow range of skills, mainly of linear-type thought. White folks are perfectly willing to look to the past if that is where their merit badges lie, but not to ours if those pasts show disadvantage and hurdles surmounted. Of course, if their past includes a grandfather who immigrated from Ireland or a poor Baltic nation, they'll remind us of that over and over, overlooking the business dynasty the family established in between."

"A dynasty that may have taken real energy and talent to set up," Rodrigo pointed out, "but that nevertheless was aided by the advantage white skin conferred."

"So you're saying we can't be concerned just with distributing the pie fairly. We have to ask who set the table, invited the guests, and made the place cards."

"Exactly," Rodrigo exclaimed. "And the place card example is perfect. Conservatives would probably be irritated at the suggestion that merit is comparable to etiquette. But in some ways it is. All cultures have utensils for eating, but they vary and no one set is necessarily better than any other. (Rodrigo indicated a group of diners on the other side of the restaurant who were seated on cushions and using their fingers instead of the more usual chairs and silverware.) All have ways of assigning places to guests. In some, tradition prescribes who sits where; in others, place cards are used. Much the same is true of merit. Each society is organized in a particular way and has rules—which they call merit—to ensure that their organizational system continues undisturbed. But the organization and the assignment of roles is, to a very large extent, arbitrary. Move the basketball hoop up or down six inches and you radically change the distribution of who has merit.[26] Add items related to love, compassion, or intercultural awareness and you have a completely different SAT."

"But Rodrigo, if two candidates have exactly equal merit for a job, and one is white and the other is black . . ."

"They're not equal," Rodrigo interjected. "The black probably has come further. They are equal only if you arbitrarily decide that overcoming advantage is not a component of merit. Many whites get inheritances; most people of color do not. Whites often receive artfully crafted letters of recommendation. When a teacher proposes an extra credit assignment that allows them to receive an A-minus in an honors course, a neighbor gives them a summer job, or their father stakes their first home mortgage, they consider that normal, not a part of race and class advantage. Yet it is. You might even consider it a form of affirmative action—a system of benefits and resources awarded without regard to merit."

"There are exceptions," I pointed out. "The black middle class is growing. And the minority old-boy network looks after its own, as well."

"I know there are exceptions," Rodrigo replied. "But all too few. Ones of another kind—what I call 'cultural exceptions'—come up much more often."

"I'm not sure what you mean by the term."

"I think we were speaking of this before. Take a case close to hand. Law school teaching candidates are supposed to be hired because of their teaching and scholarly potential. But merit, like most legal terms, gets applied against a background of cultural assumptions, presuppositions, understandings, and implied exceptions, most of which operate against our people.[27] Return to our two candidates for a faculty position, one white, the other black. Let's suppose both served on the law review and dutifully wrote the same well-researched note, heavy on case analysis. Both made the finalist round in moot court, and so are likely to be good teachers as well—to whatever extent one can predict that."

"But the white gets the job, right?"

"Usually, yes. It turns out that the white had a more pleasant demeanor, was deemed better at small talk, went to a well-known private school. The black seemed tighter, a little intense. The white comes recommended by a more well-known professor. The white ends up getting the job."

"But isn't the solution, then, to assure that *true* meritocratic criteria are applied and not those other self-serving, counterfeit ones? Wouldn't it be better to insist that appointment committees steadfastly refuse to look at these other race- and class-based traits—ones that do not bear at all on teaching fitness, but simply render the candidate more familiar, more comfortable, more like one's own kind?"

"That would be a start," Rodrigo conceded. "But the number of presumptions and implied exceptions is virtually infinite, including things like dress, hair, intonation, demeanor, sports played, and so on. One's checklist would have to be very long indeed. And then, there are all those 'common-sense' and 'emergency' procedures."

"I'm not sure what you mean."

"Imagine a hiring committee that starts out the season entirely fair-minded and meritocratic. It draws up a picture of the ideal candidate—Supreme Court clerk, graduate of a top school, author of a superbly crafted student note. It reminds itself, over and over, that it will hire, or at least take seriously, any candidate that meets those specifications, white or black. It posts ads and sends letters to faculty and alumni around the nation telling them of its needs."

"And you're going to say," I interjected, "that such a committee will hire very few folks of color."

"It will hire few candidates, period," Rodrigo replied. "There are only a handful of such candidates out there. A few come through and interview, but turn their offers down—even the black candidate, the superstar with Thurgood Marshall-type credentials who unexpectedly decided to go to work for a community legal organization. Now it is February, slots remain open, including the position teaching Corporate Tax and Securities that they are desperate to fill. By now there are few candidates on the market with the superstar, formal credentials, the written-down ones that the committee started with in September. But there are several with credentials slightly lower than that. They still haven't found jobs, but are quite able lawyers, intelligent people. And they are known to the school's faculty. One of them remembers Joe, the smart lawyer he practiced with at the big firm; another remembers Martha, with whom she clerked for Judge X. The school makes a phone call, an interview is arranged, and a month later Martha or Joe has a job."

"Despite lacking the school's formal criteria—the Paul Freund/ Thurgood Marshall ones it started out with." I was silent for a minute, absorbing Rodrigo's point. Then I added: "And all the candidates hired the second way are white, right?"

"Exactly," Rodrigo replies. "Every blue moon, a law school will hire a Thurgood Marshall-type black under the superstar, formal criteria. Although even then, half the faculty and students will persist in believing he or she got a helping hand. But folks like us are never hired the second, informal way the school resorts to in February when it is under pressure and the dean is screaming that the hiring committee has not filled the Trusts and Estates or the Tax slot. That's the trouble with nonformal processes—they favor people we know, people who are like us. And in the hiring committee's case, those people are white."

"The net result is that white people have two chances of getting hired," I summarized, "by being superstars and satisfying the ostensible, on-the-books hiring criteria that institutions start out with in September or by means of the informal route the school resorts to in February or March when the season is almost over and the harvest is not yet in."

"Every now and then a school hires one of us with credentials just short of the Thurgood Marshall-type—say, somebody who graduated fifteenth in his or her class and had a gilded three years as star trial attorney in the district attorney's office. When this happens, everyone—including my friend Kowalsky, I'm afraid—will go around muttering about the iniquities of affirmative action and un-fairness to innocent whites."

"I've seen this happen," I said. "Sometimes I try a second tack. I point out that many of their most esteemed colleagues, hired under either the meritocratic criteria or the second kind, fall woefully short on any standard of professional excellence. One hasn't written any-thing in fifteen years. Another is such a notoriously weak classroom teacher that his enrollments are close to zero."

"Hmmm," Rodrigo said. "I think we have a couple like that at my school. And what happens when you point this out?"

"They always say that there's a reason. The first professor wrote the definitive work on nonprofit corporations twenty-five years ago and is obviously germinating another, equally good one. The notori-ous classroom teacher is simply demanding, or else has other talents, perhaps delivering great annual lectures to the bar, which is good public relations for the school."

"So merit criteria end up being applied against a host of back-ground forces—meanings, excuses, understandings, practices, no-tions of what any commonsense institution would do—that favor whites. Whites were in a position of power long ago, years before the merit criteria were written into the faculty code. That code naturally is interpreted against the backdrop of these forces. And so, even the most scrupulously fair-minded appointments committee ends up hiring whites and passing over blacks."

"I once served on the university-wide admissions committee. It was fascinating. It turns out that my university, like most others, has a host of express quotas and a like number of preferences:[28] drop-kickers, quarterbacks, legacy candidates whose parents are apt to give money if Johnny or Sally gets in, musicians, ROTC scholarship holders. Many of these individuals have SATs lower than those of the straight admits.[29] Then there's the geographic preference.[30] Our school likes to have students from far away, even though they all watch the same TV programs, study from the same textbooks, and write the same biographical essays. Hardly anyone sees these quotas and preferences as immoral, unfair to innocent nondropkickers, or worries that they might stigmatize the poor quarterback who enters with credentials lower than those of the National Merit scholar. None is seen as a derogation of the mighty principle of merit, although that is what they are."

We were both silent for a minute while the waiter picked up our empty plates and asked whether we would like to see the dessert menu. We looked at each other, Rodrigo nodded enthusiastically, and I said, "Let's have a look."

A minute later I said to Rodrigo, "You seem to have given quite a bit of thought to this. But you said you had a series of considerations concerning the way merit criteria are applied. The ones you have mentioned so far seem to me to be intrinsic to the concept itself or to the language game of which it is a part. I'd love to hear your ideas regarding merit's application. But before we move on, is there more you have to say about the first part, the discursive or logical aspect?"

"No, I'm just about ready to move on," Rodrigo said, looking around to see if the waiter was nearby. I marveled at my young friend's appetite while wrestling with my conscience over whether to have dessert or not. "Just one more thing."

"What is it?"

"We previously observed that conquering nations, like elite groups today, always impose their own merit criteria on the people they subjugate." I nodded. "Ideas about merit and notions of cultural superiority have always been used to justify conquest and colonialism. Recall, for example, the white man's burden of Kipling, the Conquistadores who brought the blessing of Christianity to Native Americans, the wrath of Allah that fueled the invading Moorish armies, and, in our time, banana-boat diplomacy that installed puppet regimes in Latin America to bring the people the miracles of democracy."

"Yes, go on."

"What I wanted to mention is that less idealistic nations, those with less normative zeal, were much more reluctant to impose their own merit criteria, and, as a result, were less oppressive victors.[31]

The early Romans, for example, did not demonize their slaves. They did not have to. The Romans were not Christians, and so had no need to paint their slaves as base, unsaved heathens. They did not, in other words, have to deem them normatively bad, lacking in merit. Our society, on the other hand, does need to do so, in order to justify our own bad acts. Thus, we demonize our enemies in war, and our own minority populations as well. We employ backwards reasoning: the subjugated must be bad, we treated them so badly. And we are more prone to this rationalization than a more cheerfully secular group of conquerors, such as the Romans. Merit-based ideas help us live comfortably despite the discrepancy between our ideals of brotherhood and equality and the reality of the poverty and blighted lives that we see in minority and poor populations all around us."

"Whites hate merit plans," I mused, "when they are applied against them. School teachers' unions oppose merit plans with a passion. And don't even try to get a law faculty to take seriously the idea of doing away with tenure and evaluating every professor on a year-to-year basis."

Rodrigo smiled in appreciation of my suggestion, then said: "That's all I have under the first head. Ready for the application?"

"That and dessert," I said, which made Rodrigo smile even more.

Rodrigo's Third Reason: Merit Rules Disadvantage Minorities and the Disempowered Even When Applied by the Most Fair-Minded of Administrators

"Those look great," Rodrigo said, staring eagerly at the dessert tray. "What's that one?" he asked the waiter.

The waiter explained and withdrew after taking our orders, a variegated flan for Rodrigo ("They have something similar in Italy"), and for me a banana pudding that the waiter promised was low in calories.

After the waiter disappeared from view, I said, "So, Rodrigo, you think that merit operates to harm and disadvantage minorities not only in its structure, but also practically, in the real world? I assume you mean something other than the ordinary disparate impact that the Supreme Court finds insufficient in employment settings except when an extremely overgeneral exam is used to screen out, say, state plumbers or custodians."[32]

"I am familiar with that line of cases. I was thinking of something even more pernicious. Earlier, you and I were talking about the canonical effect of certain words and social practices. There is nothing more canonical than merit. A canonical practice or meaning resists change almost by definition, for it is one of the prime mechanisms we apply to determine when change is desirable."

"That means that our notion of merit is very slow to change," I said. "I agree with that. Look how laggardly our acceptance of multiculturalism has been, and how campus curricular reform has sparked such resistance."

"In part that's because changes in courses required and books assigned come with the implied statement that these new authors and subjects are worth learning about. Persons who believe that only the Western greats are properly on that list naturally protest."[33]

"Take a case we discovered at my old school. My friend Ali and I were on a faculty-student committee charged with revising the first-year curriculum.[34] I was the LL.M. delegate, Ali the alternate. We were doing some fact checking in the placement office when we discovered something interesting. The minority students, many of whom had been admitted under affirmative action programs and with lower indices, were graduating at virtually the same rate as the rest of the class. Not only that, they were getting jobs and passing the bar at similar rates and even making more money—not a lot more, but still more. Moreover, a slightly higher percentage were going into prestigious jobs like teaching and clerking for federal judges. All the students, of course, were brilliant, and virtually all did quite well in later life. But the minorities were doing as well as the others and, in some cases, better. All this despite entering credentials that were, on average, considerably lower than those of the regularly admitted students."[35]

"And what moral did you draw from this?" I asked.

"I thought immediately that the LSAT must be encoding some form of cultural preference for the whites, who had higher scores than the minorities, but ended up doing little, if any, better. But most of my classmates advanced a different theory."

"What conclusion did they draw?"

"First, they were suspicious of my figures and wanted to know where I got them. When I said the placement and alumni affairs offices, they were dumbfounded. Many of them insisted the results must be the product of affirmative action in wider society—judges and employers applying the helping hand to the less qualified minority, and so on."

"And that's what you mean by the canonical function of merit, right?"

"Yes, Professor. The whole point of the canon is to defend itself, to insist that countervailing evidence justify itself in terms of the canonical idea. So, when the ostensibly less-meritorious minorities did well, it must be attributable to a further derogation of merit, namely favoritism in later life. Canonical ideas resist change, insist that new evidence be interpreted in light of them, a near-impossible task for the proponent of social change."

"Merit goes along with what is canonical, placed at the center, with the 'I.' If those others are succeeding, it must be because they are getting unfair help. Canonical narratives of all kinds exist largely for that purpose: rationalizing and justifying the way things are.[36] That and making them seem right and true," I concluded.

Rodrigo nodded. Resolving to play the devil's advocate as long as possible, I added, "But Rodrigo, what about when you and I grade bluebooks. Aren't we applying merit criteria? Don't we apply merit criteria every day in life? Say I go to the grocery store and buy a dozen Grade A potatoes. Am I guilty of buying into a canonical sin, of reinforcing the status quo? I have to eat, and I want to eat the best quality potatoes. What's so wrong with that?"

"Nothing," Rodrigo replied, taking a last bite of his flan and scrutinizing the bottom of his dish to see if there was any more. "But grading people, especially for something as long-term as a job or seat in law school, differs radically from grading potatoes. When the grocer grades potatoes, the potato is static. It will be bought and eaten within a short time. The grocer properly applies a freeze-frame approach, looking only at the potato as it is now—its color, texture, shape. It is irrelevant how far the potato has come or how far it is likely to go in the future. People, however, are dynamic. Imagine a super-potato from another planet. Would you like to buy and eat one merely because right now it resembled all those other ordinary ones sitting in the grocer's bin?"

I smiled at Rodrigo's example, and he continued as follows: "I'm sure you've had the experience, Professor, of attending a reunion of the black or minority law students' association ten years after graduation. I attended one the other day. It was impressive."

"Half the alums were commissioners or judges," I guessed.

"Exactly. Others were partners of major firms. One was a law professor at a school even more highly ranked than my own."

"It happens every time. Yet the law school persists in treating affirmative action candidates as disadvantaged and likely to fail. It offers them special help and tutoring sessions."

"Which many are glad to have," Rodrigo said. "I went to a few myself in the early months of my LL.M. program. Even though I got decent grades in law school, I was struggling to get the hang of the American legal system. The sessions I attended were quite helpful."

"But then you transcended them," I said. "You caught up. You joined the other potatoes in the bin, and even went them one better."

"Oh, I don't know about better," Rodrigo said, a little impatiently. "I may have a modest talent for writing and exploring unorthodox ideas. I'm not so sure I'm a better potato. Maybe I just work harder and am willing to take more chances."

"You're Rodrigo," I emphasized. "And I, for one, am glad you're around. And, I might add, very happy you entered the teaching profession. That way, at least we get to see each other on occasions like this rather than once every ten years at your class reunion dinner."

"Merit recedes for us, as I once put it in a conversation with Ali, while it proceeds for whites.[37] We have our accomplishments explained away while the others have their golden status continue long after their initial advantage, gained at Mom's and Dad's knee, has worn off and their accomplishments become quite ordinary. Like the hypothetical professors you mentioned earlier, Professor."

"I wish they were hypotheticals," I said ruefully. "But they are based on actual cases. In a fair world, blacks would hold about 10 percent of most of the desirable jobs. But they don't, and so-called merit criteria, operating as they do, are one of the principal tools by which those numbers are kept down."

"One thing troubles me, though," Rodrigo interjected. "Whites still allow us a token few—if not 10 percent of faculty jobs, then 2 or 3. Wouldn't a ruthless adversary, one who dominates all the councils, one who gets to draw up all the job descriptions, arrange matters so that we got none of the good things in life?"

"They need tokens," I said, "so that things don't appear too inequitable, so that they can tell themselves and each other that things are improving for blacks. Theoretically, the numbers could become so suspicious as to call for an explanation. But courts don't like statistical proof of discrimination and lean over backwards to avoid finding prejudice in numbers that anyone would think bespeak it.[38] There could always be another explanation, such as lack of interest.[39] But I think there is a deeper reason why courts don't intervene."

"I bet I know what you are going to say," Rodrigo interjected. "Courts don't review the criteria themselves. They police only the periphery, the application. They never consider whether merit criteria themselves are skewed, only whether merit is tested in a rational way, one related to the job at hand. Conventional merit that may be deeply biased against minorities goes unquestioned. It's like announcing you're going to hang someone and then, when he or she complains, pointing out that you're using a nice, sanitized rope. Any criteria could be job related. And, of course, all the job descriptions are written by the majority, which happens to be white."

"I think I could use an example."

"I ran across a great one in a magazine I found on the plane here. An ad by U.S. English, which opposes bilingual education for Hispanics and others, was entitled, 'Why a Hispanic Heads an Organization Called U.S. English.'[40] The ad explained the group's position by employing the rhetoric of equal opportunity. Even though it wishes to force everyone, including the foreign-born, to stop speaking their native languages and struggle along as best they can in English, the organization described itself as entirely egalitarian." Rodrigo fished out the ad and read: " 'On the job and in the schools, we're supporting projects that will ensure that all Americans have the chance to learn the language of equal opportunity.' "[41]

"Equal opportunity?" I asked. "That sounds like Orwellian doublespeak."

"Not really," Rodrigo replied. "If you adopt the organization's view of linguistic merit—namely, speaking English—their position is quite consistent. Once you accept that, everything else follows, including the part about equal opportunity.

"Of course, one might hold that it is better to be bilingual than monolingual," I said vehemently, recalling my own struggles to learn Italian early in life and then more recently in preparation for a trip to

Italy. "One could hold that speaking more than one language is an advantage, a sign of a cultured person."

"In that case, the organization and its agenda would appear vulgar and xenophobic. But if your mission"—Rodrigo looked again at the ad—"is preservation of our common bond through our common language," Rodrigo said as he took another look at the ad, "then speaking other languages, by definition, threatens that goal."[42]

"I'll take cosmopolitanism," I said. "But it is odd that the organization urges repression of linguistic minorities under the banner of equal opportunity."

"It's all in the definition," Rodrigo replied. "If your goal is forcing everyone to speak English, then your program will seem to you like equal opportunity. It treats native speakers of English and immigrants alike: everyone must speak the official language. And this is true in general. If you exclude from the definition of merit what another group values, likes to do, and does well, they will naturally turn out to be meritless. And your actions in coercing them to learn what you deem important will seem well intentioned, fair, and just— a favor of sorts to the benighted."

"So, you believe that merit is not only biased, it's also undemocratic because it inexorably leads to tyranny of the majority. But surely we need some criteria. Otherwise you'd be calling for lazy, unqualified people to get desirable jobs—people who don't deserve and haven't earned them."

"Not at all," Rodrigo replied mildly. "Slackers get jobs right now. The economy of this country is sinking, its productivity and quality of life at one of the lowest rates ever.[43] The workforces of many Asian countries are as productive as ours, and their children attend school for more hours and earn higher scores on standardized tests.[44] Our traditional merit criteria are ensuring mediocrity. It's quite alarming."

"And you think that our preoccupation with merit is the cause?"

"It's one," Rodrigo replied. "Unless constantly revised, modernized, and renegotiated, merit causes complacency, causes meritlessness, like the British aristocracy, a millstone around Great Britain's neck. The more absorbed in 'merit' a system becomes, the worse it will fare in world competition."

"Perhaps we can get to solutions for our misguided emphasis on merit later. But I think you were hinting earlier that one cause of

this complacency or sluggishness displayed by the meritorious victors, the phenomenon we now see in the West's slipping economic
position and lost markets, is that merit has an apologetic effect of
some kind. Could you explain this a little further?"

"Sure. Merit rules reassure life's victors that their wealth and
favored positions were deserved. Looking around them, upper class,
suburban folks might feel guilt, might feel uncomfortable over the
large numbers of poor and black people leading blighted lives as a
result of slavery and racism, on the one hand, and economic dislocations and loss of jobs, on the other. If they can persuade themselves
that their own comfortable positions were fairly won, then they need
not feel responsible. They won because they were entitled to win;
the others lost because they did not work hard, or lacked the brains
or other meritorious qualities necessary to achieve success. All neutral, marketplace mechanisms have this function. And it's self-de-
feating because it reduces competition and enables those who are
currently comfortable—if only because of Daddy's inheritance—to
become lazy."

"It produces a slack people," I added.

"So it does. And so we have come full circle once again," Rodrigo
replied. "Oh, here comes our waiter."

"Would you gentlemen like some coffee?" the waiter asked.

"A cappuccino for me—double, if you have it," Rodrigo said.

"Decaf," I said. As the waiter retreated, I said, "I gather you think
this is one reason for the West's current predicament."

"Yes," Rodrigo replied. "And as world conditions change, it is
doubly ironic that we end up demonized and excluded from merit
and life's bounty. For it is our skills and talents that the United
States needs more desperately than ever if it is to solve its environmental crisis, learn new patterns of social responsibility, and acquire
new approaches to family organization and caring for the aged.[45] All
these tools and practices are within the repertoire of minority groups.
We could teach whites lessons of incalculable value, ones that might
help arrest the country's decline. But they deny and reject, demoniz-
ing the very thing that could save them." ·

"A sad irony that I'm afraid will become apparent only too late," I
said somberly.

"Oh, great! Here's our coffee!" Rodrigo exclaimed.

After we had sipped our beverages briefly, Rodrigo continued. "Are you ready for another paradox, Professor? I was thinking about this the other day."

"I have all the time in the world," I said. "They wanted me to be on a second panel tomorrow, but I demurred. I'm too old for double duty, I said. So I'm limiting myself to just the one speech. You've got me as long as I'm vertical and responding to stimuli—which in my case," I estimated as I looked at my watch, "is probably ten o'clock."

"It's a little after nine. Let me know if I'm wearing you out. I find these conferences stimulating and could probably go on all night. But you've been traveling today, plus you just gave a great twenty-minute speech. Let me know if we're overdoing it."

"I will," I said. "Please go on. I love paradoxes. What's your new one?"

"I call it the paradox of disbursed merit. Michael Shapiro coined a similar term in connection with biomedical technologies.[46] Disbursed merit is the idea that society is capable, in many ways, of distributing qualities and skills that are constitutive of the very idea of merit. For example, law school itself probably boosts a student's LSAT. That is, if most of our students retook it after two or three years of training in case analysis, they would probably score higher than they did when they took it the first time. The old adage, learning to think like a lawyer, probably has at least a grain of truth in it. The same is true of many other highly selective callings. The best athletes make training squads and Olympic teams. They thus get more practice time, access to coaches, trainers and physicians, diet help, and so on, and so rapidly increase the gap between themselves and their less-favored competitors. Movie stars, already beautiful, earn the money to buy cosmetic surgery and become even more attractive. The haves increase their lead over the have-nots, and not just because skill, intelligence, and beauty are at a premium in our society. It is also because the resources that they enable you to command permit you to buy further increments of skill, intelligence, and beauty. This enables the haves to become more meritorious, richer, and better able to buy merit-enhancers, in an endless chain."

"I agree that's how things work. But I'm not sure I see the paradox. Isn't that the inevitable result of any competitive, marketplace-oriented society? The rich get richer. It's always been that way."

"The paradox lies in the moral irrationality of rigorously applying merit criteria to distribute regimens, programs, or medicines that can give the beneficiary a boost in an attribute that forms a part of, or is a pre-existing element of, those very same merit criteria.[47] It would be like a paint store that sold yellow paint only to owners whose houses were already yellow. If law school can boost anyone's LSAT and can make practically any intelligent person into a competent lawyer, then it becomes irrational to insist on a high LSAT as a condition of entrance."

"To resolve that paradox, then, we would need to turn to other distributive principles, such as equity, utility, reparations, and the like to make the entrance determination. Once society develops the means radically to increase a person's merit in a particular regard— whether it be intelligence, strength, beauty, analytical ability, or health—it becomes pointless to continue to distribute the benefit based on the preexisting possession of that very same attribute. I gather that's what you mean by your paradox. And I think I agree with it," I said. "You may be onto something."

"It's not only a paradox, Professor. It's a potent argument against overreliance on merit, particularly in educational settings. It seems to me to set an important limit upon the meritocratic ideal, one that should give even conservatives pause."

"Did you mention it to Kowalsky?"

"I did. He resisted less than I expected. On his own he pointed out that distributing increments of merit based on merit criteria could create dynasties. Merit is a resource attractor in our society.[48] If we limit distribution of merit-conferring attributes and skills to the brilliant and talented, then we guarantee that they will corner the market, so to speak. Kowalsky loves market theory."

"To some extent this is happening now," I pointed out. "The wealthy set their children up in business, provide them with trust funds. The well-educated see to it that their kids get the best possible educations, sometimes with an assist from legacy programs instituted by the educational institutions. In America, a small percentage controls an overwhelming portion of the net wealth; this may be part of the reason."

"Professor, do you recall our earlier discussion about how merit is context-dependent—how it all depends on what society values?"

"Yes. You gave the example of the hoop in a basketball game. You also mentioned women's roles in group situations."

"Well, it just occurred to me that many of the qualms you, I, and other progressive people have with the idea of merit, aside from its disreputable history, relate to its interdependency."

"Do you mean the contextual quality we were talking about before, or some other kind?"

"I mean that which arises by virtue of the social construction of the notion of a person. Most people can be made to agree that persons do not exist in a vacuum; rather, we are coterminous with our social surroundings. Someone who lived his or her entire life on a desert island would scarcely grow up to be anything we would recognize as a person. We all derive our identity, in large part, from the social practices, roles, and expectations of the culture into which we are born. These include the premiums that we place on certain things as constitutive elements of merit."

"And I assume you mean the same is true of demerit, merit's opposite?"

"I do. That's part of the reason why I think society's toleration of the ubiquitous imagery in popular media and the press of minorities as criminal, stupid, vicious, and sexually licentious is worth addressing."

"I assume you would include hate speech. That runs your argument directly counter to the First Amendment. Our friends in the ACLU would not like that."

"All I am saying is that the social construction of demerit, like that of merit, raises serious problems and needs to be addressed. I have a feeling there are the same irrationalities and inequities built in on that side, as well. But that's a subject for another time."

"I agree," I said, looking at my watch. "I'm afraid I need to be getting back to the hotel soon. Much as I love this place and have enjoyed our conversation, Rodrigo, an old man like me needs his sleep. And I do have that early plane to catch tomorrow morning."

Both of us were silent for a moment. The waiter materialized, coffee pot in hand. "Would you gentlemen like refills?" he asked. We each looked at the other. "I believe there was one final point about history that we were going to explore," Rodrigo said, noncommittally. "I'm going strong, but you've had a long day."

I hesitated. The coffee looked good. Just then Rodrigo looked past my shoulder and with a shock of recognition said, "Kowalsky! What are you doing here?"

I turned to see a strikingly pale young man, about Rodrigo's age, with a neat suit, short hair, and an alert, sparkling expression. I half-stood, Rodrigo introduced us, and I invited Kowalsky to sit down. It turned out that he had just arrived to take part in a panel on tenure the next morning. "We were just now discussing merit," Rodrigo said. "Would you care to join us?"

"I'd be pleased to," Kowalsky said. "Although I'm just here for a snack. Looks like the two of you are nearly finished."

"Please stay," I said. "Rodrigo was going to give me the last chapter of a conversation he says was inspired by you. He was going to review the history of merit and meritocracy in the United States and draw some lessons." I turned to Rodrigo. "I hope I'm not putting you on the spot."

"Oh, no," Rodrigo replied. "Laz and I tell each other everything. Nothing scandalizes him, even my most wild-eyed radical ideas. He loves debate and, as you will see, is capable of holding his own on anything. Right, Laz?"

The pale young man smiled and said, "We'll see. I get as much out of Rodrigo's challenges as he gets out of mine. I'd love to hear what you have to say." He gestured toward the waiter, ordered a spicy dish—I complimented him on his choice—and Rodrigo began.

In Which Rodrigo and His Friend Debate Merit's History and What It Means for Today

"I'm really happy you showed up, Laz," Rodrigo said. "I didn't know you were coming. The Professor and I were talking about some of the same things you and I discussed the other day."

"Still resisting merit, eh?" Kowalsky said. "Ironic—the most brilliant member of our faculty, and you're still at it, deconstructing your own talent and distinction. I think you liberals are just uncomfortable with your own smarts, your own status. Such levelers. Too bad." Kowalsky smiled warmly to let us know he meant nothing personal.

"Touché," Rodrigo replied good-naturedly. "But even if you are right about liberals on a personal level, there still remain a host of irrationalities and problems with merit, even more than the ones you and I were talking about before. The Professor and I developed them further just now. If you like, I can bring you up to date when we get home. Actually, what flight are you on? Are you flying home tomorrow?"

It turned out that the two young scholars were indeed on the same flight. They quickly made plans to phone the airline and change their seat assignments to sit together. "I've got the 800-number somewhere," Rodrigo said. "Maybe I'll do it as soon as we get back to the hotel." He caught the waiter's eye, indicated we would indeed like coffee, and resumed his colloquy.

"I'm sure both of you know how the early anthropologists, up to the period of Franz Boas, were fascinated by the idea of proving racial differences, particularly ones having to do with intelligence and cranial capacity."[49]

"Most of these have been discredited," Kowalsky said quietly. "No one of my acquaintance or political persuasion would give them any credit today. That was a disgraceful chapter in our history. I hope you are not going to tar the entire idea of merit with the brush of the early extreme pseudoscientific meritocrats."

"Though few may subscribe to the crude versions of those early race-IQ theories," Rodrigo said, "the history of the idea is still relevant today. In many respects today's most strident meritocrats are the straight-line descendants of the late nineteenth and early twentieth century ones. And in some respects, their agenda and arguments are exactly the same. Consider the current SAT, administered by the Educational Testing Service for the College Board. Until recently, the test had items about oarsmen and regattas. It contained questions about polo and mallets.[50] It is eminently coachable. The director of one of the prominent test-coaching companies, which charges between five hundred and one thousand dollars for its services, recently admitted— boasted, really—that his organization was able to boost the score of the average test-taker by 185 points.[51] Thirty percent improved by 250 or more.[52] Because of the high price charged, the children of the wealthy are more likely to be able to take the course."[53]

"I must admit I took such a course myself," Kowalsky said. "Twice, in fact. Whether it helped my score or not, I don't know. But my parents were not at all rich, as you know. I saved up the money because I wanted to do well. If poor kids are disadvantaged by the test, is not the solution to eliminate those test items that are unfair and to make sure that the cram courses offer scholarships for poor kids who can't afford them?"

"That would be a start," Rodrigo said a little dubiously. "But I think the whole enterprise ought to come under scrutiny. The test's principal originator, Carl Campbell Brigham, was an out-and-out white supremacist who published a book in 1923 entitled *A Study of American Intelligence.* In the book, Brigham cautioned that inferior immigrants and minorities were swamping the country at the expense of those with superior European genes. He warned against interbreeding and urged that we close our borders. Two years later, he became director of the College Board's testing program. He based the first test on Madison Grant's *The Passing of the Great Race.* Its purpose was to confirm the superiority of white test-takers pure and simple. It is no different today: merit is up-to-date bigotry.[54]

"I had not heard about the SAT's history. That's appalling," Kowalsky said. "But I'm not sure what it has to do with today. No one advocates those distasteful notions any more. And isn't merit the best protector blacks have against intolerance? How else can you dispel negative stereotypes except by succeeding, being successful, demonstrating your merit?"

"That's just what we are prevented from doing," Rodrigo replied. "Remember those test items about regattas. They actually had an item like that on the version of the LSAT I took. I knew what the word meant because it's similar to one in Italian. However, if I'd been a smart but poor ghetto kid, I might have failed that item. Fairness, including fairness in testing, is always a contested concept, always relative to someone's interests, perspectives, and purposes. It does not stand outside experience in some external realm. It's a matter of what we deem important. And the 'we' is generally those who are in a position to assure that their own merits, values, standing, and excellence remain untouched."[55]

"I still think you are putting too much emphasis on early history," Kowalsky said. "The test may have been biased back then, and maybe a regatta or two creeps in even now. But ETS has professional test validators, experts who comb the items for bias. And surely you cannot say there are no differences in legal aptitude or ability. You're a teacher! Rodrigo, you see those differences every day, every time you teach a class or grade a bluebook. What's wrong with trying to see that legal education is not wasted on those who simply can't get it, on whom it won't take hold? You do no favor by admitting someone who has so little talent for analysis that every law school class is a torment, every exam a humiliation. And if they don't pass the bar, they've wasted three years."

"We were talking—the Professor and I—about bar results, jobs, and so on, before you came in. I can bring you up to date on those things on the plane back, if you want. But I'd like to return to history, if the two of you don't mind. And no, Laz, I don't think that the history of an idea is irrelevant to its current understanding. Some of the modern conservative and neoconservative writers sound themes remarkably similar to the now-discredited ones from that rougher, more overtly racist era." Rodrigo pointed out the book his friend had been carrying that now lay on the booth seat next to him. "Jared Taylor is an example,[56] but some of the more moderate conservatives and neoliberals are saying much the same thing."

"Patrick Moynihan says that blacks in the urban underclass are evolving into a new and different species, cut off from the rest of civilized society and developing mores and a culture of their own, passed down from mother to son. Speciation, he calls it," I remarked.[57]

"And he's a Democrat!" Rodrigo exclaimed. "Then there's Arthur Schlesinger, from the same party. His recent book, *The Disuniting of America*,[58] tells how the recent ethnic upsurge is tearing the country apart. He argues that multiculturalism and identity politics are weakening Anglocentric culture, our common bond. He deplores that we as a nation are getting away from the old ideal of assimilation that encouraged immigrants and minorities to shed their ethnicities in favor of WASP culture and tradition. He says this is not only bad for the country, but also for minorities. For the American tradition is 'the unique sauce of individual liberty, political democracy, the rule of law, human rights, and cultural freedom.' Collectivist cultures, by contrast—and by those he means us, I'm afraid—'have stamped with utmost brutality on human rights.' He considers them tribalistic, despotic, superstitious, and fanatical. It is absurd that society is asked to give those cultures equal respect. White guilt, he says, can be pushed too far."[59]

"I've read that book," Kowalsky said. "And it is possible that the author himself goes a little too far. Other cultures, including my own, have given America much of what it has to be proud of, ranging from some of its best music to its top scientists, and even," he noted as he gestured toward his plate full of steaming dolma-type delicacies, "its finest food. Yet, I think he has a point when he says that the American synthesis has an inevitable Anglo-Saxon coloration.[60] If so, he is not amiss in portraying racial separatism and separate dorms for blacks as forms of balkanization."

"I'm not so sure why it has to be that way," Rodrigo replied mildly. "*The Passing of the Great Race*[61] echoed some of the same themes, warning of chaos and disorder. Immigration continued, yet the evils the author warned of did not come to pass. Some of the 'English-Only' people sound some of the same alarms. Their theory is that English ought to reign supreme, that its sacred texts, including the King James Bible and Shakespeare, are the only guarantors against barbarism, which of course is not true.[62] The problem is that there is a match, virtually a one-to-one correspondence, between the new writers and the old ones who wrote tracts about white supremacy. Lawrence Auster's 1990 book[63] warns that we are seeing the end of Western civilization in recent immigration reform acts,[64] which modestly relax the previous restrictions against immigration from the Third World. Richard Brookhiser, senior editor at the *National Review*, has written in his book, *The Way of the Wasp*,[65] that Anglo traits such as conscience, antisensitivity, industry, and success must be preserved over the opposite ones that minorities and foreigners bring, namely, self, creativity, gratification, and group-mindedness. If we allow the former traits to be submerged by the latter, America is sure to lose the way.[66] These ideas resemble nothing so much as those of Henry Pratt Fairchild in *The Melting Pot Mistake*,[67] a 1920s-era tract against immigration. So, you see that today's meritocrats and test advocates have much to live down. Both their current and their old champions base their arguments, implicitly and explicitly, on racial superiority and xenophobia. Carl Campbell Brigham, in *A Study of American Intelligence*,[68] studied racial differences in mental traits. Based on a survey of army test results, he concluded that Negroes were 'very inferior' and warned against integrated education because Negroes were incapable of taking advantage of it. He became director of the SAT, which failed to repudiate his teachings, and, indeed, the ETS library bears his name!"[69]

"So, Rodrigo," I said. "You are saying that an appeal to a unity based on Anglo-Saxon values is inherently racist."[70]

"Yes, and so is pandering to fears of balkanization. As a recent author put it, ideas are only intelligible within the particular circumstances that gave rise to them and in which they are circulated. Thus, an appeal in today's climate to national unity, assimilation, or against balkanization is deeply racist."

"So is one to merit," I added, "for the same reasons."

"Rodrigo, you two have me half convinced," Kowalsky conceded. "But only half. The history you recounted is certainly distasteful— although no more so than other chapters we could name, including express quotas against Jews at top universities, and 'No Irish Need Apply' rules that were in effect in certain Northeastern cities for at least as long as the repulsive testing and IQ theories you mentioned. And I'll remind you that one still hears Polish jokes even today. But I still think that merit, properly applied, can serve as the best guarantor against racism and bias. Look at sports. As you yourself pointed out, blacks dominate, simply because they're faster and have more drive.[71] Other spheres could yield in similar fashion. Look at you, for example. You and Barney are two of our most recent hires and among our best by any measure. *Global* standards of merit, like the SAT, may be unfair, overbroad, and prone to the kinds of abuses you detailed. But I don't see how you can deny *local,* or contextualized merit—speed in a hundred-yard dash, teaching ability in a law school, spelling ability in an editor. You liberals believe in contextualizing everything. Isn't that the solution to your problems with merit?"

Rodrigo replied: "That may help somewhat. But merit still excludes, and in an especially pernicious way. The Professor and I were discussing some of these things before."

At the mention of my name, I shook my head, recognizing with a start that the relaxed reverie into which I had lapsed was drifting perilously close to dozing.

"The Professor is looking tired," Rodrigo said. "He's had a long day. Maybe we'd better call it quits for now."

"I'm going strong," I protested. "I just need another cup of coffee."

"We'll walk you back," Laz said, taking my elbow as I stood up. "I've finished my food, and my colleague and I both have early sessions tomorrow morning."

Exit Rodrigo on a Note of Race-and-Class Reconciliation

Our meeting broke up. We walked in near silence back to the hotel. Rodrigo spoke only once, to remind his friend to ask him about something later. Within ten minutes I was in my hotel bed, sleeping the sleep of the dead. I saw Laz and Rodrigo only briefly, at a distance, the following morning in the hotel lobby. They were engaged in an animated discussion. But I had a feeling I would hear from the two young scholars, one conservative, one radical—yet seemingly best friends. My hunch turned out to be true. Only two days after I got back, I received a lengthy letter from Rodrigo in my law school mailbox. Written on long computer paper (his trademark), it contained a torrent of words, concluding with the following:

> And so, Professor, after our long talk on the plane back home, we each realized that the other was both right and wrong. After hearing more of Laz's story, I've concluded that European ethnics can experience headwinds just as great as those our people suffer, the element of skin color excepted. (Did I tell you that Laz, despite his obvious brilliance, went to a community college?) Much cruelty and unfairness are perpetrated under the banner of class, which is often as great a disadvantaging factor as race, and nearly always a cross-cutting one.[72] Moreover, affirmative action merely shifts the cost of racial remedies onto those least able to protest—blue-collar whites like Alan Bakke or Laz's siblings—neatly exempting the high-achieving son or daughter of a blueblood family.
>
> For his part, Kowalsky finally came around to my and your position that we cannot accept merit standards as they are, pressing only for the occasional, limited affirmative action exception—rather, we must fundamentally re-evaluate merit standards and the way they are used. He also agrees with our conclusion that affirmative action generates its own pool problem through a sort of self-fulfilling prophecy. He added that the West's slipping economic position is especially troubling, as it is likely to close off opportunities not just for blacks, but also for upwardly-mobile white ethnics. He said his people have a kind of 'second sight' or double consciousness, like ours. They are outsiders to some extent. But they also have seen the way entire cultures can sink, as in Eastern Europe, with their superstructure, leadership, and cultures essentially intact.
>
> For my part, I agreed—somewhat reluctantly to be sure, but Laz's

logic is unassailable—that minorities ought never, except in the nar-
rowest circumstances, accept affirmative action. Doing so splits the
poor community along color lines and reinscribes the current merit
standards just that much deeper. It also reinforces the belief that people
of color are unworthy and need affirmative action, when the reality is
that society needs them and their genius at least as much as we need
society.

So, Laz and I declared a pact, a sort of truce, which we plan to
publicize to our groups and to everyone who will listen. We'll start by
holding a conference. The general idea would be that minorities will
foreswear affirmative action unless it also includes poor whites. White
ethnics and people of color—those who join the new coalition, at any
rate—would agree to work together to subvert and replace the array of
standards, social practices, and old-boy networks that now hold back
the progress of both. We believe the critique of merit, far from being a
sour-grapes venture, leads inexorably to a bold, hopeful coalition in
which two numerically large groups—minorities and ethnic (that is
non-WASP) whites—work together to lift the yokes of racism and
classism that oppress each, and that end up, as we've seen, linked.
Until now this linkage between racism and classism had not been
demonstrated. Now that it has, will you and your friends join us in the
last, the final, and the most important, subversion of all? Here are a
range of dates we are thinking of for the conference. We're getting the
money for your speaker's fee. Will you come?

Rodrigo's letter was accompanied by a neatly typed sheet of computer paper, entitled "Tentative Conference Program," which included the following events:

First Day: Reconstructing Affirmative Action. Convenor—
Laz.

Morning. Keynote address. On the need for a new race/class coalition. Ask the professor or someone of his generation.
The Critique of Affirmative Action. Panel and respondents. Discuss the history and current status of affirmative action. Supreme
Court jurisprudence. Critical perspectives. What is wrong with the
doctrine, and where do we go from here?
Break-out sessions: Pair lefties and righties. Assign a reporter to
report back to the group.
Lunch. Address by Laz.

Afternoon. Working groups. Tentative assignments: How to persuade minorities to foreswear affirmative action based solely on race. Devising new social programs and objectives that will include poor ethnic whites and immigrants. Legislative reform. New judicial standards of review.

Late PM. Plenary session: Round-table—Laz plus the reporters: Contours of the New Pluralism—Race and Class in the Nineties and Beyond.

Second Day: Reconstructing Merit. Convenor—Rodrigo.

Morning. Keynote address. On the need for new approaches to merit. Ask the professor if he wants this one? If not, get someone of his generation. Duncan Kennedy or Derrick Bell?

The Critique of Merit. Panel, respondents. Discuss history and role of merit, including IQ test; Equal Protection challenges, case law. Critical perspectives: what is wrong with conventionally defined merit—paradoxes, inequities, the need for reform. How merit standards burden both minorities and ethnic whites.

Break-out sessions: Pair people of opposite persuasions, backgrounds, races. Each group designates a reporter who reports back to the group.

Lunch. Address by Rodrigo.

Afternoon. Working groups: The social construction and reconstruction of merit. Mechanisms by which conventional merit standards oppress both blacks and poor whites. Programmatic considerations—a writing competition; sponsor test cases?

Late PM. Plenary session: Rodrigo plus the reporters. Who really has merit? Why current standards flunk, and where we should go from here?

Press conference on the new black/white coalition and program.

4

American Apocalypse

In Which I Pay a Surprise Visit to Rodrigo's Law School

Hee-hee, I caught myself muttering under my breath with a childish excitement unbefitting someone my age, as I walked up the last few stairs to Rodrigo's fourth floor office. In the past, my young *enfant terrible* had made a practice of dropping in on me unexpectedly, materializing as though out of nowhere. Now, courtesy of a board meeting of a public interest organization I had agreed recently to serve, I found myself in Rodrigo's city. With a little time on my hands, I had caught a cab to his law school to see how he was doing. And here I was, knocking on his door and feeling more than a little conspiratorial.

"Professor! What a surprise! Come on in. What brings you to the Midwest?"

"Quite a turnabout, isn't it?" I beamed, stepping inside and shaking his hand warmly. "I'm here for a board meeting. I hope you're not too busy for a few minutes with your old professor."

"Never," he replied, motioning me to have a seat on his office couch. "Let me just get rid of this call." Rodrigo picked up the phone, which was lying receiver up on his desk. "And make that five rooms with no feather pillows, please."

"Oh," I said. "You must be working on that conference. I saw the signs on the doors."

"Yes. It's the regional 'People of Color' meeting. It started this afternoon. I'm the local arrangements person. Two professors from Rutgers are in charge of the program. The last two weeks of my life have been one round of pillows, special meals, and late registrations. People are still checking in, even though we just had the opening session."

"Are you doing all this by yourself?"

"Giannina is helping out. So is Laz, my conservative friend to whom I introduced you a while back.[1] And the staff in the dean's office has been great."

"I went to the Critical Race Theory workshop last summer," I said. "I'm something of a senior statesman. This isn't the same group, is it?"

"No, although a few of the same folks are attending. It's not quite so high-powered—mostly young professors who read each other's papers and offer support."

There was a rattle outside the door. Two uniformed young people stood expectantly behind a gleaming cart. "Right down there, in the faculty lounge, please," Rodrigo indicated. Then, to me: "Those are the caterers. We're having a reception in exactly . . . (he looked at his watch) forty-five minutes. Can you join us?"

"I wish I could. Unfortunately, I have a dinner tonight with the board. But our meeting tomorrow finishes at noon. Maybe I'll come by if you allow drop-ins."

"For you, of course," Rodrigo replied graciously. "Here's a program. The afternoon session starts at one. When do you fly back?"

"Seven-thirty," I said, scanning the program. "What did I miss at the opening session?"

"Not much. The dean gave a speech. Then the Rutgers people spoke, summarizing developments on the national scene since last year's meeting."

"Emphasizing the conservative surge and attack on affirmative action, I imagine?" I asked.

"Yes, the whole panoply of right-wing advances. It was sobering, to say the least. They described the way conservatives have been rolling back affirmative action in the workplace[2] and diversity programs on college campuses.[3] They outlined the attack on minority scholarships,[4] ethnic studies programs,[5] and professors of color.[6] They reviewed how the religious Right has been opposing gay-rights ordinances[7] and school curricula that discuss sexual orientation,[8] demanding religious education and prayer in schools,[9] and urging official recognition for religious holidays.[10] They detailed how conservatives have been reversing women's reproductive liberties,[11] electing local officials with a back-to-basics approach to public education,[12] building prisons, and supporting tough-on-crime measures.[13] Conservatives also have held the line on military spending, even though the world is at peace.[14] They've been enacting repressive immigration measures, English-only laws, and referenda aimed at depriving immigrants of public services.[15] They've been reforming the tort system to cut back on recoveries by consumers injured by defective products and doctors who commit malpractice,[16] reducing social welfare for the poor and desperate,[17] and curtailing support for the arts."[18]

"Sounds chilling, especially when you hear it all at once," I said. "How did your friend Kowalsky take all this?"

"It's funny. I sat next to him. He was actually smiling and nodding approval over some of the remarks, even though everyone else was frowning. Afterward, he got into a furious argument with Jody Elmour. In fact, they're probably in the faculty lounge right now, having it out."

"*That* should prove interesting. Elmour is one of the most brilliant young scholars of color in the country. I loved his Stanford article. And Kowalsky is no slouch, either."

"He'll be back tomorrow," Rodrigo said. "We can ask him how it came out. They were arguing about prayer in schools, but before they left, Laz asked me to remind him to tell me his theory about a race war."

"I hope I get to sit in. He's smart and always gives a good account of himself. You're lucky to have him as a colleague."

"I agree," Rodrigo added. "For my part, though, I want to pin him down first on something that he strongly believes in, namely neutral principles. He thinks it's the solution for everything, and I can't seem to get him to realize how colorblind jurisprudence simply maintains racism and the status quo. He keeps saying that a system that treats blacks and whites equally in every respect cannot possibly be racist."

"He does, however, believe in affirmative action, as I recall," I added.[19]

"He does, so long as it's aimed at reversing the legacy of discrimination and denied opportunities for blacks, something he feels very strongly about. He also thinks affirmative action should apply to poor whites, and he doesn't understand why it should apply to veterans and the handicapped—especially if they're rich and cannot prove intentional discrimination. But aside from that, he thinks the law does all it can and should when it achieves formal equality—that is, treats everyone according to a single, uniform standard. He keeps saying that the law protects individuals, not groups, and that it's unfair to make working-class or ethnic whites pay for the sins of Southern aristocrats and plantation owners, sins they had no hand in perpetrating. He also keeps coming back to the way in which affirmative action benefits people of color like me, who have suffered no great hardships in life, and leaves out people like his family, who immigrated from an Eastern European country and had to struggle to survive."

"How are you going to answer him?"

"I was just formulating my response when you walked in. I have a few ideas. But before I start, can I offer you a cup of coffee? I have a new espresso maker. It's a little like yours, but smaller. Giannina has been after me to cut down. She says it makes me too hyper."

"Funniest thing," I said, smiling, to reassure my young protégé that I appreciated his high-energy manner. "I'd love a cup. Decaf if you have it."

"I do. Laz is in here a lot, and he's a decaf fan, although I hate the stuff myself." As my young friend busied himself measuring out the beans and water and setting the dials, he began:

In Which Rodrigo Critiques Neutralism, Conservatives' Stock in Trade

"I'm thinking of telling Laz that there's nothing really wrong with neutral principles, so long as we allow for redress for past oppression.[20] But I'll go on to tell him that many conservatives advance the principle hypocritically. They don't really believe in treating blacks and gays and women equally, at all. I'd love to hear your reaction, since I'm sure that if there's any weakness in my argument Laz will find it."

"I'll do my best. Go ahead."

"I'm thinking of demonstrating that the two principal arguments neutralist conservatives advance against affirmative action, namely that it punishes innocent whites and benefits undeserving blacks, are bogus.[21] If I'm right, there's little about these programs that conservatives should oppose. And I believe the same holds for other areas in which conservatives are mounting the neutralist attack. My critique consists of two parts. I could run it past you, if you have the time."

"I do, I do. Please start. How long do we have until your reception?"

"Oops. Only forty minutes," Rodrigo said, looking at his watch. "Your coffee's ready. Cream and sugar?"

"Not My Fault"—The Conservatives' First Argument

As I stirred my beverage, Rodrigo began: "As always in social relations between races, what looks ordinary turns out to be exceptional, and what appears exceptional ordinary."

"I think I agree," I said. "But I could use an example."

"With affirmative action," Rodrigo replied, "white folks are constantly telling us that it is unfair to saddle them with responsibility for what happened long ago. They themselves never owned slaves or operated a whites-only lunch counter. So why should they have to make sacrifices so blacks and Mexicans can get jobs or places in university or law school classes? They admit that the things that were done to blacks were terrible. But they insist that those who committed these atrocities are dead, and so the moral debt that America once owed the slaves and children of slaves is simply not repayable."

"I hate to say this, Rodrigo, but that sounds like a pretty good argument to me. I assume you have some kind of response?"

"Suppose white America were a corporation and the victims were DES kids. A harm to one generation can easily cause foreseeable harm to the next one, and so the law has held."[22]

"But that addresses the other side of the equation, Rodrigo—the plaintiff side. Today's white folks are saying that they don't deserve to be defendants—that we are suing the wrong party, so to speak. Those who did unspeakably evil things to us are no longer present."

"That's why I used the analogy of the corporation. No one would argue that a corporation should get off the hook merely because its board of directors has changed or its chief executive retired. The responsibility runs to the corporation and so we allow the DES kids to seek redress against the firm that manufactured or marketed it, even though it is many years later and the principal characters have changed. And the same is true of other kinds of corporate liability — it doesn't end just because the cast of characters has changed."

"And, in the case of the country, those directors never include us, of course, and always happen to be white. But, I wonder about your analogy. Are you saying that a country is like a corporation?"

"Of course it is," Rodrigo replied. "It's just that we're not used to assigning guilt that way. White victims, like most of the DES kids, elicit sympathy. And we are glad to recognize white-on-white responsibility. Black-on-white is another matter."

"But there are differences between a corporation and a country," I insisted. "Corporations need to be able to do business, enter into contracts, and so on, over time. No one would deal with them if they couldn't be held liable."

"But the same is true of countries. They borrow money, issue bonds, and enter into treaties, all intended to be in force much longer than the life or term of the person, usually the chief executive, who borrows, issues, or signs them."

"But those go to specific instruments, like a bond, that everyone understands are to be enforceable for their duration. Moral debts are different, don't you think?"

"They're different, of course, but no less enforceable — assuming, of course, that the will is there. The United States required that Germany make reparations to Israel and the victims of the Holocaust, even though the Nazi government had been disbanded and most of its leaders executed or imprisoned. We made reparations to our own Asian-Americans who were interned during the war and to Indian tribes whose lands were taken, in some cases a century or more ago. If there is any difference between our case and those, it lies in the direction of even greater equity. The dominant culture is prepared to accept responsibility running to a second or third generation if that second or third generation is white or Japanese, but not if it is black."

"So you are saying," I summarized, "that there is nothing that formally bars a program of redress for us. What stands in the way is the implicit conviction that blacks are simply worth less—that harms to them are less worthy of redress than harms to others. Since we are unworthy of full consideration, harms to us are like stepping on an insect or a dog's tail. Anyone who feels deep distress over what happened to us would be considered abnormal."

"Even current civil rights law shows that. Nowhere else in the law of remedies do you see requirements like intent,[23] strict causation,[24] and narrow tailoring of remedies.[25] Nowhere else do you see excuses such as business necessity allowing one to perpetrate a clear-cut harm on another.[26] We are not entirely without redress. Rather, it's that mainstream society does not take the need to redress our injuries as seriously as it does injuries to its own."

"And that is what you mean, I take it, by law's bogus neutrality."

"Exactly," Rodrigo replied. "Or, rather, by the disingenuous quality of the conservative argument. We could easily keep in place—strengthen, even—measures like affirmative action without violating any moral rule that we also apply elsewhere."

"It just occurred to me that the United States insists on the most meticulous form of justice for the MIAs, most of whom are white. Even though most or all of them are surely dead, we persist in order to provide surcease for American families. And we continue punishing Vietnam as a nation because it drags its feet about returning the ashes. But what about the other half of your equation, Rodrigo? Not just the perpetrators of slavery and racism are gone. Conservatives insist the victims are, too. How do you deal with that?"

The Other Half of the Conservative Argument—The Middle-Class Son or Daughter of the Black Brain Surgeon

"That's another argument you hear. It's considered a clincher, but, like the first one, it's only trotted out against us. In property law, fraud actions are routinely permitted for one cheated out of an inheritance, even though the fraud took place before his or her birth."

"And you mentioned the DES cases before," I added. "In those, we allow the now grown woman to sue for her medical injuries, even though the manufacturer's negligence occurred before she was born, when they produced or sold the defective medication to her mother."

"Right. And I'm not sure you know about this, Professor, because it's not your field, but there's a whole new branch of tort law called wrongful life[27] and wrongful birth.[28] These are for preconception harms and ones that take place while the fetus is *in utero.* These cases allow the child to sue the doctor who was negligent, for example in not counseling the forty-five-year-old mother of the risk of Down's syndrome, even though the child was not yet in being, or in some cases even conceived."[29]

"Yes, I've heard of those cases," I said, with a slight edge of irritation. "Even at my age, we're expected to keep up, Rodrigo."

Rodrigo blushed slightly, then went on. "What I meant, Professor, was that you don't teach torts. I know you're very widely read. So I'm sure you've read about the new second-generation Holocaust-survivor syndrome that doctors are documenting.[30] I expect we'll have test cases soon."

"Are you suggesting that there should be a battered-slave syndrome, or something similar? I'm not so sure how far you'll get with that."

"It makes perfectly good sense, even though the actual victims of direct slavery are no longer in the world. Slavery wasn't so long ago. Charles Black, for example, tells how he learned to play the harmonica from a man who had been a slave.[31] And the social devastation and destruction of culture, family, language, and ties that accompanied slavery surely has effects even today. Black people have to read diligently to learn about their traditions and their forebears.[32] They rarely receive inheritances; many white people do.[33] One reason is that blacks started out poor. There were no forty acres and a mule for freed blacks.[34] Indeed, after Reconstruction ended, a system of Jim Crow laws subjected blacks for fifty years to conditions little better than those they suffered under during slavery.[35] As recently as 1960, law schools only had a token representation of blacks. Several national law schools even had express rules against admitting blacks; a number of schools had not graduated one in their entire histories."

"Past discrimination cuts down on the competition. White people today have an easier time getting ahead because of it," I added.

"I'm sure you've heard the pool-is-so-small argument from whites," Rodrigo said.[36]

"Of course. Many of them use it against us in connection with higher-level hiring, such as law school faculty positions. Faculties can't be expected to desegregate all at once because the pool of available, college-trained black professionals is so small. What they rarely observe is that white culture made it that way. The smallness of the pool, if true, ought to be an argument in favor of affirmative action. Instead, perversely, it is offered against it, at least in any effective, quick-acting form. It's often struck me as odd that no one seems to notice this. They go on blithely citing the argument as though the pool became so small all by itself, like some natural misfortune. But a meteorite didn't hit us; racism and slavery did."

"That's what I meant earlier by how neutral principles work," Rodrigo added. "They look neutral only to the person who applies and cites them as a matter of faith. Anything familiar seems true. Recovery for preconception torts now seems familiar. But harms to blacks because of the country's inception and what took place then— that seems strange. But the cash value of neutral principles, at least as applied to us, is that we are treated poorly, denied jobs, refused compensation—and find our mistreatment justified by flimsy excuses like the pool one."

"A new legal theory, pragmatism, says we should look to the cash value of theories," I added, "not their elegance, rhetorical quality, or the way they make you feel good."[37]

"On that basis, neutral principles fail miserably, except as a justification for white supremacy."

"At which they're highly successful," I added wryly.

"Many white folks deny any sort of collective debt, reasoning that they are personally innocent of racial wrongs. They fail to notice that they benefit from the system of racial injustice that existed earlier in a raw form, and today in a more refined, veiled one. Many internalize and unconsciously subscribe to racist value systems, according to which our people are dangerous, lascivious, lazy, and stupid.[38] These stereotypes are embedded in millions of psyches and find expression in thousands of plots, scripts, children's stories, and narratives. They render us one-down in daily transactions, including many that clearly matter, like interviewing for a job or applying for an apartment.[39] Despite their denial of this collective debt, white folks, especially conservatives, very much want blacks to obey the law and Constitution that their iniquitous forebears laid down—a Constitution that contains no fewer than six clauses designed to protect the institution of slavery."

I straightened up on Rodrigo's couch. "I think I see what you are saying. Law-and-order conservatives want to deny any social obligation stemming from the racist behavior of the early Colonials and Southern plantation owners. But they are happy to remind us that we owe obligations to the document and nation that they set up. We owe obligations arising out of that social contract, but no obligation is owed to us arising from the abuse we suffered in connection with it. Ahistorical young conservatives want the benefit of social compliance from blacks with a system that provides young whites with security, schools, and liberty. But they don't want to pay for it by recognizing a debt they owe blacks arising from their forefathers' wrongs."

"It's illogical," Rodrigo added. "A little bit like arguing for a moral bankruptcy or forgiveness program for white society, while still insisting that blacks, who receive much less benefit from the surrounding culture, obey all its laws and codes of conduct. Logically, any obligations blacks owe, stemming from the same transaction, should be canceled as well. Our system is based on continuing consent to a scheme laid down in the past.[40] If a corporation borrowed money to set itself up, it can't simply repudiate it later on the ground that the original treasurer died."

We were both silent for a moment. Then, I said, "Rodrigo, you know as well as I that there is a companion argument that conservatives marshal against affirmative action and other programs for blacks. It's related, I think, to the neutrality arguments you just discussed. But it's a little different."

"And that argument is . . . ?" Rodrigo asked.

"I don't know if we have the time to address it. When does your reception start?"

Rodrigo looked at his watch. "Fifteen minutes. But don't worry. Laz and Giannina said they would be there. If I'm a few minutes late, nothing will happen. Just make sure you're not late for your dinner. What's the third argument?"

Affirmative Action vs. the Merit Principle

"It's that affirmative action violates the merit principle, since it allows individuals who lack the usual credentials to get a job or place in a law school class. Merit is one of those neutral principles, like the two you just addressed—the requirements of a guilty offender and a deserving victim—that conservatives love to trot out."

"I've talked about that with Laz. He's much more open to reason than you might think. But other conservatives are less so."

"How do you answer the objection, then?" I asked.

Rodrigo downed the last of his coffee, and gestured to ask if I would like more. I shook my head no, so he continued. "The argument is closely related to the first one. It holds that not only are middle-class blacks living today not the victims of racism, since American society is now formally equal, but that affirmative action's *operation* derogates from the sacred principle of merit. The boost that blacks get ensures that jobs and places at universities are filled with people less qualified than the ones who would get in otherwise. Blacks end up getting slots that should go to more highly qualified whites."[41]

"We talked about this before, I think," I said.

"The first time we met, and then again later. We agreed that merit criteria never operate as neutrally as they are supposed to. They end up applied against a background of expectations, pre-understandings, and exceptions that assure that the more familiar candidate wins out, even though they have little, if any, connection with the criteria we advertise on the job descriptions. Private universities operate legacy programs under which sons and daughters of the alumni get in under criteria much less stringent than others.[42] When we hear about this, we nod and make allowances: 'But of course . . .' we say. They also admit athletes and musicians for the school band under much lower standards than the other students.[43] No one considers those cases of affirmative action, or worries that the star quarterback will end up feeling stigmatized. Schools employ geographic preferences according to which applicants from far away are admitted with lower credentials.[44] This is supposed to enrich the entering class, even though all the students watch the same TV programs and study from the same textbooks in high school."

"Are you saying that all this is unjustified? Isn't it natural to favor one's own kind?"

"Perhaps it is," Rodrigo conceded. "We certainly do it all the time. White folks, for example, hire each other's kids to mow their lawns. They write artfully crafted letters of recommendation for each other, something that happens for very few blacks. When a favorite student approaches a teacher about extra credit work that enables him or her to change a 'B+' to an 'A-' in an honors class, that doesn't seem like affirmative action, but it is. The entire system of favors, courtesies, and informal networking that goes on every day, and from which our people are almost entirely excluded, is really a form of affirmative action: It enables people to get grades, jobs, entrance to desirable schools, and so on, without regard to formal merit."

"But people of color network and help each other out all the time, too," I pointed out.

"True—but merit becomes an issue only when a handful of us start getting ahead. When a few paltry blacks or Mexicans get into a law school because of affirmative action, conservatives are outraged. *That's* what I mean by 'unprincipled,' they say, neatly ignoring the letter of recommendation, inheritance, or stake from their father that enabled them to buy their first house."

"Merit is white people's affirmative action, as we said before," Rodrigo added.[45]

"White folks point out that we weren't enslaved, as though that is a killer argument. Yet they weren't enslaved, either."

"And, nevertheless, benefit from an enormous system of interlocking favors and informal practices that assure that they get ahead. White folks are the true affirmative action babies," Rodrigo said.[46] "The merit charge is not only hypocritical in overlooking how whites benefit from non-merit-based favors and exceptions, it overlooks how merit often fails to work for us. Even when a black or Mexican acquires all the standard earmarks and accoutrements of merit, such as high test scores or occupational prestige, he or she still ends up excluded and marginalized."

"Ellis Cose wrote a splendid book on the subject."

"I was just reading it," Rodrigo said, pointing at his bookshelf. *"The Rage of a Privileged Class.*[47] Roy Brooks showed the same thing—blacks of all income groups are worse off than whites, have more frustration, experience more discrimination, suffer more illness, are hassled more by the police."[48]

"We both know the dismal statistics," I added. "College-educated black men earn only a few dollars more than white high school graduates.[49] Only black federal judges are regularly impeached and charged with corruption.[50] The police stop and arrest conspicuously successful blacks, those driving Porsches or emerging from commuter trains, for example. There are few black full professors at universities[51] and not a single black CEO of a Fortune 500 corporation."[52]

"The reason is not hard to see," Rodrigo continued. "The black who evidences merit, who is a neatly dressed commuter, for example, or is driving an expensive car late at night, strikes everyone, including the police, as anomalous, as out of place.[53] Wealthy or extremely successful blacks end up facing *more* challenges and hate stares than the middle-income black letter carrier or custodian who goes home to a house in an all-black neighborhood at the end of the day."[54]

"Norms never work," I summarized. "We were talking about this once before.[55] And the same is true with the neutralist one. We give lip service to the idea that we should treat all persons with equal respect. But when a police officer stops the black executive who is jogging near his home in a wealthy neighborhood late at night, this seems to us normal and understandable. We're not offended. Rather, we sympathize with the police. After all, blacks *are* responsible, in a statistical sense, for a large proportion of the crime, we reason.[56] It's a lamentable truth, and so the police must, unfortunately, act on it for the safety of all of us."

"And when they do, it strikes everyone as perfectly understandable, neutral, and nonracist," Rodrigo concluded.

We both started. Someone was knocking at the door. "Come in," Rodrigo said. A pale, smiling young man dressed in a neat suit stepped inside.

"Laz! Come in. You remember the Professor, don't you?" Rodrigo said.

"Of course. Welcome to the law school," Kowalsky said, extending his hand and shaking mine firmly. "I hope you're here for the conference."

"Unfortunately, I can't stay. I'm here for a board meeting. But I'll try to drop by tomorrow," I said. "I bet your reception is about to start."

"The Program Chair is about to speak. But there are plenty of seats if you'd like to join us. And there's more than enough food."

"I'd better be going," I said, standing up. "I have a dinner meeting soon. But I'll see the two of you tomorrow. I want to hear your theory of a race war," I said smiling at Rodrigo's young colleague.

"Rodrigo quotes me too much. But I'll be happy to run it by you. When do you think you can make it?"

"My meeting ends at noon."

"How about a quick lunch?" Rodrigo suggested.

"I'll do my best," I said.

Welfare Leeches: In Which Rodrigo Critiques the Conservative Program of Welfare Reform

My board meeting went a little long, so that by the time the cab dropped me at Rodrigo's school the conference had already broken for lunch. An empty seminar room, except for neatly arranged piles of papers and programs, greeted me. Just as I was wondering where everyone had gone, I heard a pair of familiar voices from behind me. Rodrigo and Kowalsky were walking down the hall, engaged in animated conversation.

"Professor! We were wondering if you would make it. Are you still interested in lunch?"

"Very," I said. "These legal services meetings are truly bare bones. All I've had since last night is coffee and a bagel. I'm starved."

The two young friends consulted quickly, then Rodrigo said, "How about Southwestern, Professor? We could walk over to this little place in the shopping center across the street. Everyone else is eating in the conference center. We've got almost an hour and a half before the next session."

"Are you sure we shouldn't eat with the group?" I asked.

"I'm positive," Rodrigo replied. "Giannina is sitting in with them this time. All the others have meal tickets, since they are staying in the conference dorm. The three of us aren't, so we're taking turns."

"It's formal equality," Kowalsky said, smiling. "My favorite legal principle, as I'm sure you've heard."

"Shopping center food sounds fine to me. It'll save some time, plus, I love Southwestern. I'd like to hear how you made out in your discussion with Elmour. And you agreed to tell us more about your theory of race riots."

Kowalsky was silent for a moment. Then, "Oh, you mean a race war. I'm happy to do so, although it doesn't exactly make my fellow conservatives look good. It's just a hypothesis," he explained, as we waited for a break in the traffic.

"Laz is an equal opportunity trasher," Rodrigo said, giving his friend an affectionate clap on the back. "He's as tough on mean-spiritedness in the conservative camp as he is on looseness and lack of rigor on our side. Here we are."

A few minutes later, we were studying the menu in what turned out to be a plain but attractive natural food restaurant. "Not bad for a shopping center menu," I said. "What do you recommend?"

"Southwestern food is their specialty," Rodrigo replied. "I'm having the menudo. Giannina loves this place."

"I think I'll try that myself," Kowalsky said. "And to answer your question, Professor, Elmour and I had a great talk about church-state law. He made a number of good points at my expense, although it turns out we're not as far apart as you might think. It seems his father was a Baptist minister. Oh, here's our waiter."

I quickly scanned the menu while my two young friends placed their orders. "What do you think of the grilled vegetables?" I asked. "I've been cutting down on meat. Doctor's orders."

Rodrigo made a sympathetic face and said, "I've never had it, but everything here's good." I nodded to the waiter: "I'll have that," and he departed.

After a short pause while a second waiter put down our chips and salsa, I asked, "How was this morning's session?"

The two young men looked at each other. Then Rodrigo spoke up: "It was about welfare cutbacks—or reform, as our conservative friends like to say. Elmour and one other person were on the panel. They reviewed the Republicans' proposals and also the failed efforts, beginning in the sixties and early seventies, on the part of liberals to have subsistence declared a fundamental right.[57] It was sobering, to say the least." Then, after a pause, "I think Laz was the only one in the room who wasn't frowning."

We both looked over at Laz, who replied evenly: "I have no problem whatsoever with that. The Constitution doesn't guarantee happiness, or even that you won't go hungry. It guarantees only the right to pursue happiness. If some people don't want to work or are content to be poor, that's their business, not the government's. Poverty is a great incentive to find work. I would exclude, of course, the helplessly disabled and single mothers with infants. Everyone else should rise or fall according to their merits. I don't mean to be heartless, but that's our system, and it's responsible for our having the highest standard of living in the world."

"Fifth highest, actually," Rodrigo interjected.

"Depending on how you count," Kowalsky quickly retorted. "And don't get me wrong. I agree with many of the points made this morning connecting poverty with social pathology. Conservatives are no fonder of crime than you liberals are. We just don't think that rewarding single mothers for having more babies and paying people for not working is the way to fight it."

"But your people are cutting job training and aid to schools," Rodrigo replied. "How are the poor going to pull themselves up without the training and education the more fortunate provide for their children almost as a matter of course?"

"Basic education I have no problem with," Kowalsky replied. "Although I wish some of you liberals would consider supporting alternative schools and voucher systems for those who want to opt out of the cookie-cutter one-size-fits-all approach."

"We might support those programs," I chimed in, "if your people were a little more accommodating on basic social support for the desperately poor. You seem to be more reasonable on this point than some of your fellow conservatives, I must say. Murray and Herrnstein, for example, write that we are doomed to suffer a large and growing underclass.[58] If we don't hold the line on welfare and overreproduction on the part of the poor, we will end up being swamped with people and debt."

"We're already swamped in debt," Laz quickly replied. "The national debt now stands at more than 4.8 trillion dollars, the most of any industrialized country. Our annual deficit is so big that the conservative Congress is finally thinking of doing something about it."

"But welfare for the poor constitutes only a small part of the federal budget. Less than one percent, according to an article I was just reading," I pointed out.

"Other federal handouts account for much more," Rodrigo added quickly. Then, looking over at Laz he asked, "Would you favor cutting the military budget? We're at peace, but your conservative friends want to give the military as much hardware as usual, if not more." Rodrigo looked up brightly and motioned to the waiter, who was passing nearby. He whispered something, then looked up to hear Kowalsky reply:

"National security is one of those areas we can't very well privatize or pawn off on individual initiative. You liberals get excited when citizens want to own guns or form militias."

"Touché," Rodrigo replied, grinning. "But that's only one area of federal handouts to fat cats. Thanks," he said to the waiter who had just brought a telephone. "Let's see if this works." He fished in his briefcase for a moment while mumbling something almost inaudible: "You won't believe how much."

After a second, Rodrigo said, "There! Where were we?"

"Welfare costs and fat cats," I prompted.

"Right. Giannina and I were just starting to do this before. Do you want to see how much money this country spends on welfare for the rich and middle class?"

"I'd love to," I said.

"I've been urging the elimination of protective tariffs for U.S. industries for years," Kowalsky quickly interjected. "They're a form of handout and are bad for the economy."

I looked over to see what Rodrigo was doing.

"I got this last month," Rodrigo explained, indicating the tiny laptop computer he had just pulled out of his briefcase and connected to the restaurant's phone line. "It's great on planes." Rearranging our food, which had just arrived, he punched in a few numbers, then: "Here we are. Just like Giannina found before. Social Security, a form of welfare for middle-class widows, many of whom haven't worked a day in their lives, 22 percent of the budget—almost forty-five times more than aid for dependent children, the program conservatives want to cut. And, oh. Look here." His fingers practically flew over the keyboard. "Another big one—Medicare, 11 percent. Neither of these is aimed at the poor. They're entitlement programs—giveaways, really, and they total almost one-third of the federal budget."

"I didn't say I favored those programs," Kowalsky replied a little defensively. "I'm against welfare for the rich as much as for the poor. For example, hardly any conservatives in Congress are urging that we take a look at the national farm surplus program. I favor cutting that. It's wasteful and sets up exactly the wrong sort of incentive. It rewards farmers for not producing. There's no excuse for it. Quotas, too. Latin American and Caribbean sugar is much cheaper to produce than the American kind. Sugar quotas are in effect a subsidy to American industry, and so on for all the others."

"Let's take a look," Rodrigo said and performed new magic on his keyboard. "Hmmm. It's a big one, too. Look at that—$9.8 billion a year on farm income supports, according to the Congressional Budget Office. Compared to that, the SBA's $500 million and the $675 million the feds spend on cultural agencies are 'chicken feed,' as one commentor put it. The same writer points out that for many farmers, annual supports are so large that they are the farmers' biggest single source of profit. Payments sometimes go to farmers who agree not to plant crops at all. Other times they go to prop up crops that otherwise are not profitable."

"Absurd," Kowalsky agreed. "A form of welfarism we should drop as soon as possible."

"And it's nearly as large an item as AFDC, the main federal program for poor families in need of relief," Rodrigo replied. "If conservatives are really in favor of neutral principles, they should be as indignant over this form of giveaway as over welfare handouts to single black mothers. And, hold on a second. Here. Giannina was looking for this before. $1.4 billion for price subsidies for big sugar farms alone. That's almost as much as we pay for heating fuel subsidies for the poor."

"Which House Republicans want to cut out," I added.

"I might keep that in myself," Kowalsky added quietly. "I've been cold in the winter. It's nothing any human should have to tolerate."

"Oh, and look. They also want to eliminate $377 million for legal services for the poor. Yet at the same time, the current budget provides $700 million for alcohol fuel producers, who otherwise could not compete. Congress would leave in a $400 million tax subsidy for entertainment expenses for businessmen but cut $281 million for tuition grants for national service volunteers. The Republicans are defending a loophole that allows wealthy people to renounce their citizenship to avoid taxes. $400 million a year in revenues lost, according to the Democrats, who want to close it."

"I'm against most forms of corporate welfare," Laz replied, his voice rising slightly. "It's just as bad as the other kind."

"Look here." There was no stopping Rodrigo now. Ignoring his meal, which was growing cold, he went on: "Two billion a year helping high-tech companies build a space station that will benefit no one except themselves. Oil companies get to keep their favorite tax break, to offset their so-called intangible drilling expenses—another $1.2 billion a year." Click, click, click. His fingers flew over the keyboard, as they had on two other occasions. I wondered whether I would ever acquire his technological wizardry. I started too late in life, I thought, gloomily. "Let's try this other data base.... Ah! I thought I'd find it here. The taxpayers help the Department of Agriculture to the tune of $110 million a year advertising abroad such U.S.-made delicacies as McDonald's Chicken McNuggets, Pillsbury muffins, and Sunkist oranges. They even tried to sell Gallo wine to the French. It didn't work. Oh, here's another big one—the federal mortgage interest deduction, which benefits mainly middle-class homeowners. More than—let's see—nearly a third of what we pay at all levels, state and federal, for welfare subsidies for the poor. Throw in food stamps and it's . . . still one-third the amount. And, oh my—twenty billion to bail out Mexico, mainly for the benefit of U.S. investors and Mexican oligarchs."

Rodrigo was furiously scribbling figures down on the napkin. "If you two will give me a second, I think I can come up with a total."

We honored his wish. "I've got it," Rodrigo announced, looking up. "If you add in all the figures I just mentioned, plus tax breaks for those unproductive industries . . . . Let's see . . . how many U.S. citizens are there?"

Kowalsky and I looked at each other. "About 260 million?" Laz asked.

"Assume 280. There are all those illegal aliens, as your buddies like to call them. Divide out and you get . . . . Well, look at that. It looks like we pay quite a bit more for welfare for the middle class, the wealthy, and industrialists than for the country's poor—three times more, in fact."

"Since there are fewer rich people than poor or lower middle-class ones," I added, "it looks as if we, as a society, end up paying a good deal more per person to keep the rich afloat than the poor."

Rodrigo disconnected the telephone wire, handed it back to the waiter, and snapped his computer shut.[59] "What do you think, Laz?"

We were silent for a moment. Then Kowalsky said quietly, "It looks to me as though the real welfare leeches in our society are middle-class retirees on Social Security, veterans, investors, and corporations with strong lobbies. They feed from the public trough at least as much as welfare mothers or little black kids in Head Start programs. Yet they do not see themselves as parasites at all. It's all a matter of perspective, as you Crits like to say, although in the case of Social Security widows, at least their husbands worked at some time, if only in the past. And the farmers we help are doing something, even if only letting their fields go fallow."

"Of course, a black welfare mother is doing something," I interjected, "namely, raising her child. And even if the father is not working, black America worked long hours without pay not too long ago, when we were all in slavery."

"I have no quarrel with that," Kowalsky added. "I think all the freeloaders should stand on the same footing, corporate or individual, black or white, middle class or poor alike. We should scrutinize and ruthlessly cut every program that is not absolutely essential for national security or to save someone's life. Any more than that and you sap individual initiative. Not to mention add to the tax burden of all the rest of us. It's bad for the market and bad for our national economic health. There is no excuse for it, any of it."

"Yet, we're thinking of cutting relief only for the already poor, and eliminating programs like job supports, Head Start, race-targeted college scholarships, and affirmative action that are crucial for upward mobility for the community of color,"[60] Rodrigo summarized. "What do you think is going on?"

The waiter arrived to clear our plates. "Would you gentlemen like coffee or dessert?"

Rodrigo looked at his watch. "I wouldn't mind some. We've got a little while." The waiter laid down the dessert menus and took our orders for coffee.

Kowalsky leaned forward in his booth. "As you know, I'm an equal opportunity critic. I have a theory, although I'd like the two of you to agree not to represent it as any more than that. I don't want to seem too hard on some of my fellow conservatives."

Both Rodrigo and I nodded. "We'll take it in that spirit," I promised. "What's good here in the way of dessert that my doctor wouldn't disapprove of?"

Kowalsky and Rodrigo looked up sympathetically. "You could try the yogurt *frullato*. Giannina recommends it," Rodrigo suggested.

"Okay." The waiter took our orders, frullato for me, buñuelos with powdered sugar for my two young friends, and departed.

Kowalsky's Theory: The Upcoming Race War

"Good choice, Professor," Kowalsky said. "You can have a bit of my confection, if you like." He reminded us of our promise, then began:

"Have you ever wondered why my fellow conservatives seem bent on eliminating affirmative action? I mean not simply cutting it back, but eliminating—destroying it entirely?"

"As an issue, you mean?" I asked.

"Exactly," Kowalsky answered. "We all know what reasons they give for opposing it. I subscribe to some of them, as you know, although in my opinion they call for restructuring, not eliminating the program."

"I give up," Rodrigo interjected "Why do conservatives want to put an end to affirmative action?"

"I was thinking about this yesterday, after my argument with Elmour. In a way, affirmative action is the perfect issue for the Right. It never goes away. It reliably delivers votes. And it enables people like me to point out how unprincipled you liberals are and how we are morally superior. You fall right into our hands every time. It's been the perfect vote-getter, year after year. Yet, my fellow conservatives across the land are trying to get rid of it, decisively and forever. Initiatives in California and other states, bills in Congress . . ."[61]

"And those three Supreme Court decisions just this last term," Rodrigo interjected.

"Right," Kowalsky replied. "Making it harder for states to redraw voting districts so as to increase minority representation,[62] making it easier for school districts to end desegregation plans,[63] and applying the higher, constitutional compelling interest standard to federal affirmative action[64]—all these are evidence of the same thing. The political Right is prepared to destroy affirmative action once and for all."

"And you think this means something more than just muscle-flexing?" I asked. I was curious where the young conservative *wunderkind* was going.

"I do," Kowalsky continued. "Otherwise the Right would opt for a series of gradual cutbacks, and not sweeping measures like California's Civil Rights Initiative. Affirmative action enables the Republicans to argue that they are the defenders of the just and the true. It reliably causes indignation on the part of working-class and ethnic whites, who can be led to believe blacks are getting away with something."

"Even though our levels of school drop-out, unemployment, suicide, poverty, and infant mortality are the highest in the country and approaching those of the Third World," Rodrigo added.[65]

"And your people still lag in undergraduate and graduate enrollment,[66] middle and upper management jobs,[67] and virtually every circle that matters—except sports and entertainment. As I said, it's a perfect issue. It enables my side to rally the troops and depict liberals as the cause of unhappiness and job insecurity on the part of blue-collar whites, like my family," Kowalsky added.

"And I suppose you have a theory for why they are acting as they are?" I asked.

"I think they are gearing up for a race war," Kowalsky said quietly. "It's not a conspiracy, exactly. Rather, I think there is a general sense that it's time to pick a fight. Caucasians will cease being a majority in this country about midway in the next century.[68] At that point, numerical and voting power should, logically, shift to groups of color—blacks, Asians, and Latinos. White opinion-makers don't want this to happen. So, they're gearing up for a fight. It's one of the oldest tricks in the world—provoke your enemy until he responds, then slap him down decisively. You get to impose your regime and sleep well nights, too, because you can maintain that it was all his fault."

"So, right-wingers are trying to increase minority misery to the point where we react, to the point where violence breaks out?" I asked incredulously.

"Yes, like the sixties. Only this time, it will be different. The rebellion will be put down, like before. But this time, instead of enacting sympathetic rules and laws to ameliorate black poverty and racial injustice, like the Civil Rights Act of 1964, the country will put in place repressive measures increasing police surveillance, criminalizing sedition, and providing for martial law. We will then sail into the next century secure. Whites' political and economic power will be assured by a host of new laws and executive orders, a little like South Africa. The new redistricting decision is just the first of many measures that will prevent blacks from ever obtaining political power. And gatherings, organizing, and street marches will be ruthlessly put down. The U.S. will have a system of apartheid, in effect, with whites wielding power over a large but powerless black and brown population of laborers and domestics."

"And the idea is to provoke this confrontation before it is too late?" Rodrigo leaned forward, his expression serious.

"Yes, it would need to be done fairly soon, before power passes peacefully," Kowalsky replied. "That's why you see everything we were talking about earlier—welfare cutbacks, which are calculated to increase blacks' misery. Voting-rights retrenchment. Withdrawal of scholarships, which enabled future black leaders to get a college education. Attacks on 'big government'—which is seen as an employer and defender of minorities. And, most of all, elimination of affirmative action."

"I used to think all we had to do was wait," Rodrigo said, somberly. "That demography would produce a peaceful change of power sooner or later. You've given me pause."

"A great convulsion, in which whites decisively put down a black insurrection, would be exactly what's needed," Kowalsky said. "And one doesn't need to resort to conspiracy theories to understand the host of anti-black and anti-poor measures that are taking place right now. Whites have simply decided enough is enough—it's time to take a stand. If millions across the country, and conservative elites at dozens of think tanks and institutes have the same sense—that it's our turn—and act on it, it produces the same thing. Something must be done, everyone agrees tacitly. And so the product is a coordinated campaign. It may have started already in California, our most ethnically diverse state."[69]

"Laz," I burst in. "I used to think leftists were paranoid, always afraid that the government was spying on their meetings, acting in league with big business, and so on. Of course, some of that turned out to be true. But this idea of yours goes further than anything I've heard. For one thing, our legal system and Constitution would never stand for it. We have the Bill of Rights, the Fourteenth Amendment."

"All of which can be overridden by a compelling state interest, as you well know, Professor," Laz replied levelly. "Do you have any doubt that the current Supreme Court would find one if civil unrest broke out in every city across the nation?"

"*Korematsu* could be a precedent,"[70] Rodrigo pointed out. "The Supreme Court could hold that emergency measures like curfews, surveillance, sweeps, and even the detention of leaders of color are justified. We baited the Indians at Wounded Knee until they responded. Then we wiped them out.[71] Unfortunately, there is more historical precedent for Laz's grim scenario than any of us would like."

"Our Latino friends would cite the zoot suit riots in the 1940's, when America went through a wave of anti-immigrant, nativist sentiment,"[72] Laz added. "Roving gangs of Anglo sailors started the riots. When the Latinos in Los Angeles and other cities responded, we threw them into jail, charging them with breaching the peace and provoking civil disorder. Congress then instituted Operation Wetback, in which tens of thousands of Mexican-Americans, many of them legal immigrants or even citizens, were rounded up and deported to Mexico."[73]

"Most Republicans oppose arms control," I pointed out. "Some even favor assault weapons,[74] even though there is absolutely no use for such weapons other than to put down a civil insurrection." And with a chill, I remembered: "And Republicans in think tanks and everywhere favor keeping the military budget high, even though we are at peace and have no major enemies anywhere in the world. I still think it's crazy, but what other use can there be for all that hardware than to prepare for an upcoming domestic war and fortress America?"

"People of color rarely support guns," Rodrigo added quietly. "Right wing militias are virtually always all-white, so assault weapons create firepower among the white minority.[75] Even elite groups are arming themselves, hiring security guards, and retreating behind gates and walls. Right-wing fundamentalists have always had a morbid fascination with apocalypse. Formerly, they defined it in terms of H-bombs and nuclear Armageddon. They preached fear of communists, the other main group that possessed these weapons. Now they don't talk in terms of H-bombs, but of race war."[76]

"It seems to me very possible that we will have one," Kowalsky added. "They know this, are prepared for that possibility, and want to make sure that their group wins."

"For the first time, there is a religious theory for white supremacy," Rodrigo interjected. "It combines with the pseudoscientific one—I'm thinking of books like *The Bell Curve*—to produce a mentality among whites that holds that they are entitled to remain on top, no matter what the population statistics and numbers show. Consider all the interest in our own Civil War, for example. One network recently aired a series on the subject.[77] There are new books, including some excellent ones by Shelby Foote.[78] Why else would there be such a revival of interest if people were not starting to think, at least on an unconscious level, that a new one is coming up?"

I looked at Rodrigo. "In South Africa, whites did amass weapons in preparation for armed resistance. And fundamentalist white churches there preached that whites had a spiritual imperative to preserve their control over the country. And that series you mentioned, Rodrigo, in several hours of installments featured mainly white heroes. There was only a little on Frederick Douglass and other black figures who opposed slavery and argued that the Union should fight to end that scourge."

"Other recent books about the civil rights revolution do the same thing," Rodrigo replied. "Jack Greenberg's book,[79] for example, emphasized the role of whites in controlling the course of the desegregation campaign. 'Look how much whites have sacrificed for blacks,' these books seem to say. This way of presenting history legitimizes white anger now. Blacks are depicted as ingrates who don't appreciate all that good white liberals have done for them. This enables liberals, and the Democratic Party, to look the other way, or even join in the mass reaction against black gains. During the period just before the Civil War broke out, the South drafted local boys and armed them. That's how they got an army. The near future could witness the same thing."

Kowalsky added: "We are seeing the beginnings of that now in the militia movement.[80] Private groups are buying weapons, training in the woods, developing their own ideology and leadership structure. They keep in touch by E-mail and conventions. They interpret every move by blacks and their supporters as anti-American, as an attack on them and their values. That's the advantage of an ideology that demonizes the other side. If you decide at the outset that X is an enemy, your enemy-creation will let you interpret X's every action as justifying your visiting violence on him. That's the lesson of Chief Sitting Bull and Wounded Knee. It's also that of Japanese internment and the *Korematsu* case, which held, based on the slenderest evidence, that the mere existence of Japanese citizens living peaceably on the West Coast was a threat to national security.[81] You try your best to provoke the other side into responding. When they don't, you simply declare that milder and milder actions on their part are provocations. Eventually their mere existence is an outrage that cannot be ignored, as with the Japanese."

"We've seen that historically," I conceded. "But do you really think this could happen today? Laz, I think you are going too far. Your theory may be a useful *interpretive* approach to understanding much of what is going on, all the goading and stiffening of the spine. Many whites are uneasy and spoiling for a fight. As a *psychological* hypothesis to explain all the muscle-flexing and general ugliness—on that level, what you say makes much sense. Threatened people often look to pick a fight, to reestablish who's boss. But you surely don't think we are preparing literally for a race war, do you?"

"Only time will tell," Laz replied. "The FBI may have done something similar in the Idaho standoff. Federal officials provoked the family until they reacted and then shot Randy Weaver's wife.[82] Of course, in that case the shoe was on the other foot. But conservatives learned the lesson all too well. As your Huey Newton once said, 'It's not paranoia if they really are out to get you.' Hate crimes are increasing. Incidents of campus racism as well.[83] Every major city reports Rodney King-type incidents in which white police beat black men to death. One just took place in San Francisco.[84] And African-American columnist Carl Rowan recently described how white racism operates inside many political departments, including the elite federal Alcohol, Tobacco, and Firearms agency, which held a 'Good Ol' Boys Roundup' earlier this year in the hills of Tennessee.[85] It featured T-shirts with Dr. Martin Luther King's face behind a target and O. J. Simpson's in a noose. Another showed white cops arresting a black, sprawled across a police car, under the heading 'Boys on the Hood.' A lawsuit bought by black agents featured evidence that ATF agents frequently used the word 'Nigger' and placed Ku Klux Klan cards and other paraphernalia prominently in their offices. I'm afraid that my theory may come literally true, and at a broad national level. You mentioned earlier the hope that our institutions—the law, the police—would serve as a bulwark against white supremacist repression. I'm afraid they may prove to be among the most enthusiastic supporters."

The waiter arrived offering coffee refills. "Not for me," I said. "Sobering as this is, I need to be moving along soon. And you"—I looked at Laz—"don't you have a panel starting any minute now?"

"It only takes a couple of minutes to walk back," Rodrigo said, looking at his watch. "Are you all ready for your talk, Laz?"

When his friend nodded, Rodrigo went on. "To summarize, then, it's not just wild-eyed patriots and white supremacists now who are talking about holding the line, saving America as a white society, and resisting the changes that would otherwise take place when the numbers of blacks and browns exceed those of whites, as will happen soon. The cruder elements are arming, while conservative churches are preaching a return to early values—thinly veiled references to race—thus laying the theological basis for a race war. Conservatives across the board are taunting blacks and liberals, calling us balkanizers and tribalists and barbarians. They are dismantling affirmative action and ethnic studies programs on campuses, while cutting programs of critical importance to the inner city poor. Laz, you may have a point. It does look like a coordinated effort to prod blacks, to provoke us into lashing back, so that mainstream society can respond with armed force."

"Don't forget that there will be legal and constitutional change accompanying the armed put-down," Laz added. "Constitutional amendments and new laws will assure that there cannot be a second uprising, ever. We have already seen the start. Bills authorizing the building of new prisons and the hiring of new police officers, reviving the death penalty, and providing for mandatory sentences for crimes associated with the black underclass are only a beginning. I hate crime, as you know, and think these measures are not a bad idea. But they're aimed just at you, which any self-respecting conservative should detest. English-only laws and ruthless immigration measures make things hard for Chicanos and other immigrants of color.[86] Congress is even considering abolishing U.S. citizenship for the children of undocumented immigrants.[87] One proposal would amend the Fourteenth Amendment, for the first time in its history, to provide a narrower grant of citizenship.[88] The thinly veiled purpose of the amendment is to keep America white."

"Laz," I said. "I wonder if you are familiar with the new eugenics movement, which advocates controls on breeding for the black underclass. New books by conservatives sound the alarm. Our best citizens, as they call them, have only a few children per family, while immigrant and black populations have too many, with the result that our precious national gene pool is deteriorating.[89] Supposedly, we are losing several IQ points per generation. The new eugenicists include Nobel Prize winners like William Shockley, prize-winning educational psychologist Arthur Jensen,[90] and writer and columnist Ben Wattenberg, whose *Birth Dearth* sold well in conservative circles."

Kowalsky added, "And someone whose other ideas I respect, John Tanton, in a secret memo written a few years ago but only recently publicized, sounded the cry for whites to mobilize in the face of engulfment by what he saw as inferior races. I brought his 'Witan IV' memo right here, just for you. He wrote: 'As Whites see their power and control over their lives declining, will they simply go quietly into the night? Or, will there be an explosion?' He also asked, 'Will the present majority peaceably hand over its political power to a group that is simply more fertile?' and '[i]s advice to limit one's family simply advice to move over and let someone else with greater reproductive power occupy the space?'[91] Cordelia Scaife, a respected conservative philanthropist, went over the edge, in my opinion, when she sponsored a reprinting of Raspail's novel, *Camp of the Saints*,[92] which features North African hordes sweeping over and destroying civilization."[93]

"*That* I didn't know," I said. "But I was reading somewhere that early twentieth-century laws criminalized abortion, in part because doctors wanted to control midwifery, but also because late-Victorian women were beginning to rebel against their role. They were having fewer babies, which alarmed male legislators. Today, something similar is taking place. Middle-class white men, and some women, want to take away the right to abortion. Black women are having too many babies, white women too few. The equation is changing."

"And in a way that threatens white supremacy," Rodrigo added. "There are very few black women in the right-to-life movement, and surprisingly few Latinos."

We were all silent for a moment. Then Laz spoke up: "You see, I said I was an equal opportunity critic. I support much of what my fellow conservatives say and do, but not this. I felt I had an obligation to tell the two of you. I still believe in neutral principles, in rewarding hard work, and in treating all persons with similar respect. Everyone in our political system deserves the right to be treated as an individual and to have his or her fundamental humanity respected. But I'm alarmed at some of the steps my fellow conservatives are taking. There are better ways to recall America to its individualist roots than to goad already suffering populations, mired in slavery and Jim Crow laws until not so long ago, into what will prove to be a bloody and decisive defeat."

Rodrigo looked at his watch and drained his coffee cup. "As morbidly fascinating as I find all this, I'm afraid we had better be going. I'll just sign the check—it's on the law school, by the way—you're a speaker, Laz, and you an honored guest, Professor—and we should head back."

We walked in silence back to the law school, broken only by my commenting about being glad Laz believed in equal treatment—otherwise we would not have heard his critique of his own movement—and Rodrigo's request that Laz try to rein in a certain copanelist, who I gather was famous for longwindedness, so as not to exceed the time limits. ("We might want to save some time to discuss some of these broader issues," he said.)

As luck would have it, the afternoon's panel turned out to be technical, having to do with changes in the law of sexual harassment in the workplace, and a little outside my field. I listened as best I could, but my attention kept returning to our lunchtime conversation and its interpretation of events occurring on a wide spectrum of activities and encompassing a broad range of actors, organizations, and writers on the Right. I recalled that our conversation had begun with a simple riddle: Why are the conservatives trying to get rid of affirmative action, the goose that (for them) laid and reliably continues to lay the golden egg? I thought about how Laz had drawn our attention first to the draconian rollbacks conservatives are advocating in welfare—rollbacks which go far beyond those necessary to save the budget or provide the poor with an incentive to work. He, and Rodrigo too, pointed out the strange way in which conservatives manage to exempt their favorite industries, the military, and high-income people from cutbacks. I recalled Rodrigo's lightning display of technological wizardry, which culminated in the conclusion that the rich are the main beneficiaries of governmental largesse.

I recalled how Kowalsky had then offered his chilling explanation for all this: namely, that conservative consciousness has now reached a tacit decision—not so much a conscious conspiracy as the overall effect of a group mentality—to push blacks and the poor until they respond. Their response would then provide the justification for harsh measures and perhaps a race war. Otherwise, how can one explain, for example, the conservative campaign to end affirmative action, a program that until now had provided them with benefits, both rhetorical and political? How else explain recent Supreme Court decisions reversing a legacy of Warren Court solicitude, or measures like California's Proposition 187, the upsurge in eugenics and similar proposals to limit reproduction on the part of poor blacks? And how else can one explain the advent of militia groups and fundamentalist religion calling for a return to and defense of traditional values? I reflected on the picture that emerged, like a photograph emerging from the darkroom tub, over the course of our conversation. I wondered if society was really headed toward a conflagration aimed at assuring that power does not change easily and peaceably as minority numbers begin to exceed those of whites a few decades from now. Was Kowalsky, the brilliant young "equal opportunity trasher," too hard on his fellow conservatives? Or would elite whites achieve much the same thing by stirring up division among outgroups, minorities, and Jews, so that the next race war would be between minorities fighting for the scraps, much as happened in South Africa before the moment of reckoning?

I did not see my two young friends much more that day. After the afternoon session ended, both were engrossed in herding all the conference attendees over to the dormitory facility for a barbecue, then an impromptu session in one of the lounges on "an important matter that just came up." I wondered if that matter had to do with the substance of our noontime conversation, and if so what the other conference participants would make of Laz's and Rodrigo's hypothesis. I even wondered, in passing, about Kowalsky's motives in spelling out for us how his fellow conservatives' actions might produce a racial showdown. The brilliant young conservative seemed genuinely sympathetic to minority causes and the poor. But why had he brought the news to us and to the conference of young, left-leaning professors of color? Was it out of concern and sporting justice? With a shudder, I realized that any overreaction on our part— sounding the alarm to our communities, or arming, for example— could at the very least subject us to withering criticism as alarmists and demagogues. It could even, paradoxically, bring about the very repression against which Kowalsky warned.

I arrived at the airport with my head spinning and a tablet full of notes. While walking down the nearly deserted concourse to meet my late-evening flight back home, I roused myself from the introspective daze I had been wrapped up in since getting into the shuttle outside the law school, which Kowalsky had been kind enough to call for me. There, in front of my eyes, in a display behind the locked window of a small concourse bookstore, I saw for sale *The Turner Diaries*, which deals with an upcoming race war, and is authored by a right-wing novelist. I noted the price, publisher, and order number posted on the display and resolved to buy and read the book as soon as I got home.

5

Cosmopolitanism and Identity Politics

In Which Rodrigo and I Meet on the Inspection Team

"Good timing," I commented to Rodrigo as we waited to hail a cab in front of the airport. "I'm glad we managed to coordinate our arrivals."

"Me, too," said my young friend. "How was your flight?"

"Fine. And yours?"

"I barely made it. Laz had to drive me to the airport. We were talking, and I lost track of the time."

"That was quite a conversation we had last time," I said. "Despite his cheerful demeanor, Laz knows how to spin a dark tale."[1]

"That he does," Rodrigo agreed. "And the disturbances that broke out in California, and the referenda being voted on right now across the nation restricting immigration, welfare, and citizenship all show that Laz's prediction is right on pace.[2] Here's one."

We gave the driver the address, and as he started up, Rodrigo commented, "Do you realize this is one of the law schools I applied to for my LL.M. just a few years ago? And here we are on the AALS site inspection team for their reaccreditation."[3]

"I didn't know that," I said. "But I'm glad you wound up where you did. It let us get acquainted. Plus, you met Giannina that way, too, didn't you?"

130

"I did. It worked out well all around. Just like our flights."

"And this inspection team. I must confess, though, I accepted the assignment only when they told me who was on the committee. I've served on so many of these it's lost its appeal. But when I learned you were on this one, I changed my mind. Ever since you took that job in the Midwest, we see each other all too infrequently. Look— that must be the court building."

"District court," the cabbie said. "That's where they tried that serial killer last month. They had press coming in from everywhere."

After a short but enlightening exchange with the cabbie, who turned out to be an amateur crime buff, on juror selection, forensic evidence, and the after-hours habits and tipping practices of journalists compared to lawyers, Rodrigo turned back to me and said: "I agree. It *is* all too infrequent. I keep wishing you'd get on E-mail, Professor. You're one of only a few of my friends who isn't. It's really easy to learn and saves on the phone bill."

I was about to say something about old dogs and new tricks when the driver asked: "Will you gentlemen be needing help with your bags?"

"Oh, we're here. That was fast!"

We paid the driver, carried our bags inside, and fifteen minutes later were sitting in the hotel's nearly deserted coffee shop admiring the view.

"Quite a skyline, isn't it?" I asked.

"It is. Reminds me a little of Milan's."

"You *are* a cosmopolitan person," I said. "I keep forgetting how well traveled you are. Which reminds me. I was about to ask you something—if you have the time. Do you need to call Giannina?"

"She has her aerobics class this evening. We agreed I'd call"— Rodrigo looked at his watch—"about an hour from now. What's on your mind?"

"I was reading about a new critique of identity politics—what you and I would call civil rights. It's based on the idea of cosmopolitanism and takes a number of forms. Since you are an extremely cosmopolitan person, Rodrigo, I wondered what you would think of it."

"Do you mean the idea that focusing on one's narrow ethnic or national identity is dangerous in a nuclear world? I know that version. Martha Nussbaum and others have written that narrow nationalism is a luxury humanity can no longer afford.[4] She favors universalism, not surprising from a neo-Aristotelian. Todd Gitlin has written in a similar vein."[5]

"There is that version," I admitted. "Although I was thinking of a different one. Jeremy Waldron, a well-known legal writer at Berkeley, came to similar conclusions but on different grounds. He wrote not so much about the nuclear threat as the kind of costly squabbles and incessant demands that go on under the banner of 'identity politics,' as he calls it. I have a copy of his article with me."[6]

Rodrigo was silent for a minute. "No, I don't think I've heard of that version, although I'd love to. I do consider myself a cosmopolitan person. But I'm also a racial activist, as you know. I believe that society needs to incorporate outsiders, the sooner the better,[7] as we've discussed before."

"That's why I thought you'd be intrigued by the critique. Waldron is the principal spokesperson, although there are others.[8] The basic idea is that identity politics is inconsistent with cosmopolitanism. The cosmopolitan person is one who refuses to define himself or herself in terms of a location, ancestry, or even citizenship or language. Rather, he or she picks and chooses from a multitude of sources. He or she may eat Italian food one day, Indonesian the next, take his vacation in South America or Tibet. The cosmopolitan does not consider his identity compromised when he or she learns Japanese or Spanish, listens to arias by Verdi sung by a Maori princess recorded on Japanese equipment, or studies Buddhist meditation and Japanese or Korean management techniques. This person, according to Waldron, 'is a creature of modernity, conscious of living in a mixed-up world and having a mixed-up self.' "[9]

"Sounds a little like me, all right," Rodrigo admitted, a little ruefully. "Except for the part about identity politics. How does he derive that from the cosmopolitan ideal?"

"Two or three ways," I replied. "He considers intense loyalty to one's narrow group dangerous and likely to lead to militancy and war.[10] He also says it is costly, since it entails rescue operations and propping up dying cultures that demand subsidies and handouts from the more modern ones that surround them.[11] Backward cultures want to have it both ways, he argues. They want to be allowed to survive, to maintain their primitive ways. Yet, that very survival needs financing by the more advanced societies that have modernized and joined the industrial world of commerce and ideas. An indigenous culture's holding onto its time-honored condition 'may be something that particular people like and enjoy. But they no longer can claim that it is something that they need,' "[12] I read, looking down at the xeroxed article in my lap.

"Is he the writer who compares ethnic politics to living in Disneyland?" Rodrigo asked.[13]

"The very one," I replied.

"Laz was starting to tell me about him. But then something happened and we had to cut short our conversation. He was smiling, so he may have been baiting me slightly. So, it's the same writer."

"I'm sure it is. He writes that preserving small backward groups, like pygmies living in rain forests or nationalist American blacks who want to live in the black community and go to all-black schools, is as artificial as a Walt Disney theme park. For Waldron, the disappearance of such an identity group is no great loss. 'It is like the death of a fashion or a hobby, not the demise of anything that people really need,' " I read.[14]

"But one of the tenets of nationalism, at least of the African-American variety, is not to be dependent on whites but to develop one's own resources and institutions, like banks, schools, and political organizations," Rodrigo replied.[15]

"I doubt that would stop Waldron and his friends. The 'Cosmo Boys,' as I call them, believe that any degree of separatism is practically impossible to maintain in today's world,[16] and almost wholly undesirable even if you could do it."

"I suppose any ethnic community would need police forces and the implicit promise on the part of other groups not to attack it," Rodrigo conceded. "It would also have to have streets, highways, and air traffic crossing it, telephone wires, and so on. To that extent it would require peaceable interaction with the outside world."

"That's not all," I added. "Commerce is now globalized, as is communication. 'Modern persons,' according to Waldron 'have intercourse in every direction.'[17] We read and are shaped by the same books, the same newspapers, the same influences. Pollution crosses boundaries. A flood or famine in one part of the world affects another. Depletion of a resource in Brazil changes twenty industries in the United States, Germany, and Korea. The problems of the world today are not those of a Zulu villager, or even a race reformer like yourself in the Midwest.[18] Liberals should recognize these things and stop devoting so much energy to the narrow agendas and parochial concerns of local groups that are, in any event, bound for oblivion."

"Bound for oblivion? Those other things may indeed be happening, but why oblivion?"

"Because the modern citizen is inevitably cosmopolitan. Bankers in The Hague and in New York or Buenos Aires today live much the same life—drive the same cars, read the same reports, send their children to the same type of school.[19] Maintaining one's own distinct culture today may be a 'fascinating anthropological experiment,'[20] but it requires 'an artificial dislocation from what is actually going on in the world.'[21] It can be preserved only by artifice and subsidy. It is inauthentic and contrived. A digression from what is really going on. Those are Waldron's words, not mine, but do they not contain a grain of truth?"

"I think I'm beginning to understand," Rodrigo replied. "Indians demanding protection of their lands, women and children demanding respectful treatment, and cultures insisting on protection of their sacred grounds all ought to be evaluated from the perspective of how these demands would be seen by a cosmopolitan member of the larger society. If to him or her, the demands seem unreasonable, costly, and artificial, they should be rejected. This *is* an interesting critique, Professor. Now I can see why you wanted to tell me about it."

"And do you not think it has some force?" I repeated.

"I'm not so sure. It's a variant of the neutral-principles attack we were talking about last time.[22] It declares one perspective—that of the cosmopolitan, big-city citizen of the world—the baseline. It then pronounces the small group's demand a request for special treatment."

"Even if it consists merely of the demand to be allowed to continue to exist," I observed. "The special and the ordinary trade places."

"Exactly. We could just as well proclaim the mode of life of an Indian community—self-sufficient, not bothering anyone, living in peace with the land—the baseline. Then, the behavior of a polluting industrialist would be seen as a demand for special treatment."

"Inauthentic, expensive, and a luxury we cannot afford," I added. "One can turn the critique around."

"It smuggles in a value premise," Rodrigo said. "Life is becoming a certain way. Therefore, groups that wish to preserve another way are acting unreasonably."

"Just the way worldly people, educated at the best universities, disdain theme parks like Disneyland."

Rodrigo was silent for a moment, then added: "Or at any rate don't think they should receive state money. But the troublesome thing about this new critique is that it comes from international law and cross-national studies, an area of law that outsider groups had thought was friendly to our concerns."

"It has been until now. The U.N. has been holding hearings on Indian claims, taking testimony from groups throughout the world.[23] Several international resolutions and treaties now protect native groups from theft of their lands and cultural patrimony.[24] Member nations are required to protect native groups from extinction, from forced relocations, and from any governmental action that would endanger their language, religion, or customs."[25]

Rodrigo sighed. "I'm afraid it's an instance of what we were discussing before with U.S. civil rights law. When the self-interest of powerful groups dictates that a rain forest be razed or an Indian reservation relocated so that the lands can be mined or used for development, new meanings are read into laws to enable the dominant group to accomplish what it needs. Neutral principles never work for us, especially in the face of a determined effort by the empowered group. Redress for blacks was fine, until it began to impinge on the prerogatives of elite whites. Then a new principle— no reverse discrimination, or color-blindness—clicked in.[26] It's not so surprising, then, that international law is turning out to work the same way."

"So cosmopolitanism is the limiting principle in international law?"

"It's one. I would not be surprised if more were in store. And the sad thing is that the cosmo boys, as you call them, cite some of my heroes." Rodrigo picked up the article which he had been eyeing. "Tagore, Salman Rushdie.[27] Those were, indeed, brave writers and men of the world. They were above petty factionalism. Rushdie got into serious trouble with his own religion, as you know, when he wrote a book that some Muslims considered sacrilegious.[28] Neither of them was *against* his group, however. Neither labeled his people a Disneyland. Rather, they identified with all of humanity."

"There's a big difference," I agreed. "But the critique of particularity and identity politics has a second strand. Are you familiar with John Merryman's position on cultural artifacts?"

In Which Rodrigo and I Discuss Aztec Calendars and Cultural Patrimony

"I am," Rodrigo replied. "And in some ways it is like Waldron's critique, although perhaps not so disparaging. I assume you are thinking of his famous 'Elgin marbles' article?"[29]

"That and others," I replied.

"Then we are thinking of the same thing. Merryman, a well-regarded expert on comparative and international law, is also the author of a proposal that would divest cultural property of much of its current protection."

"I hope we understand the same thing by cultural property," I said.

"As I understand it," Rodrigo explained, "it is anything of archeological, historical, artistic, or ethnological importance going beyond the functional, monetary value of the thing.[30] For example, an Aztec calendar may be worth $20,000, but a desk calendar from a stationery store only $2.00. Cultural property is essential to the self-understanding of a people or group. Without it, the people would be bereft.[31] An Aztec calendar is such an example. A 1994 Porsche is not. A Renoir painting probably is not."

"And you've read about the internationalist critique of cultural property?"

"Yes," Rodrigo replied. "And it seems to me closely related to the cosmopolitanism one. Recently, native groups have been asserting themselves against museum curators and collectors that have been coming to their countries in search of artifacts. They have been asking authorities to enact laws against this type of trade.[32] And, they've succeeded in getting the U.N. to enact a treaty providing a degree of protection.[33] American Indians have been asking for the return of sacred objects now in museums. Collectors and museum curators hate the whole idea."

"So does Professor Merryman, who holds that it stands in the way of a cosmopolitan, internationalist spirit, not to mention the free market."[34]

"I read his article," Rodrigo interjected. "He uses as an example the Elgin marbles from the Greek Parthenon, but now residing in the British Museum. He argues that they are of value and interest to all of humanity. They can be seen and appreciated by anyone. So, why should the Greeks have a unique claim to them—assuming a willing buyer ready to donate them to the British Museum?"[35]

"I believe he also has a law-and-economics argument, does he not?" I asked.

"He does," Rodrigo replied. "He reasons that if a buyer of Indian relics, say, or the Elgin marbles, is willing to pay more for them than a Greek citizen or an Indian on a reservation, it must be because he or she values them more and is therefore a more appropriate owner. Of course, his argument overlooks that the Indian nation may be deeply attached to the object—which may have a unique role in its religion—but be unable to match the wealthy collector's offer. It also overlooks that white society may have had a direct role in producing that state of affairs."

"I agree," I said. "And it also overlooks that the object may lose much of its meaning when taken out of its original setting. An Indian fetish may serve a religious purpose when kept in a hogan. When displayed in a cabinet in the study of an Anglo collector, it becomes a mere curiosity. Before, it was a part of living culture; now it is a dead museum piece."

"Nevertheless, Merryman is an important player. And, of course, the museum lobby and the wealthy collectors love what he is saying."

The waiter materialized to ask if we cared to order dinner. "They fed us on the plane," I said. "How about you?"

"The usual inedible in-flight snack. I could use a bite, if you could," my lanky friend said. The waiter brought two menus and disappeared.

"So," I summarized, "you think that the cosmopolitan ideal's appearance at this time in history on two fronts—identity politics and cultural property—is no coincidence. Clamorous indigenous groups now beginning to assert themselves are getting in the way of business as usual. The outsiders were just starting to get somewhere, finding a body of law that seemed responsive to their needs. So, just as happened in the U.S., we see the hook, the backlash. Writers find a countervailing principle to limit the gains minorities hope to achieve."

"And," Rodrigo added, "notice a further parallel with U.S. civil rights, where conservatives marshal ringing declarations about equality of opportunity, the sanctity of the individual over the group, and the odiousness of race-based treatment. In the cases we have been talking about today, grand principles come into play as well. The cosmopolitans talk about transcending parochialism and self-interest, and about the unity of all mankind. They warn about the dangers of petty nationalism, about the superstition that fueled the attack on Salman Rushdie. They conjure up pictures of religious rivalries and village strife."

"It's very neat," I added. "A small, beleaguered group goes, hat in hand, to international authorities. It invokes principles such as self-determination and protection of linguistic and cultural minorities. It has high hopes. But then, their adversaries pull out a principle of their own. This principle cancels out the one the small group based their claim on, denies it any moral high ground. Their concerns are depicted as petty and small, their wishes selfish and uneconomical. The race reformer—defender of indigenous rights—comes out looking like a petty tyrant."

"And the intriguing thing is that the critique is also addressed to liberals, not just fellow conservatives. It tells them it's all right to oppose identity politics and civil rights, things that already make some of them uneasy. It gives them a principle they can latch onto, namely cosmopolitanism. Who could be against that? Everyone believes it's good to embrace other cultures, languages, customs, and cuisines, to be tolerant and eclectic rather than narrow and nationalistic. It's the perfect banner under which to launch a counterattack on rowdy, raucous identity politics."

"One can invoke it to browbeat insurgent groups, oppressed for ages but now beginning to assert themselves, into silence. One can scold them for not being modern. One can tell them to get with the program, modernize, cast off their petty local concerns and stop bothering us with demands for protection and respect. Be like us. If they refuse, we call them parochial. We tell them they want to live in Disneyland."

"If the critique has its way," Rodrigo said, "Indians insisting on the return of plundered sacred objects and minority groups demanding protection of rituals and practices would all be evaluated according to how these demands would be seen by a cosmopolitan, well-traveled man or woman of the world.[36] If to such a member of the larger culture these demands seem petty, frivolous, troublesome, or backward, the larger society would be justified in rejecting them."

"I think you have put it fairly," I said, pointing to the essay. "In fact, in the final pages, Waldron says not only that the major powers are *justified* in rejecting such demands. He implies that it would be immoral for them to give in. Far from being 'cozy and attractive,' group allegiances today are as apt to build on 'ancient hatreds of one's neighbors as immemorial traditions of culture.' "[37]

"He translates the cry for relief into an expression of tribalism, equates respect for an ancient culture with abetting balkanization and bloody wars. He portrays a small group asking for relief so that it does not die out, as the aggressor, the one placing unreasonable demands on larger society. Group harms become practically incoherent, a case of insistence on a preservationist, sentimental program. So, we get to turn them down and to feel just at the same time."

"I'm reminded again of the analogy to U.S. civil rights law," I said. "And of those conservatives who insist that affirmative action and other provisions that benefit minorities are reverse discrimination. Whites must be treated the same as blacks. A measure that disadvantages a white is just as bad as one that disadvantages blacks. Of course, affirmative action is designed to redress three-plus centuries of slavery and Jim Crow laws, something whites never had to face. Neutral, color-blind jurisprudence obscures all that, and merely asks what is happening right now, at this point in history. And if the answer is that a white, somewhere, is being disadvantaged, well, that's unconstitutional discrimination."

"So, like neutral principles in civil rights law, cosmopolitanism points us only to a narrow range of considerations—namely, what is happening at this moment. The uniqueness of the group's history and culture is lost. It is like a freeze-frame: you get to see only the group as it exists today, making this absurd and economically inefficient demand. You can easily think, as Waldron did, that it is white, mainstream society that is being imposed upon."

"But when you look at the group's history," I said, "a different story emerges. You begin to see why they place such a premium on their language, religion, or way of living on the land."

"You certainly do," Rodrigo agreed. "In many cases, these are people whose way of life was almost destroyed by colonizing nations—the very ones they now appeal to for relief. Of course the colonial power does not want to look into the past, for there it would find, prominently displayed, its own iniquity. That is why it loves neutral principles and ahistoric approaches like the cosmopolitan ideal. Neutral principles cannot easily capture and deal with asymmetric events, like A harmed B. In fact, that's their charm."

The waiter stopped by our table. "Are you gentlemen ready to order?"

Neither of us had looked at the menu. "How about a hamburger?" Rodrigo suggested.

"The consummate cosmopolitan meal," I said. "You go ahead. I'll just have a refill," I told the waiter, pointing to my glass.

The waiter disappeared with our orders and Rodrigo continued as follows:

In Which Rodrigo and I Develop Answers to the Cosmo Boys

"How, then, shall we reply to the cosmopolitans and those attracted to their message?"

"There's no easy reply," I answered. "Tolerance and cosmopolitanism are valid ideals. They can serve as a brake on narrow nationalism and self-interest. They can enlarge our view, make us think about the consequences of our actions for the larger community. They can make this a safer world."

"Not to mention that cosmopolitanism is fun. It's great to enjoy Middle Eastern food and read Latin American magical realism. I'm stuck in the Midwest, but Giannina and I manage as cosmopolitan a life as possible. In fact, we're hoping to go on vacation together to a small island off the coast of Chile to meet a colony of Mennonites who moved down there last century. It's the *use* the cosmo boys make of their principle, namely to put down nationalist and cultural claims, that we both find troubling."

Rodrigo gestured almost imperceptibly in the direction of a handsome couple, the man wearing a turban, the woman a sari, speaking to each other softly in Oxford-tinged English. We were both silent for a moment. Then, I spoke up: "I agree, the use is wrong. But what's the answer?"

Rodrigo leaned forward in his booth. "I think the answer must take a form that the cosmopolitan will identify with and understand. We must appeal to cosmopolitan self-interest."

"How?"

"One possibility," Rodrigo said, "is to point out that cosmopolitanism and its opposite, parochialism, exist in dynamic tension. They both threaten and reinforce each other. The cosmopolitan person needs the breadth of experience and opportunities, the broad palette, that only respect for native claims makes possible. To take Waldron's example of the opera singer, if colonial society had wiped out, or reeducated, Maori culture, Waldron could not enjoy the arias he favors today. Cosmopolitan individuals not only like to visit European capitals, many of them enjoy going on safari in the Serengeti or trekking in Nepal. They enjoy staying at an Amish settlement on vacation, eating Indian food, and reading their children fables written by South American writers. How could they enjoy these things if their very sources were wiped out?"

"So you are saying," I summarized, "that cosmopolitanism requires a degree of its opposite. Otherwise the world becomes bland as the major capitals increasingly sport the same hotel chains, serve the same food, music, and entertainment. Cosmopolitanism by its own terms requires at least some of the exotic."

"A bit of Disneyland, as Waldron put it," Rodrigo added. "But there are other reasons for resisting it as well."

"Such as?" I asked.

"Driving out older cultures may deprive the so-called advanced ones of a source of information they vitally need—not just to pique a jaded taste—but for their very survival. We were talking about this before, Professor."[38]

"The first time we met?"

"I believe so. Answers to questions now troubling the industrialized West may lie in the repertory of non-Western nations or groups.

Old age care is a serious problem in the U.S., yet other societies do a better job of it than we. The American Indians' ideas about land and wildlife may provide new ways of looking at our environmental crisis. Japanese management and personnel practices strike a better balance between efficiency and humanitarianism than our own. Other societies do a better job of providing child care than we do. And so on. If we drive out these cultures or force them to conform, secrets needed for our own survival may be lost."[39]

"Those are valid self-interest-based reasons for resisting any program that would let minority and indigenous cultures die out, and cultural patrimony be bought up by the collector with the fanciest price tag. But are there any reasons of *principle?* I mean, other than where the critique leads you?"

"There are," Rodrigo replied. "I jotted some down as you were talking. Cosmopolitanism may be fine as a personal principle or guide to life. But it fails as a principle of politics. Waldron's use of it is reductionist, in other words. As a theory of education or personal development, it's fine, even exemplary. We want the young to grow up appreciating different cultures, languages, and cuisines. So, for purposes of raising children, designing a curriculum, choosing textbooks, hiring teachers, and so on, it is certainly one value among others that we ought to promote."

"But it doesn't work for politics, you say?"

"No. Cosmopolitanism cannot take account of injustice and the need for reparations. It cannot tell us why a culture might be sensitive about protecting its language, religion, marriage ceremonies, or sacred relics. It is too present oriented, too caught up in the individual. It cannot tell you what harms need redressing. It cannot tell you anything about the redistribution of social goods and influence. It has no theory of inequality. It offers at best weak protection for oppressed groups."

"A thought-provoking argument, Rodrigo. But you said there were others."

"A second is that cosmopolitanism offers a weak bond. Historically, the worst excesses stem from the universalizing urge—one thinks of Christianity, Maoism, Leninism—while the most impressive rescue operations in history, for example that of ten million Russian Jews by the nation of Israel, or West Germany's bailout of seventeen million bankrupt neighbors, stem from nationalism and the idea of kinship."[40]

"I believe we were getting at something similar before when we pointed out that cosmopolitanism is a thin, weak spring for action. It is almost entirely abstract. It points the reader toward a neo-Aristotelian ideal, namely of the universal man or woman. It is like a Platonic form, what every person has in common. Regional and personal differences are erased. Perhaps that accounts for why Martha Nussbaum is so attracted to it."

"She's a neo-Aristotelian," Rodrigo replied. "And I'm sure your next question is going to be, What's wrong with that? One problem I see is that the universal person—the cosmopolitan citizen of the world—is apt to be white, male, Western, and a member of the educated elite."

"That's a criticism some have made of Aristotle's politics, as well as of the neorepublican revival,"[41] I pointed out. "Aristotle believed in politics by deliberation. But it turns out that the participants he had in mind for his town-hall system of politics were Athens's aristocracy of landed white elderly men."[42]

"And you and others have pointed out," Rodrigo added, "that neorepublicanism, which emphasizes dialogic deliberation about the common good, lends itself to domination by a well-educated elite with little place for outsiders.[43] But cosmopolitanism also lacks life. It lacks blood. Although it has a superficial appeal—I mean, everyone likes the idea of spicy, exotic cuisine and attractive ethnic blankets, masks, and artifacts—what will sustain and give richness and depth to the cosmopolitan life? What holidays will the cosmopolitan celebrate? What national birthdays? Someone who draws from all cultures, picks and chooses from among many, will lack strong attachment to any particular one."[44]

"I agree," I said. "I'm glad you are cosmopolitan. Your broad education, your wide travels and experience, have brought life and new perspectives to our discussions. But you seem to have a strong sense of who you are. You are an African American, a radical, and a race reformer. You have a well-developed identity. You draw from other sources, bodies of literature, and cultures, without losing touch with your social and political commitments."

In Which Rodrigo Accuses the Cosmo Boys of a Category Mistake and Also with Suspicious Timing

Rodrigo waved off my flattery. "I think the best that can be said, Professor, is that cosmopolitanism is one of those principles that works well in good times and when no structural inequality or historic injustice is present. In that respect it is like the conservatives' color-blind principle. There is nothing wrong with being color blind, so long as it is not your only principle, your only approach to racial justice. It works well only in settings—such as discussion among equals—where there is no need to take account of race or redress the past."

"So, one can perhaps say this," I summarized. "One should be a cosmopolitan in one's personal life—at least to the extent one can without neutering oneself. One should embrace tolerance and a broad outlook when it comes to education and the raising of the young. But in politics one cannot rely on it alone. In particular, it is a serious mistake, even in cosmopolitan terms, to invoke the principle to turn a deaf ear to small, historically oppressed groups crying for relief."

"In other words, lead your personal life like a Salman Rushdie or a Tagore. But in politics, heed the message of Martin Luther King, Cesar Chavez, Benazir Bhutto, or Malcolm X."

"Agreed," Rodrigo replied. "We should always choose principles that will reduce inequality, not deepen it."

"In fact, I was just thinking about this before you spoke. Do you think there is something odd about the timing of the cosmopolitan counterattack on nationalist politics?"

"I do. Many formerly backward countries that suffered under the yoke of colonial oppression are beginning to emerge from it. Many are beginning to develop. They have the beginnings of industry, are starting to contribute to pollution and the international environmental crisis. Their populations are booming, and the dislocations of the labor market that accompany rapid development are causing a migration—both legal and illegal—of many of their citizens to the more developed countries. If developing countries can be persuaded to adopt international standards of environmental protection, ones laid down by the large powers, this will slow their development somewhat but also help ease the global pollution problem, something the advanced countries very much want to happen. The same is true of immigration. The developed countries want to get the others to abide by immigration laws under which the poorer countries will send only engineers, doctors, scientists, and other highly trained and employable people. This will of course cause a brain drain, but will greatly help the more advanced countries."[45]

"Your theory may have something to it," I said. "Developing societies, like minority groups of color in the U.S., need protection first, and the opportunity to assimilate—*mongrelize*, as Salman Rushdie puts it—later.[46] If the world community does not afford them the chance to do this, cosmopolitanism will injure them, set back their development, while it aids the cause of the most privileged."

"In counter-Rawlesian fashion," Rodrigo interjected.

"My point exactly. But what about the balkanization problem, Rodrigo? Is that not a serious concern? Certainly the world needs less feuding, fewer old scores getting settled by blood and fire. Is not cosmopolitanism a brake against that, at least?"

In Which Rodrigo Rephrases the Balkanization Problem and Issues a Warning for Progressive People

"I'm not so sure," Rodrigo demurred. "Balkanization properly understood refers to small countries squabbling senselessly over old grievances, settling scores that really should not matter. It does *not* come into play when a small country wants to assert its independence, its cultural uniqueness, against one of the major powers. That is not balkanization but national self-determination. From the perspective of the highly educated academic, like Waldron, Merryman, Tagore, or Rushdie, nationalist politics and identity activism may appear the opposite of the serene, worldly view they like and prefer. But poor nations and oppressed groups need protection, need self-identity, first. They need to cure their histories of smashed cultures, stolen lands, plundered patrimony, and damaged self-esteem. Only then can they begin thinking of entering the world community on equal terms and becoming cosmopolitan."

"And do you see a moral in all this, Rodrigo, for progressive people? I mean, besides watching out for the cosmopolitan wolf in sheep's clothing?"

"I do," Rodrigo replied. "It is that there is no safe haven, in law or anywhere else. We began by discussing the way disadvantaged groups and minorities have been turning, ever hopeful, to international law in an effort to redress grievances that are not easily tackled locally. African Americans invoke the genocide convention in hopes of stopping the high arrest, incarceration, and execution rate of African-American men. Antihate speech and antipornography activists invoke several conventions in hopes of getting nations to toughen their stance against assaultive speech and incitement to hatred. And, of course, indigenous groups on several continents have been taking their cases to the U.N. in hopes of protecting land, patrimony, and culture. But as soon as this happens, the countermove materializes. Law generates a counterprinciple—cosmopolitanism—that cancels out the ringing human-rights provision the small group is invoking."[47]

"An old story."

"So there turns out to be no structure of thought, no law or body of doctrine that will serve as a magic wand, causing one's problems to roll away. There is no banner—not even antidiscrimination law—that cannot be flipped, turned against one. There is no such magic principle. But that is not to say, Professor, that there are no universal truths."

Rodrigo was silent for a moment. So I asked, "Do you have a few in mind?"

"Pain is feared everywhere. All people desire preservation and self-respect. Everyone needs a kindred group and culture. Disneylands are tawdry and bad, but not just for the reason Waldron mentioned. They contain demeaning symbols and stereotypes, of which their managers are blissfully unaware until called to their attention. The cosmopolitan ideal is useful only when it concedes these things, acknowledges its own limitations, and its backers refrain from using it, as a principle of politics, to suppress those who are already lowly and seek only respect, security, and dignity."

I was about to pin Rodrigo down, somewhat halfheartedly, on his surprising embrace of these universalisms. I would have commented, as I had done before, on how he seemed to a have a spiritual—or at least a universalist—side, after all. But any further conversation was made impossible by the arrival of the bustling, efficient chair of our inspection committee. ("Oh, there you are. I've been looking for you. I left messages on your room phones but I'm glad I found you. Can we talk?") I heard, with a sigh, that I was to be responsible for the library inspection tomorrow morning, starting with a meeting with the entire staff at 8:30. Rodrigo was assigned the plum job of interviewing the junior faculty. The chair gave us each a two-hundred-page packet in a three-ring binder ("These are supplementary memoranda the school filed just last week. Try to read them by tomorrow, if you can").

"Well, that was fun while it lasted," Rodrigo remarked as we said goodnight to the chairperson. He bolted the last of his hamburger, and we stood up and headed over to the elevators, our new reading material in hand. "Waldron does have a point," I heard him say, as I pointed out the elevator signs, mine for Tower West, where I was staying, Tower East for my young friend. "Life in the West is increasingly becoming the same. This hotel has the same design as one I stayed in in Des Moines just last month. I bet your room has a TV clicker on a central computerized console and a view of the courtyard and parking lot."

"I wouldn't be surprised," I said. "Although I wouldn't have minded a nationalist touch here or there. Maybe I'll find a foreign-language TV channel before going to sleep. I'm trying to brush up my Spanish."

"Well, goodnight, Professor," Rodrigo said.

"Happy bedtime reading," I said.

Rodrigo smiled slightly, waved good-bye, and disappeared into his elevator.

6

Citizenship: How Society Rejects the Very Persons It Most Needs

In Which Rodrigo Does Not Let Me Get Away Unscathed

"Professor! What are you doing?"

I looked up from my labors to find Rodrigo, to my great pleasure, standing in my doorway. He was looking concerned.

"Come on in. It's good to see you. Thanks for the card saying you were coming. I called, but your secretary said you'd already left."

"What are all these boxes?"

"I'm packing up. It's time for me to move on to other things. I was going to write and let you know."

"So the rumors I've heard about your retiring are true, then?" Rodrigo asked, worry written all over his face. "You're our rock of Gibraltar. Why are you leaving so soon?"

"Please sit down," I said, gesturing toward my couch. "Just push those things out of the way. I'm glad enough to take a break. This is hard work for an old man. You never realize how many books you have until it's time to move."

"I went through the same thing last year when I took my first teaching position in the Midwest. Giannina asked me to move some of her things to my new place because we're splitting time between the two cities, as I think you know. But tell me about this move of yours. Where are you going? Are you really retiring for good?"

"With a little help from some people you know, namely our friends in the Immigration and Naturalization Service. The same folks who gave you a hard time before when you wanted to return to the U.S. from Italy."[1]

"Did they ever. At one point, I was afraid I'd never get back," Rodrigo recalled. "It took a little doing on my part, along with some help from a friendly service agency and a certain United States senator."[2]

"I remember very well," I said. "I, and many of your friends here, were afraid we'd never see you again."

"But now tell me, how on earth is the agency giving *you* a hard time? You're a U.S. citizen, are you not? You've been teaching law here, I assume, for nearly forty years. And were you not born in the United States?"

I sighed. "All those things are true. It's a long story. Are you sure you want to hear it?"

"Of course," Rodrigo replied. "And I'd like to do what I can to help."

"I'm afraid it's beyond that," I said, a little resignedly. "But you're a good friend, so I owe you an explanation. Can I offer you—oops, I was about to offer you a cup of coffee, but I just packed my espresso machine. I could make you some tea. I still have my collection of bags around here somewhere. Here they are. And there's hot water next door in the faculty lounge."

"I accept," Rodrigo answered, getting up to accompany me, cup in hand, to the lounge. "But I'm more interested in the hot water you're in. What's happening?"

As we walked back to my crowded office, littered with the paraphernalia of many years of teaching—boxes of teaching notes, unfinished manuscripts, memorabilia, and the ever-present blue books—I began:

"I got a letter from the INS the other day, asking me to come in for what they called an office interview. I'm sure you read about the new measure that passed last month, amending the constitutional grant of citizenship?"[3]

"I did. It's one of a host of anti-immigrant rules that have been enacted or proposed recently, tightening up the border, requiring the speaking of English as a condition for citizenship, voting, or participation in political life, and denying naturalization or green-card status to people who were entitled to them before, such as family members.[4] When the citizenship amendment passed, I checked to see if it applied to me. It didn't, so I breathed a sigh of relief. I never thought it would pass, even when the California legislature proposed it to Congress some years ago."

"A lot of people didn't, including me," I replied. "After all, the Fourteenth Amendment, which formerly granted citizenship to any person born in the United States, had never been amended in its entire history. It's the cornerstone of equal protection and due process. It also spells out who can be a citizen. But now everything seems to be under reconsideration. A new wave of nativism is sweeping the nation, even more intense than the ones we've seen at various points in our history, when we saw the country enact anti-Japanese or anti-Chinese measures, and round up and deport even legally present citizens of Mexican descent."[5]

"All this is deplorable," Rodrigo replied. "But how on earth does it apply to you? Professor, you're not someone who sneaked across the border. You speak perfect English, indeed are a distinguished professor and writer. You have never been on welfare or committed any crimes. So what exactly is the INS's grievance with you?"

"As I said, it's a long story, and you mentioned you wanted to help. You can't. I appreciate the offer. But my mind's made up. I've already bought a Winnebago, in fact."

"I can't believe this," Rodrigo replied. "You're our saving grace. Dozens, maybe hundreds of young professors look to you for advice and counsel, not least of all, myself. You've been my adviser, mentor, and sounding board. You've been—if you don't mind my saying— my 'straight man,' my alter ego, my interlocutor. Without you I couldn't have gotten my ideas out."

"You give me too much credit," I demurred. "You'll do fine. You're very brilliant. And we'll keep in touch. I promise I'll write."

"I can't believe this," Rodrigo said. "See what I'm reduced to? I'm repeating myself. First I heard, just last week, that my sister Geneva is getting ready to retire. Now you! Professor, this is a kind of death. That's why I'm so distraught. I wouldn't exist without you. Do you have the letter the agency sent you? There must be an avenue of appeal. On what grounds do they want to deport you?"

"They don't say anything about deportation," I replied. "And the letter is already packed up. Basically it says that they have information that may bear on my entitlement to United States citizenship, namely that my father may have been an illegal alien at the time I was born. They have a few questions about that and also about the status of my mother. They asked me to bring my birth certificate, records of any foreign travel or residence I may have had, and of any service in a foreign army. They also asked me to bring a copy of my parents' marriage license."

"Was your father in fact an illegal alien?"

"I think he may have been," I replied. "He's a proud man, and so I've never asked him directly. But he immigrated from Aguascalientes, Mexico, at the age of fifteen with no money and no friends in the U.S. to sponsor him, at least that I've heard of."

We both started. The phone was ringing. It was my moving company. I listened, then said, "Ten-thirty would be fine. Just drive up to the loading door. My office is Room 1201."

"It's funny, Professor," Rodrigo continued. "I've never asked about your ethnicity, although from your appearance and identification with us, I assumed you might be black. But your name sounds Latino. I had no idea you might have a citizenship problem. You are one of the most eminent civil rights scholars in the United States. The very idea that we might lose you, that the government might deport you . . ."

"They didn't say anything about deportation. I'm deporting myself," I said quietly.

"But their letter is spurring you, I assume?"

"It does have something to do with it, I must admit. But it's the entire panoply of anti-immigrant measures and propositions, English-only laws in effect now in several states, and Proposition 187-type measures that have already been enacted in California and elsewhere denying education, welfare, and other forms of support to illegal and in some cases even to legal immigrants."

"Giannina said something like that happened to her neighbor, a cleaning woman. She had to move."

"It's the new eugenics movement and books like *The Bell Curve*, which encourage society to look at people like you and me as threats to the national gene pool . . ."

"But your daughters graduated from Swarthmore and Minnesota. They were honors students. Professor, you shouldn't overreact. First of all, they're not talking about you. And second, we can fight this thing. I'll represent you. We must ask for a hearing." Rodrigo was pacing my office nervously, stopping only now and then to take a sip from his tea cup, balanced precariously on the arm of my sofa, which was cluttered with books and boxes in preparation for the van's arrival tomorrow.

"That's all true," I conceded. "And I shall miss my daughters very much. But they, like you, can come visit me in my new country. And, as I mentioned before, there's always the mail." I took a plaque down from the wall and placed it carefully in a padded box.

In Which Rodrigo and I Take a Last Look Around, and Discuss Expatriation

"The mail. Great. I get to keep in touch with my mentor by mail. I bet it takes only three weeks from wherever you're going to be." Rodrigo's voice was filled with disappointment.

"Rodrigo, I can see you're wrought up. And for my part, I'm cramped and tired from packing all these boxes. How would you like to go for a short run? It'll be my last around this campus. We could run off our excess energy while I show you some of my favorite places."

"I'd love to," Rodrigo replied. "In fact, you kind of promised me you'd go running one time before. But I didn't bring any equipment."

"I'm pretty sure I've got a second set right . . . here," I said triumphantly, rummaging behind a filing cabinet. They'll be a little big in the waist, but if you just pull the drawstring, I'm sure they'll fit. Oh, and what size shoe do you wear? I have an extra pair of elevens."

"Elevens are perfect," Rodrigo replied. "I have big feet." We changed clothes and I admonished Rodrigo to take things easy on an old man. A minute later we were on our way out the door.

"This *is* a beautiful campus," Rodrigo exclaimed as we rounded a corner and came upon a group of Gothic buildings surrounded by tall trees. "But tell me, Professor, what was the date of that letter you got from the INS?"

"I've already packed it. And thank you very much for your kind offer, Rodrigo. The prospect of free legal representation from a lawyer of your brilliance is the one thing that might possibly tempt me to make a fight of it. And, on substantive grounds, I think I might have a chance. But I'm not going to fight it. I spent six years in Mexico when I was a teenager. I have colleagues in that country. The atmosphere there is in many ways freer than it is here. There is no wave of nativism. No one there looks upon someone like you or me as a potential welfare cheat, merely because of the color of our skin, or a perpetual, irresponsible breeder of defective children. Watch out for that sprinkler."

I could see Rodrigo was taking mental notes. "Professor, you say you're not going to fight this, but you may change your mind. Hundreds of your fans are going to be upset—no, bereft—when they hear you are leaving. You have been a beacon to all of us. You have many of your best years ahead of you. When did you live in Mexico?"

"I'm huffing and puffing already. Could we slow down? I was twelve years old. My Dad decided to pack it in and move back to his home country. He had spent nearly twenty-five years in the U.S., marrying my mother, a U.S. citizen, you will be happy to note." (Rodrigo did.) "Although whether my birth came before or after their marriage and my father's subsequent naturalization, I do not know and have never asked. My father is a man of fierce pride and exceptional intelligence, a self-taught engineer. We moved around a lot when I was young. I never knew whether this was because he and my mother were trying to stay one step ahead of the INS, or whether he changed jobs frequently because of racism. I know he was ambitious and wanted to get ahead. But he looked very Mexican—even more than I—and spoke with an accent. When I was twelve and he about forty, he announced we were all going to Mexico."

"How did you take that?" Rodrigo asked.

"It was quite a shock at first. I had to learn Spanish. But my Dad prospered. He caught the first wave of national economic development and became moderately successful."

"And what was it like for you?"

"Wonderful! I grew up bilingual and bicultural, attending an American school where half of my classes were in English, the other half in Spanish. Some of the kids were expatriate Americans, like me, the others, Mexican nationals from Mexico City."

"It sounds a little like the base school I attended in Italy," Rodrigo commented.

"It must have been similar. This was during the years immediately following the Hollywood blacklist. Let's go this way. There's something I want to show you. Anyway, half of the friends I went to school with had names like Trumbo, Buñuel, Butler, and Maltz. I didn't know this at the time, but many of them were sons and daughters of parents who had left the United States to escape persecution. Many parents continued writing under pseudonyms. Most were leftists. It was a fascinating community."

"Sounds like the United States did Mexico a great favor by sending them some exceptionally talented people."

"They did. And whether they're doing other countries a similar favor now, I can't say. I am leaving, however. As in the fifties, when a host of creative people from Los Angeles and the writing community found that the air was freer elsewhere, I'm going to try it out. Not try it out, actually. I'm leaving permanently—as permanently as these things are, that is."

"Professor, you're an institution. We need you here. You should fight this thing. What good will you be, sitting and enjoying yourself in some foreign capital? I really need to look at that letter. I hope the time for an appeal has not passed. You may have missed the date for your interview, but I'm sure I can get them to schedule another."

Rodrigo seemed genuinely upset. "Slow down a little. You keep picking up the pace. Relax yourself, and let me tell you a story. It's one of the oldest in the world: old, battle-scarred veteran steps aside. It's time. It's that simple. I've been laboring in the trenches of civil rights struggles for nearly a half century. I'm tired. It's time for people like you to take up the cudgel. You need me less than you think. I'm flattered that you think I'm indispensable. But I need a new challenge. The government's letter only served as the occasion for my doing something I'd been thinking about for some time."

"Do you have enough money to retire?" Rodrigo asked.

"I do. I have my university annuity any time I want and social security clicks in only a year from now. My daughters are all grown up. I'll be fine."

"But, Professor, you'll be out of touch. How can we reach you when we need you? Retire if you must. But stay in the States where young scholars can at least seek you out. You could write books, give an occasional speech—if your time and energy permit, that is. Are you planning to sell your condo?"

"It's in escrow."

Rodrigo's face fell. "So, you're really planning to do it then?"

"I am. I'll travel around Mexico. I've always loved art. I have friends there, both in law and the art world. In fact, I'm meeting with some people in Chiapas just next month. And if things don't work out for some reason, I can always come back."

"I'm not sure you're right about that, Professor," Rodrigo replied with alacrity. "I wish you'd let me check. Suppose you miss the meeting the INS wants to schedule. If you then just take off for another country, they may take that as evidence of intent to renounce your U.S. citizenship. A line of Supreme Court cases holds that denaturalization is possible if a person has indicated such an intent.[6] That way, even if the facts of your birth, your father's status, his marriage, and so on ultimately do not bear out the INS's suspicion that you are not a citizen—if you are one, in other words—they may still denaturalize you.[7] That's why it's incredibly important that we go to the hearing. I wish you would hunt for the letter when we get back."

"You make a valid point, technically speaking. But my mind is made up."

"Professor, I'm sure we could prevail. The agency always has discretion. The facts in your case seem to me not black and white. Your absence from the country took place at an early age and was beyond your control.[8] Unlike me, you never served in a foreign army. The facts of your father's entry are probably lost in time. By the same token, you cannot possibly be expected to produce your parents' marriage certificate. You have an unbroken line of residence in the U.S. You are a respected teacher. You have two outstanding children, and have never, I assume, been on welfare. You have friends and allies. The letters will come pouring in. We can fight this."

"Rodrigo, I am a law professor. All my life I have taught my students to uphold the law. What kind of example would I be if I flouted it now, or argued facts that I cannot prove, in order to get what I want? The country has decided it doesn't want people like me.[9] It has changed the rules for citizenship and, as I read the new measure, made them retroactive. They apply to me, or very probably do. I could argue for an exception, throw myself on the mercy of the agency, flood the hearing officer with letters. But this would be to ask for special advantages not available to other, less well-connected people. The agency must be holding hundreds of hearings across the country right now. Why should I expect to be treated better than others?"

"So you're going to leave quietly. Professor, you've always been a fighter. What about Martin Luther King? What about legal instrumentalism? What about civil disobedience?"[10]

"I have been a fighter, as you say, but for causes I believe in, and on behalf of others. Also, I have never counseled anyone to break the law. The law is my profession. I love it. I believe we must bow down even to unjust laws because, unless they are clearly unconstitutional, they are the will of the people. And fighting a single unjust law is not the same as fighting a change in the country's very self-definition.[11] I'm not so sure that is something one is entitled to do. Look at that fountain."

"Gorgeous. But civil disobedience aside, this law may be unconstitutional. I'll fight it. I'll represent you and argue it all the way up to the Supreme Court."

"Rodrigo, how can a provision of the Constitution, as the new measure is, be unconstitutional?"

"It would take a novel argument, based on the structure and meaning of the document as a whole. That way, if a new provision, such as this new clause amending the Fourteenth Amendment to deny citizenship to persons like you, is out of harmony with the rest of the document, as I believe it is, a court could strike it down."

"And do you believe the current Supreme Court would?"

"There's always a chance. It's true the Court is conservative—it has made it easier for school districts to terminate a desegregation order[12] and harder for states to redistrict to increase the chances of a minority candidate.[13] It has also applied the more restrictive, compelling-interest standard to federal affirmative action.[14] But I still think we would have a fighting chance. The Court may treat citizenship more solicitously than it does, say, voting rights or affirmative action. It is a more basic aspect of our political life. I would expect it to look closely at a measure like this, as with any of the other new measures that are part of the nativism movement."

"It seems to me there was an earlier Supreme Court decision on citizenship."

Rodrigo winced. "You're right—*Dred Scott vs. Sandford*,[15] in which the Supreme Court held that a slave had no rights which the courts were bound to respect. But that opinion is notorious.[16] The Supreme Court today would never issue anything similar. It has its own reputation to think about—its standing in the world community, its place in history."

"But justices rarely decide cases in ways that are too far afield from the country's general mood and temper. And that mood today is distinctly antiminority and antiforeigner. There are a dozen measures making it difficult for immigrants to come here. We cut off social services to them once they are here and deny them the right to an education. We enact English-only laws, and deny naturalization to anyone who can't speak and write English. Affirmative action is under attack, as is multiculturalism on campuses.[17] Cutbacks in welfare and proposals to limit it for families who have too many children are thinly aimed at people like you and me. In a climate like the present one do you really think the Supreme Court would strike down an amendment, enacted by the people, aimed at denying citizenship to newcomers and even long-term residents?"

"We'll attack the measure for being retroactive. It changes the rules for citizenship for people who have been here all their lives."

"Do you mind if we walk a little? I don't see how you do it. You're talking a blue streak and running what must be seven-minute miles at the same time."

Rodrigo obediently dropped to a walk. "It's true," I said. "Ex post facto laws and bills of attainder can sometimes be struck down if they violate settled expectations or seem vindictive in character.[18] But this is an act of the people. It amends the basic document. No, Rodrigo, I'm afraid your case is harder than you think. You might lose, even if I allowed you to file suit on my behalf, which I won't. And on the substantive challenge—to the constitutionality of the measure that narrows citizenship for native-born offspring of aliens— you know as well as I how difficult it is to challenge a measure enacted by the people as a whole, or their representatives."

"Alas, I'm well aware," Rodrigo replied. "Referenda and direct ballot petitions are extremely difficult to set aside. It's almost impossible to prove a racist or sexist intent on the part of thousands or millions of voters voting in the privacy of their ballot boxes.[19] Judicial deference is at its highest when a law comes into existence this way, as opposed to agency rule-making or legislative enactment. Courts consider direct democracy the will of the people and are reluctant to find that will tainted by an illegitimate motive.[20] There have been a few exceptions, however.[21] Perhaps we could argue that one of them applies here."

"I doubt we could," I replied, "even if I were willing to make the effort, which I am not. There are two reasons for doubt. First, the country is in no mood to show generosity toward outsiders. We are in the midst of one of the most virulent periods of nativism in history. Courts cannot but heed what is going on in the wider society. Second, there has been put forward in recent years a powerful theoretical argument for closing the borders. I am sure you are familiar with the communitarian argument put forward by Peter Schuck and others."[22]

In Which Rodrigo and I Discuss the Idea of Citizenship

"You mean Schuck's article in the Columbia Law Review and his later book?"

I nodded and Rodrigo continued. "They argue that a society is entitled to engage in self-definition, to determine what kind of a people it wants to be. It is entitled to decide its traditions, principles, customs, and mode of government. They connect this argument with classical notions of the autonomy of the state. They point out that if a horde of outsiders were free at any time to enter the society and change its values, customs, norms, and practices, the society as a self-determining living thing would cease to exist. The outsiders have their own nation, their own sending country. If they want to live in a different kind of society, their recourse is either to change their home state or find a new, more congenial one willing to admit them. They do not have the right, under political theory or international human rights law, to migrate en masse to a society where the standard of living is higher and then demand that it change to accommodate them."

"Rodrigo, I am fully familiar with that argument," I replied quietly. "And I half agree with it. That, in part, is why I am going. If this country wants to adopt a nativist policy, I am entitled to argue against it. But if my view fails to carry, I have no recourse. I must leave. I am not part of this society's freely selected plan and self-definition."

"We don't know that for sure, Professor," Rodrigo said, his voice rising. "All you have is a letter inviting you to come in to talk. It may all be a mistake, a misunderstanding."

"I doubt it. The other national currents we spoke of—the English-only measures and immigration cutbacks,[23] the attacks on multiculturalism underway at practically every campus—are very popular. The new eugenicists are winning wide acclaim and writing best-selling books.[24] Society seems to have made its decision. I've made mine."

"We can take on the Peter Schuck argument, Professor. We can work together to change the atmosphere of hate and xenophobia. Even though you are a voice in the wilderness, people still respect you."

"The Schuck argument is unassailable. How would you argue that a people do not have the right to determine themselves and their own definition?"

"Easy," Rodrigo replied. "One simply takes the argument back a step. One asks *how* it is that the community came to have its current character, its current polity. If the means by which it came to have its current composition are flawed, then the community has an obligation not to remain the same, but to change itself to right the wrong that has been done."

"I could use an example."

"Sure. Suppose a community has committed genocide, nearly wiping out a minority group. Some years later, the group shows signs of making a comeback, so the wider society enacts measures designed to make this impossible. It bars their members—ones who have relocated abroad, say—from immigrating. It forbids their language, religion, and customs. It consigns them to inferior schools and takes measures to dilute their voting strength and job prospects. When challenged, the society says it has deliberated. It has consulted itself and decided it likes this self-definition, this constellation of colorations and traits. We would immediately see the illegitimacy of such a response. The current composition is tainted by the massacre, and is not entitled to respect."

"And do you think the same holds true of today?" I asked.

"I do," Rodrigo replied emphatically. "Latinos and Asians, in the main, are not the source of nativism. The strongholds are in the white community and a few blacks who only see these others as competition. Yet those other two minority groups are the very ones who have been excluded from the political community. Why would we—why should you, Professor—bow meekly and accept as inevitable a fate that was made without us?"

"I guess I'm ready to jog a little. In what sense was it decided without us?"

"Our numbers and impact have been artificially suppressed. Society doesn't allow immigration by persons who might say things the government does not want to hear. Beginning with the Chinese Exclusion cases,[25] and before that the forced relocation of Indians,[26] we made sure that foreign workers and inconvenient populations stayed where we wanted them—usually far away. Slavery, of course, brought millions of Africans here, but we made sure they had only the impact we wanted them to have, mainly through their work in the fields and grand homes of the South. Every Southern state enacted laws prohibiting teaching them to read, and, even after Emancipation, Jim Crow laws and separate but equal schools impeded their progress and ability to have any sort of intellectual or political impact on the shape of the majority culture.[27] Thus, the composition of the U.S. citizenry, as well as the content and range of ideas it has been exposed to, have been shaped by racism."

"So if we follow the Peter Schuck principle and allow the people to define themselves, we merely forward and give effect to prior racism," I summarized. "Is that your argument?"

"It is, in a nutshell," Rodrigo replied. "Citizenship is the bedrock, the basic notion of politics. The way you define it says everything about you as a people. If you look around you at the U.S. polity, talk to them, hear their ideas, you see something that has been radically shaped by racism. Racism is reflected in who is NOT there, who does NOT speak, and ideas that are never heard or taken seriously. People may grow up in this culture without a racist bone in their bodies. A person may be a good liberal, may think he or she is genuinely fair and open-minded about blacks, race, Critical ideas, socialism, and so on. But simply by virtue of having grown up in a white enclave in a world that is dominantly black, brown, or Asian, the person has had a skewed experience. Give that person a vote, ask him what sort of society he wants, and it is absolutely predictable what he will say."

"A society much like the one he has now," I said.

"Exactly. Or perhaps, if the person is progressive, one with one percent more representation of outsider persons, voices, ideas, and political power," Rodrigo added. "If you give a society the power to define itself and don't take into account what has shaped its current self-understanding, you'll get stasis. I'm not equating Peter Schuck, who is a liberal, with Brimelow,[28] Auster[29] or Herrnstein. But their arguments are similar. There's practically a straight-line connection."

"So what is the solution," I prodded.

"We should never treat preferences as exogenous, as givens. One must always go deeper than that. The most basic political question for a democracy, then, is not, what do we in fact want, but what should we want. We should force ourselves to deliberate, to confront new ideas, to talk with those who are radically Other. Professor, you are the kind of person American society needs to hear. I can't believe you are leaving. I don't want to overdo it, but this is a tragedy, and not just for me. I can't exist without you, as you know . . ."

"Oh, yes you can," I insisted.

"Well, not easily. But society needs people like you. Western society is sinking, its standard of living dropping, quality of life decreasing year by year, infant mortality, crime, and other measures of social pathology on the rise. We are being overtaken by more dynamic societies in other parts of the world. The cure for the United States' stagnation is new ideas from minority, Latino, Asian, and non-Western sources.[30] You say you have a responsibility to leave, if the American people want you to. But I think you have a responsibility to stay. You need to shape those preexisting wants, desires, and preferences, challenge the settled myopia of our age. What sort of example will you set by leaving? What will that say to all the young professors of color, minority activists, and intellectuals if you go meekly? It's a cop-out. You must stay."

In Which the Professor Exits, over Rodrigo's Strenuous Objection

"I'm leaving anyway. I'm old. Perhaps my leaving will inspire others to continue. Oh, look, we're coming up on faculty glade. Isn't it beautiful? It's my favorite part of campus. That's the Chem building over there. And that traditional-style building over there is the faculty club."

We both slowed down for a moment while Rodrigo took in the tranquil scene. "I can see how you'll miss this place, Professor."

"I will."

"You could drink the hemlock here, just as well as in Mexico. It's funny—we've always drunk coffee. You could resign your position at the law school, or change jobs, just as you've done more than once in your career to dramatize a grievance. You could go on the road, speaking at dozens of campuses and cities about the need to struggle against the conservative tide that is sweeping the country. Your place is here. Your friends won't let you starve. And you could make money from speaking or publishing, probably more than you do now from your professor's salary."

"But you're forgetting one small thing—that letter sitting in my file like a ticking bomb. You want me to speak to society, to try to persuade it to soften its current attitude of disdain and neglect toward its poor and minorities. But the letter makes one thing plain— the government doesn't want me."

"I'm sure it doesn't say that, Professor. Although you have refused to show it to me . . ."

"Not refused. I just don't know where it is right now."

"We could easily get them to send us another copy. But I'm sure it doesn't announce, 'You're deported,' just like that."

"Oh, no," I replied. "It was quite cordial. It invited me to come in for what they call a routine inventory, as though they were just checking their files. But they did say it was for a 'citizenship audit,' whatever that is. It was even addressed, 'Dear Professor.' "

"Of course," Rodrigo replied. "Letters from the field agents are invariably polite, even when the Home Office is as ruthless as can be. And we can capitalize on that. Accept their invitation to come for a hearing. I'll go with you. We'll find out what the grounds of their case against you are. Then, we'll deal with them. We'll document whatever they need documented, make arguments if your case falls in the middle ground where there is a range of discretion. We'll get letters from friends testifying to your good character."

"It's not so much my character that is at issue, but that of the country. Face it, Rodrigo, a person like me is an incongruity here. I don't fit in. And society has made clear it doesn't want to change to include people like me, or, maybe, you."

"We should struggle to change that, Professor," Rodrigo replied quietly. "Starting with your meeting. We'll talk with the hearing officer, make him or her understand that whatever the circumstances of your coming to be here, I mean be born here, you are precisely the sort of person this country needs. The officer will probably be college educated, maybe a lawyer. We'll explain about dialogic politics and why they should lean over backwards to keep people like you here. We'll point out that whatever happened to cast a shadow on your U.S. citizenship happened a long time ago and that you have been a model citizen ever since."

"I did spend those six years out of the country," I replied. "I consort with known race reformers and radicals like you. I teach my students to question illegitimate authority and challenge unfair laws, to represent the poor and outcast, criminals, drug dealers, and others who are not exactly in favor today. All this is a matter of public record. If there is a hearing or trial, it will all come out. And if they write to my father, who is an old man living in retirement in a little town outside Mexico City, he'll probably tell them to go to hell. He never approved of my returning to the States for college. And although he cheers when I publish and advocate on behalf of Chicanos, blacks, and poor people, he thinks I'm crazy to stay in this mixed-up country. Even if he has exonerating evidence and documents in his possession, he may refuse to cooperate or send them."

Rodrigo was silent for a moment. "I can see this line of argument is hopeless with you. You keep repeating over and over that we may lose, as though that's equivalent to saying that we will. And as for your leaving the United States, that is a complete *non sequitur.* All the review committee wants to do, so far as I can tell—since you refuse to show me the letter—is ascertain your citizenship. Even if they find you are not a U.S. citizen, which I doubt they will—I mean, what an absurdity in the case of someone like you who has lived an exemplary life here for nearly half a century—that is not the same as saying they are likely to deport you. For all we know, since this is brand new legislation, they may conclude that you are not a U.S. citizen but allow you to live out the rest of your life here. You could not vote or run for the presidency of the United States, but other than that, there is little you could not do that you are doing now. You could teach your classes, live in your condo—assuming we can rescind that pending sale—speak, write, meet with your friends. You could watch your children grow up."

"They are already grown up."

"Well, you could watch them go through adulthood, marry, have a family. You could be a grandfather. Don't you want to see your grandchildren?"

"That depends," I answered. "One of my friends, who is a race reformer like me, had a son who grew up to be an FBI agent. He pulled his hair out at first. But now they have a rather uneasy, long-distance relationship."

"But what about me?" Rodrigo asked plaintively. "I don't mean to be clinging or self-centered. You and I are a team, a pair. I rely on you, almost, for my very voice. I sharpen my ideas through you. You're the vehicle through which I reach whatever audience I have as a young, untenured professor with an offbeat mind. If you leave, where does this leave me? What about Laz?"

"I'm sure the two of you will find a way," I replied. "You will have Giannina, who is also a writer. You don't need me nearly as much as you think you do. Ideas have a way of getting out. They are more important than individuals, anyway."

"But this country's mood is antithetical to what I have to say. They'll listen to you, Professor. You are the softer voice. You command widespread respect—"

"Then why the letter that I got last week?"

"It's probably just bureaucracy. They were undoubtedly just checking some files on a computer and ran across your name. I doubt very much that they targeted you because of who you are. But as I was saying, you are our spokesperson. Your gray beard, years, and dignified manner cause people to listen."

"The country is set on another course. They are listening to conservative ideas. They don't want me. Maybe they'll listen to you. At any rate, it's your turn. Here we are, back to the law building."

"Thanks for the tour, Professor. It's lovely, especially the old buildings. I can see why you say you'll miss this place."

"I will, certainly at first. And I'm glad I got to show it to you before leaving. You saw some of my favorite places."

"For a guy your age, you keep up a good pace."

"I try," I said. "Would you like to shower? There's a small one on the fifth floor. Hardly anyone uses it this time of day. I'm pretty sure I have an extra towel, if I haven't packed them up."

"In a pinch, I've used paper towels before, Professor. I'm pretty skinny and I dry fast."

We rode the elevator up in silence, in the company of a late-working colleague who asked me what I was going to do for my "sabbatical." I introduced him to Rodrigo, and he seemed surprised that my young-looking friend was a professor from a well-known state university in the Midwest. "I'm getting more grizzled by the moment, or rather by the bluebook," Rodrigo replied, causing my colleague, who was notorious for returning bluebooks and grades late, to smile sympathetically.

After a quick shower, we both stood in the doorway of my cluttered office. "Can I help you with those boxes?" Rodrigo asked.

"No, I only have a few more things to pack. I can finish up in the morning. Besides, it's easier if I pack things myself. That way I know where they are."

The evening light was streaming in the stained glass windows of my office. "I'll miss this place. And you, too," I said.

"Well, write," Rodrigo said, squeezing my arm and looking me in the eye for several seconds. Then he turned, opened the door, and was gone.

Epilogue

So far as Rodrigo or any of the professor's other friends and acquaintances could tell, he completed his packing and left the next day. Out of curiosity, Rodrigo telephoned the citizenship review panel, but they declined to speak with him because of the confidentiality of the proceedings and his lack of an explicit letter of retainer or appointment as guardian ad litem. Rodrigo did not self-deconstruct, as he had declared heatedly and emotionally he might in the professor's office. Instead, he and Giannina vowed to undertake a program of joint scholarship aimed at continuing the professor's tradition and memory. Several months later, after he had returned to his law school to begin the new term, Rodrigo received the following letter on flimsy international stationery, with a series of indecipherable cancelations on the envelope, some seemingly marked "Chiapas, MX," others "Mexico DF," and one "Langley, Virginia." The envelope, which arrived slightly torn, contained several pages of notes and the following letter:

> *Dear Rodrigo,*
> You will be happy to know that I am safe and staying with friends in a small town in south central Mexico, near Oaxaca. The camper held up well, although I had to make an emergency stop in the desert on the way down when a part gave up the ghost. Detroit just doesn't make cars the way they used to. But an expert local mechanic improvised a new part out of ones on hand, and I was on my way the next day.

I move into my new place in town next month. The address is on the letterhead. I'll be near the university and the outdoor market. Please come down and visit me. This place has the best coffee in the world. I was planning on giving it up—my doctor has been after me for a while, you know—but it's so good down here it's proving difficult. Remember that time we had empanadas at that little restaurant down the street from the law school? If you come down, I'll show you a place that rivals even those. Bring Giannina. How's her Spanish? There's a writer's center in town and also one in San Miguel Allende, not too far away.

That was quite some run we had the last day. It motivated me to gear up my exercise program. I've been going out every day, despite the high altitude. The local people are pretty friendly. A puzzled man on a burro even offered me a ride the other day. It was hot and he must have felt sorry for an old guy loping down the dusty road.

I've been going through some papers and discovered these notes from our many conversations. I thought you should have copies. Remember that first one, when you had just returned from Italy and were checking out U.S. law schools? It seems like such a long time ago. We talked about your plans, and you laid out your theory of cultural change and a possible role for minorities in arresting the West's decline. I've also got notes on that second one, on law and economics, in which you put forward your remarkable thought experiment on why the free market of economic trades does not drive out racism, and the third one as well, in which I learned that, contrary to what you say, you do have a spiritual side.

Remember the time you and Giannina were feuding and I helped out? We talked about anti-essentialism, the white feminist movement, and the relationship of men and women of color. It's all there. I hope you can read my writing. (If not, ask my former secretary for help; she's had lots of practice!) We had all those talks, too, about affirmative action, that alarming one on the assault on narrative jurisprudence after which you disappeared on me, and that even scarier one with Laz on the right-wing surge taking place right now.

Make whatever use of this stuff you care to. I quitclaim it all to you— you're the author and inspiration for most of it anyway.

My own role, now that I'm a retiree with time on my hands? Like a lot of displaced and unemployed people, I've been doing a lot of thinking and talking. As I might have mentioned, last week I met with some folks in Chiapas. Leaders of the farm revolt movement. We had a lot in common. Fascinating types, and very political. I can introduce you to them when you come down here, if you do.

As for me, I'll use the apartment in town as a base, but keep on the move. The little Winnebago gets me around comfortably. I give talks, meet people, and buy pottery for my collection. My Spanish is getting better and better. Maybe I'll be back sometime, maybe not. Keep healthy, and send me drafts of your work.

Best to Giannina and Laz.

A big *abrazo*,
The Professor

Notes to Chapter 1

1. RICHARD DELGADO, THE RODRIGO CHRONICLES, ch. 9 (1995).

2. The magazine, as I learned later, was RACE TRAITOR, edited by Noel Ignatiev and John Garvey. The package also contained *Treason to Whiteness Is Loyalty to Humanity, An Interview with Noel Ignatiev of Race Traitor Magazine,* UTNE READER, Nov./Dec. 1994, at 83.

3. CHRONICLES, *supra* note 1, at ch. 9 (discussing critique of law reviews and legal scholarship).

4. *Id.* (describing role of young teenagers).

5. *Id.* (summarizing critique of storytelling scholarship by these and other scholars. *See also* Jane Baron, *Resistance to Stories,* 67 S. CAL. L. REV. 255 (1994) (on the critique of legal storytelling).

6. CHRONICLES, *supra* note 1, at ch. 1 (describing Rodrigo's deportation).

7. *Id.* at ch. 2 (describing how Rodrigo got back to the U.S.).

8. *Id.*

9. DAVID LODGE, SMALL WORLD: AN ACADEMIC ROMANCE (1984), tells the story of an ambitious academic who is abducted from the Villa Serbelloni in Bellagio, Italy (where, coincidentally, Rodrigo's Seventh Chronicle was written amid tranquil surroundings).

10. CHRONICLES, *supra* note 1, at chs. 1, 3 (Western society turning increasingly deaf ear to minorities). *See also* Cathy Scarborough, *Conceptualizing Black Women's Employment Experiences,* 98 YALE L.J. 1457 (1989) (discussing ways law creates invisibility of black women).

11. *See* Mari Matsuda, *When the First Quail Calls: Multiple Consciousness as Jurisprudential Method,* 11 WOMEN'S RTS. L. REV. 7 (1989) (suggesting that an underlying bond unites all oppressed peoples).

12. CHRONICLES, *supra* note 1, at ch. 8.

13. *Id.* at Appendix B (white-collar and corporate crime more dangerous, to life and limb, and costly—in an aggregate and a per capita sense—than street crime).

14. On the decrease in empathy generally, or the need for the law and legal discourse to be more empathic, see, *e.g.,* Anne C. Dailey, *Feminism's Return*

to Liberalism, 102 YALE L.J. 1265, 1266–67 (1993) (book review); Richard Delgado & Jean Stefancic, *Images of the Outsider in American Law and Culture: Can Free Speech Remedy Systemic Social Ills?* 77 CORNELL L. REV. 1258 (1992); Lynne Henderson, *Legality and Empathy*, 85 MICH. L. REV. 1574 (1987); ELIZABETH SPELMAN, INESSENTIAL WOMAN: PROBLEMS OF EXCLUSION IN FEMINIST THOUGHT 12 (1988). *See also* Natalie Angier, *Society's Glue: Science Examines Empathy's Role for Man, Beast*, DENVER POST, May 9, 1995, at 2A, col. 3 (leading scientist quoted as pointing out one drawback of empathy: namely, that identification with one's ingroup tends to be accompanied by dislike of other groups); Scarborough, *Conceptualizing, supra* note 10. For the view that empathy is no replacement for legality, see Toni M. Massaro, *Empathy, Legal Storytelling and the Rule of Law*, 87 MICH. L. REV. 2099 (1989). For a critique of empathy that parallels this one to some extent, but focuses on its role in liberal political theory, see Cynthia V. Ward, *A Kinder, Gentler Liberalism? Visions of Empathy in Feminist and Communitarian Literature*, 61 U. CHI. L. REV. 929 (1994).

On various definitions of empathy, see *id.* at 933–34. Rodrigo and the professor use the term in its ordinary language sense—the capacity to project or imagine the thoughts and feelings of another person.

15. On "Giannina," Rodrigo's companion and soul mate, see CHRONICLES, *supra* note 1, at chs. 3, 4, 6. Giannina, a published poet and playwright, and Rodrigo have been together for nearly two years.

16. Attributed to Antonio Gramsci, false consciousness consists of an oppressed individual or group's taking on the values and perspectives of the oppressor class, thereby becoming complicit in their own oppression. *See* GEORG LUKACS, HISTORY AND CLASS CONSCIOUSNESS (Rodney Livingstone trans., 1971); Duncan Kennedy, *Antonio Gramsci and the Legal System*, 6 A.L.S.A. FORUM 32 (1982).

17. Kennedy, *System, supra*.

18. *See* H. KRAUSS, THE SETTLEMENT HOUSE MOVEMENT IN NEW YORK CITY, 1886–1914 (1981); HANDBOOK OF SETTLEMENTS (R. Woods & A. Kennedy eds., 1970) (on the education these houses provided for their members); H. KARGER, THE SENTINELS OF ORDER: A STUDY OF SOCIAL CONTROL & THE MINNEAPOLIS SETTLEMENT HOUSE MOVEMENT, 1915–1950 (1987); JANE ADDAMS, TWENTY YEARS AT HULL-HOUSE (1980).

19. *See, e.g.*, KARGER, SENTINELS, *supra*; ADDAMS, *supra*; PEARL IDELIA ELLIS, AMERICANIZATION THROUGH HOMEMAKING 19–29 (1929).

20. Derrick Bell, *Serving Two Masters: Integration Ideals and Client Interests in School Desegregation Litigation*, 85 YALE L.J. 470 (1976).

21. *Id.* at 470–72, 482–93.

22. In other words, A, who wants to empathize with a radically different person, B, instead imagines how he, A, would feel as a B.

23. GERALD LOPEZ, REBELLIOUS LAWYERING: ONE CHICANO'S VI-
SION OF PROGRESSIVE LEGAL PRACTICE (1992).

24. *Images, supra* note 14, at 1261, 1281. *See also* Lucie White, *Seeking
. . . "The Faces of Otherness,"* 77 CORNELL L. REV. 1499, 1508–09 (1992).

25. I was thinking, for example, of how no black civil rights organization
had filed an *amicus* brief in *Korematsu* (the Japanese internment case), and
how some men of color still patronize the women in their lives. *See* CHRON-
ICLES, *supra* note 1, at ch. 6 (discussing this and other unlovely traits).

26. On double consciousness, according to which blacks see events from
two perspectives at the same time—that of the outside world, according to
which they are despised, and their own, according to which they are normal,
see W. E. B. DU BOIS, THE SOULS OF BLACK FOLKS 16–17 (1903); RALPH
ELLISON, THE INVISIBLE MAN 1–7 (1952).

27. I am grateful to Margaret Montoya for this example.

28. On Cortes's (and La Malinche's) role, see WILLIAM H. PRESCOTT, 1
MEXICO AND THE LIFE OF THE CONQUEROR FERNANDO CORTÉS 208, 228,
238, 240, 247, 274, 290, 303, 310, 328, 333, 372, 375, 424 (1900); 2 *id.* 60, 68,
94, 144, 190, 281, 338 (1900); *see also* BERNAL DIAZ DEL CASTILLO, THE
CONQUEST OF MEXICO 1517–21 (1956).

29. *E.g.,* Clark Cunningham, *The Lawyer as Translator, Representation as Text: An Ethnography of Legal Discourse,* 77 CORNELL L. REV.
1298, 1368–87 (1992) (speculating on the ethics of broadcasting a client's
stories).

30. *See* MICHEL FOUCAULT, POWER/KNOWLEDGE: SELECTED INTER-
VIEWS AND OTHER WRITINGS 1972–77 (Colin Gordon ed. & Colin Gordon
et al. trans., 1980).

31. *E.g.,* U.S. DEP'T OF LABOR, OFFICE OF POLICY PLANNING AND
RESEARCH, THE NEGRO FAMILY: THE CASE FOR NATIONAL ACTION
(1965); DANIEL PATRICK MOYNIHAN, FAMILY AND NATION (1986), which
was written in an effort to understand and help, is today considered virtually
an argument for abandoning hope for that "pathological" institution. *See also*
PATRICIA A. TURNER, I HEARD IT THROUGH THE GRAPEVINE: RUMOR IN
AFRICAN AMERICAN CULTURE (1993) (on urban myths that circulate in
the black community; author describes the myths as efforts to increase
community and empowerment, but drawing attention to them runs risk of
making the community look ignorant and ridiculous); KRISTIN BUMILLER,
THE CIVIL RIGHTS SOCIETY: THE SOCIAL CONSTRUCTION OF VICTIMS
(1988) (book by progressive scholar, based on interviews with victims of
discrimination, now used by some to argue against civil rights laws and
enforcement on the ground that they simply encourage a victim mentality).
On the possibility that "imaginative" empathy can reinforce hierarchy, see
Ward, *Kinder, supra* note 14 at 950–51.

32. *E.g.*, RICHARD A. POSNER, THE ECONOMIC ANALYSIS OF LAW (4th ed. 1992) (on the view that law should be efficient—i.e., maximize trades and transactions that will promote the satisfaction of preferences).

33. *E.g.*, ANDREW HACKER, TWO NATIONS: BLACK AND WHITE, SEPARATE, HOSTILE, UNEQUAL 50–52, 93–133 (1992); Lance Morrow, *Voters Are Mad as Hell*, TIME, Mar. 2, 1992, at 16.

34. I thought of Willie Horton, and Jesse Helms's "white hands" commercial, and also of the way many politicians have been rallying around such neo-nativist themes as immigration control and English Only, which are aimed at making life difficult for Latinos and other recent arrivals. *See, e.g.,* Anthony Walton, *Willie Horton and Me*, N.Y. TIMES MAG., Aug. 20, 1989, at 52; Richard Lacayo, *For Whom the Bell Curves*, TIME, Oct. 24, 1994, at 66; Isabel Wilkerson, *Racial Harassment Altering Blacks' Choices on Colleges*, N.Y. TIMES, May 9, 1990, at A-1; Tom Tancredo, *Make a Candidate Sweat—Ask about Illegal Immigrants*, DENVER POST, Apr. 30, 1995, at E-1, col. 1.

35. Richard Whitmore, *Adults in Poll: It's Worst Time since Slavery*, DENVER POST, May 27, 1994, at 2-A, col. 2.

36. *See* Pierre Schlag, *Normativity and the Politics of Form*, 139 U. PA. L. REV. 801 (1991); Richard Delgado, *Norms and Normal Science: Toward a Critique of Normativity in Legal Thought*, 139 U. PA. L. REV. 933, 957–59 (1991).

37. Miller & Kahneman, *Norm Theory*, 93 PSYCHOL. REV. 136 (1986).

38. On helping behavior, see Faye Crosby et al., *Recent Unobtrusive Studies of Black and White Discrimination and Prejudice: A Literature Review*, 87 PSYCHOL. BULL. 546 (1980).

39. Stephen G. West et al., *Helping a Motorist in Distress: The Effects of Sex, Race, and Neighborhood*, 31 J. PERSONALITY & SOC. PSYCHOL. 691, 693–94 (1975).

40. CHRONICLES, *supra* note 1, at ch. 1 (on the need to provide a self-interest basis for affirmative action and racial justice).

41. *Id.* On the economic-determinist (interest convergence) view of civil rights law, see also DERRICK BELL, RACE, RACISM, AND AMERICAN LAW 1–51 (3d ed. 1993).

42. On the backlash vote and role of angry white males, see Morrow, *Mad as Hell, supra* note 33; David Gates, *White Male Paranoia*, NEWSWEEK, Mar. 29, 1993, at 48.

43. *See* Richard Delgado, *Zero-Based Racial Politics: An Evaluation of Three Best-Case Arguments on Behalf of the Nonwhite Underclass*, 78 GEO. L.J. 1929 (1990).

44. On some of the cruelties committed by the early conquistadores, see BERNAL DIAZ CASTILLO, CONQUEST, *supra* note 28; on the Inquisition, see

H. KAMEN, INQUISITION AND SOCIETY IN SPAIN IN THE SIXTEENTH AND SEVENTEENTH CENTURIES (1985); on a U.S. chapter, see A. MILLER, *The Crucible, in* COLLECTED PLAYS (1957).

45. Kohn, *Between Bad and Good, Research Shows Believers No More Likely to Love Their Neighbor Than Nonbelievers,* S.F. CHRONICLE & EXAMINER, July 8, 1990, This World, at 15 (summarizing various studies of helping behavior).

46. *Id.* On the false piety of self-righteous belief, see Peggy Davis, *Law as Microaggression,* 98 YALE L.J. 1559 (1989).

47. On the gap between rich and poor, see *Blacks Still Trail Whites in Wages,* Boulder, CO, DAILY CAMERA, Apr. 30, 1995, at 9A, col. 1; CHRONICLES, *supra* note 1, at ch. 1 (Appendix D).

48. On this socioeconomic theory of racism, see, *e.g.,* J. KOVEL, WHITE RACISM — A PSYCHOHISTORY 44 (1984); GORDON ALLPORT, THE NATURE OF PREJUDICE 224–25 (25th Anniversary Ed. 1979).

49. *See, e.g.,* Robert Trivers, *The Evaluation of Reciprocal Altruism,* 46 Q. REV. BIOL. 3 (1979); B. M. DeWaal, *The Chimpanzee's Sense of Social Regularity and Its Relation to the Human Sense of Justice, in* THE SENSE OF JUSTICE: BIOLOGICAL FOUNDATIONS OF LAW 241 (Roger D. Masters & Margaret Gruter eds., 1992).

50. *See* DERRICK BELL, AND WE ARE NOT SAVED: THE ELUSIVE QUEST FOR RACIAL JUSTICE (1987) (on the way white dislike of blacks unites working-class and elite whites and keeps the former from challenging the latter).

51. Derrick Bell, *The Chronicle of the Space Traders,* 42 RUTGERS L. REV. 1 (1990), 34 ST. LOUIS L. REV. 3 (1990) (same chronicle in slightly revised form with additional commentary). *See also* Michael Klarman, *Brown, Racial Change, and the Civil Rights Movement,* 80 VA. L. REV. 7, 102–04 (1993) (on populism and its evolution into anti-civil rights sentiment).

52. Richard Delgado, *Fairness and Formality: Minimizing the Risk of Prejudice in Alternative Dispute Resolution,* 1985 WIS. L. REV. 1359; PATRICIA WILLIAMS, THE ALCHEMY OF RACE AND RIGHTS 146–48 (1991); Trina Grillo, *The Mediation Alternative: Process Dangers for Women,* 100 YALE L.J. 1545 (1991).

53. CHRONICLES, *supra* note 1, at ch. 4.

54. *See* Richard Delgado, *Enormous Anomaly? Left-Right Parallels in Recent Writing about Race,* 91 COLUM. L. REV. 1547 (1991).

55. Henderson, *Empathy, supra* note 14.

56. Herb Eastman, *Speaking Truth to Power: The Language of Civil Rights Litigators,* 104 YALE L.J. 763 (1995); Ward, *Kinder, supra* note 14, at 946 (criticizing this view as utopian).

57. On the difficulty battered wives have had in winning a legal defense of nonimminent provocation or self-defense, see Holly Maguigan, *Battered Women and Self-Defense: Myths and Misconceptions in Current Reform Proposals*, 140 U. PA. L. REV. 379 (1991). *See also* Lucie White, *Subordination, Rhetorical Survival Skills, and Sunday Shoes: Notes on the Hearing of Mrs. G.*, 38 BUFF. L. REV. 1, 4, 29–52 (1990) (client surprised attorney by successfully arguing for a novel theory of relief, for the first time, at her own hearing).

58. 426 U.S. 229 (1976).

59. On causation in civil rights cases, see, *e.g.*, City of Richmond v. J. A. Croson Co., 109 S. Ct. 706 (1989); Firefighters Local Union No. 1784 v. Stotts, 467 U.S. 451 (1984); Daniels v. Williams, 474 U.S. 327 (1986); DERRICK BELL, NOT SAVED, *supra* note 50, at 170–73.

60. On the role of the "BFOQ" (bona fide occupational qualification) in civil rights law, see, *e.g.*, MACK A. PLAYER, FEDERAL LAW OF EMPLOYMENT DISCRIMINATION 51–58 (1992).

61. R.A.V. v. City of St. Paul, 112 S. Ct. 2538 (1992).

62. On this and similar incidents and their role in justifying anti-hate speech rules, see Richard Delgado, *Campus Antiracism Rules: Constitutional Narratives in Collision*, 85 Nw. U. L. REV. 343, 348–58 (1991).

63. On this ironic juxtaposition, see Charles Lawrence, *Cross Burning and the Sound of Silence: Antisubordination Theory and the First Amendment*, 37 VILL. L. REV. 787 (1992). *See also* Mari Matsuda, *Public Response to Racist Speech: Considering the Victim's Story*, 87 MICH. L. REV. 2320 (1989) (law often fails to take account of the injuries of victims of hate speech).

64. Lawrence, *supra* at 787–95; 112 S. Ct. at 2540–51.

65. *See* RICHARD DELGADO ET AL., WORDS THAT WOUND (1993) (on the way racist, assaultive speech injures its victims).

66. *E.g.*, HENRY LOUIS GATES ET AL., SPEAKING OF RACE, SPEAKING OF SEX (1994) (depicting in often terrifying fashion the parade of horribles likely to ensue if hate speech rules are enacted).

67. *See* Sharon Cairns, unpublished manuscript (1995) (on file with author) (on the way discourse rules govern shows of emotion).

68. For a study of these unwritten rules of etiquette, see B. Bogoch & B. Danet, *Challenge and Control in Lawyer-Client Interaction*, 4 TEXT 249 (1984); Bogoch, *Power, Divorce, and Solidarity*, 5 DISCOURSE & SOC'Y 65 (1994); Cairns, *supra* note 67.

69. On this risk, see Peter Gabel & Paul Harris, *Building Power and Breaking Images: Critical Legal Theory and the Practice of Law*, 11 N.Y.U. REV. L. & SOC. CHANGE 369 (1982–83).

70. *See* Eastman, *supra* note 56, at 765–72, 778–81.

71. Bell, *Serving, supra* note 20, at 470–72, 482–93; *see also* Anthony Alfieri, *Practicing Community,* 107 HARV. L. REV. 1747, 1751 (1994); Alfieri, *White Knight* (book review), 108 HARV. L. REV. 959, 962–63 (1995) (urging that whites stay out of leadership positions in civil rights movement).

72. Eastman, *supra* note 56, at 765–72; MARTHA MINOW, PARTIAL JUSTICE AND MINORITIES, IN THE FATE OF LAW 68–77 (Austin Sarat & Thomas Kearns eds., 1991) (on effacement of minorities through the choice of story).

73. Paul Finkelman, *Not Only the Judge's Robes Were Black: African-American Lawyers as Social Engineers* (book review), 47 STAN. L. REV. 161 (1994).

74. *Id.* at 166–69.

75. Richard Delgado, *Words That Wound: A Tort Action for Racial Insults, Epithets and Name-Calling,* 17 HARV. C.R.-C.L. L. REV. 133 (1982).

76. Catharine MacKinnon, SEXUAL HARASSMENT OF WORKING WOMEN (1979).

77. Alan Freeman, *Legitimizing Race Discrimination through Antidiscrimination Law: A Critical Review of Supreme Court Doctrine,* 62 MINN. L. REV. 1049 (1978).

78. DAVID A. J. RICHARDS, THE RIGHT TO PRIVACY: GAYS, LESBIANS, AND THE CONSTITUTION (1991).

79. McCleskey v. Kemp, 481 U.S. 279 (1987). *See* Randall Kennedy, McCleskey v. Kemp*: Race, Capital Punishment, and the Supreme Court,* 101 HARV. L. REV. 1388 (1988).

80. For a discussion of recent caselaw dealing with victim-impact statements, see David D. Friedman, *Should the Characteristics of Victims and Criminals Count?: Payne v. Tennessee and Two Views of Efficient Punishment,* 34 B.C. L. REV. 731 (1993).

81. For an overview of some of this literature, see Anthony Alfieri, *Stances,* 77 CORNELL L. REV. 1233 (1992).

82. *E.g.,* Carrie Menkel-Meadow, *Portia in a Different Voice: Speculations on a Woman's Lawyering Process,* 1 BERK. WOMEN'S L.J. 39 (1985); *Is Altruism Possible in Lawyering?* 8 GA. ST. U. L. REV. 385 (1992).

83. *E.g.,* GERALD LOPEZ, REBELLIOUS LAWYERING, *supra* note 23; *Reconceiving Civil Rights Practice: Seven Weeks in the Life of a Rebellious Collaboration,* 77 GEO. L.J. 1603 (1989); *Training Future Lawyers to Work with the Politically and Socially Disadvantaged: Anti-Generic Legal Education,* 91 W. VA. L. REV. 305 (1989).

84. *E.g.,* Clark Cunningham, *A Tale of Two Clients: Thinking about Law as Language,* 87 MICH. L. REV. 2459 (1989); *The Lawyer as Translator, supra* note 29.

85. *E.g.,* Anthony Alfieri, *Practicing Community, supra* note 71; *Reconstructive Poverty Law Practice: Learning Lessons of Client Narrative,* 100

YALE L.J. 2107 (1991); *The Ethics of Violence: Necessity, Excess, and Opposition* (book review), 94 COLUM. L. REV. 1721 (1994); *White Knight, supra* note 71.

86. *E.g.,* Alfieri, *Reconstructive, supra* note 85; Binnie Miller, *Give Them Back Their Lives: Recognizing Client Narrative in Case Theory,* 93 MICH. L. REV. 485 (1994); White, *Sunday Shoes, supra* note 57.

87. Herb Eastman, *Speaking Truth, supra* note 56, at 778–81.

88. Alfieri, *Reconstructive, supra* note 85, at 2118–21, 2128–29; *Ethics of Violence, supra* note 85, at 1721–44, 1749, 1764 (we must "learn," "unlearn . . ." and "relearn" better or different approaches to our clients and advocacy).

89. Alfieri, *Ethics of Violence, supra* note 85, at 1721–25, 1729, 1733–36, 1749–50; *see also Reconstructive, supra* note 85, at 2130 (another *mea culpa* about a different client, a Mrs. Celeste).

90. *Ethics of Violence, supra* note 85, at 1731–33, 1743, 1748.

91. Bell, *Serving Two Masters, supra* note 20, at 470–72, 482–93.

92. For other self-flagellations and confessions of failure, see Cunningham, *Translator, supra* note 29, at 1300 ("I was one of his oppressors. I was his lawyer"); *id.* at 1325, 1328, 1330; White, *Sunday Shoes, supra* note 57, at 45–50; Miller, *Case Theory, supra* note 86, at 569–70.

93. *See also* Miller, *Case Theory, supra* note 86 (lawyer wanted client of color to adopt a theory of racism in defending against a shoplifting charge; client resisted, realizing this was a theory that could not win because the jury are more likely to believe the shopowner and the police); White, *Sunday Shoes, supra* note 57, at 33–37, 51 (author wanted client to speak up, be more articulate and well spoken).

94. *See* LAWRENCE TRIBE, AMERICAN CONSTITUTIONAL LAW §§ 3–10, 3–11, 3–14 (2d ed. 1988).

95. Zahn v. International Paper Co., 414 U.S. 291 (1974).

96. *E.g.,* Eisen v. Carlisle & Jacquelin, 417 U.S. 156 (1974).

97. Martin v. Wilks, 490 U.S. 755 (1989) (overruled by Civil Rights Act of 1991).

98. ELLIS COSE, THE RAGE OF A PRIVILEGED CLASS (1993). The middle- or upper-income person of color is apt to have more contacts with whites and thus more opportunities to be the victim of discrimination.

99. *See Interview, supra* note 2; *see also* volumes 3 & 4 RACE TRAITOR MAGAZINE (1994–95).

100. *See, e.g.,* 1 RACE TRAITOR (frontispiece).

101. *Interview, supra* note 2, at 85; *see also* Edward H. Peeples, *Thirty Years in Black and White,* 3 RACE TRAITOR 34, 45 (Spring 1994).

102. *Interview, supra* at 84–85. *See also* LOPEZ, REBELLIOUS LAWYERING, *supra* note 23, at 24, 31–38, 50–51, 55, 73 (suggesting various measures

by which activist lawyers can identify more fully with the client community); Alfieri, *Practicing Community, supra* note 71, at 1762–63 (same).

103. *Interview, supra* at 84–85 ("so long as the white race exists, all movements against what is called 'racism' will fail. Therefore, our aim is to abolish the white race"); *see* IAN HANEY LOPEZ, WHITE BY LAW (1995) (on the social and legal construction of the white race).

104. *Interview, supra,* at 84–86.

105. *Id.* at 85 (how to be a race traitor: six ways to fight being white); John Garvey, *Family Matters,* 4 RACE TRAITOR 23, 24–29 (Winter 1995).

106. *Interview, supra,* at 86; Editorial, *When Does the Unreasonable Act Make Sense?* 3 RACE TRAITOR 108 (Spring 1994).

107. *See* Program, *Critical Networks Conference: Race, Class, and Identity* 4 (1995) (on file with author).

108. Derrick Bell, *Property Rights in Whiteness, in* CRITICAL RACE THEORY: THE CUTTING EDGE (R. Delgado ed., 1995).

109. On responsibility and evasion, see JEAN-PAUL SARTRE, *Absolute Freedom, in* BEING AND NOTHINGNESS (1956). *See also* LOPEZ, REBELLIOUS LAWYERING, *supra* note 23, at 329; Alfieri, *Reconstructive, supra* note 85, at 1750 (both authors calling for mobilization, radical identification, opposition, and reconstruction as alternative to law practice as currently understood).

110. *E.g.,* RALPH NADER, UNSAFE AT ANY SPEED: THE DESIGNED-IN DANGERS OF THE AMERICAN AUTOMOBILE (1972).

111. On the Poor People's March and King's planned rapprochement with the poor community, see DAVID J. GARROW, BEARING THE CROSS: MARTIN LUTHER KING, JR., AND THE SOUTHERN CHRISTIAN LEADERSHIP CONFERENCE 575–624 (First Vintage Books ed. 1988).

112. Robert Kennedy, the scion of a wealthy family, toward the end of his life went to California to demonstrate solidarity with the farm workers, met with leaders of minority and poor communities, and was present at the origin of the Poor People's Campaign. ARTHUR M. SCHLESINGER, JR., ROBERT KENNEDY AND HIS TIME 790–91, 846–47, 872–73, 908, 914 (1978).

113. *See Critical Networks, supra* note 107, at 4.

Notes to Chapter 2

1. The Professor is traveling to give a speech he promised to give six months ago, which he now regrets having scheduled during deepest winter.

2. On "Giannina," Rodrigo's playwright friend and life companion, see Richard Delgado, THE RODRIGO CHRONICLES, chs. 3–7 (1995).

3. Regarding Rodrigo's LL.M. thesis and its various spin-off writing projects, see CHRONICLES, *supra* note 2, at chs. 3–4.

4. *See* Derrick Bell, *Racial Realism,* 24 CONN. L. REV. 363 (1992) [hereinafter Bell, *Racial Realism*] (putting forward the "racial realist" view that African Americans are unlikely to make serious gains in our political and legal system, but that the effort must nevertheless be made). For earlier statements of Bell's thesis, see, for example, Derrick A. Bell, Jr., Brown v. Board of Education *and the Interest-Convergence Dilemma,* 93 HARV. L. REV. 518 (1980) [hereinafter Bell, *Interest-Convergence*] (arguing for a shift in focus from the integration of the races within the educational system to the overall improvement of educational quality); Derrick Bell, *Foreword: The Civil Rights Chronicles,* 99 HARV. L. REV. 4, 13 (1985) [hereinafter Bell, *Foreword*] (using fantasy in the form of imagined chronicles to explore the myth that "racial justice can be realized without sacrificing the material and psychological rewards of racial domination").

5. *See* Alan D. Freeman, *Race and Class: The Dilemma of Liberal Reform,* 90 YALE L.J. 1880 (1981) (reviewing DERRICK A. BELL, JR., RACE, RACISM AND AMERICAN LAW (2d ed. 1980)).

6. *See generally* john a. powell, *Racial Realism or Racial Despair?,* 24 CONN. L. REV. 533, 544 (1992) (arguing that Bell's racial realism, while partly sound, is nevertheless excessively bleak and calculated to subdue reform fervor).

7. *See* Bell, *Racial Realism, supra* note 4, at 373 (declaring that "[e]ven those herculean efforts we hail as successful will produce no more than . . . short-lived victories that slide into irrelevance").

8. *See, e.g.,* JOSEPH CAMPBELL, THE MASKS OF GOD: PRIMITIVE MYTHOLOGY (Viking Press 1970) (1959) (describing how similar mythological symbols continue to reappear in different societies); JOSEPH CAMPBELL, MYTHS TO LIVE BY (1972) (examining the way myths and symbols create a firm base for the moral order of a society).

9. *See* Bell, *Interest-Convergence, supra* note 4, at 522–28.

10. *See id.* at 524 ("I contend that the decision in *Brown* . . . cannot be understood without some consideration of the decision's value to whites"); *see also* DERRICK A. BELL, JR., RACE, RACISM AND AMERICAN LAW 44–50 (3d ed. 1992) (elaborating on his theory).

11. *See* Bell, *Racial Realism, supra* note 4, at 363 (declaring that "[r]acial equality is, in fact, not a realistic goal").

12. *See* Richard Delgado, *Derrick Bell and the Ideology of Racial Reform: Will We Ever Be Saved?* 97 YALE L.J. 923, 930 n.28, 931 n.31 (1988) (book review) (delivering statistics on blacks' status in the United States); *see also* ANDREW HACKER, TWO NATIONS: BLACK AND WHITE, SEPARATE, HOSTILE, UNEQUAL (1992) (reporting further statistics on blacks).

13. *See* Mickey Kaus, *The Work Ethic State: The Only Way to Break the Culture of Poverty,* NEW REPUBLIC, July 7, 1986, at 22 (arguing that there

exists a "culture of poverty [which is] largely a black culture"); *see also* Mickey Kaus, *Bastards*, NEW REPUBLIC, Feb. 21, 1994, at 16 (discussing work-oriented welfare plans for, among others, the black underclass culture); *Workfare That Works*, NEW REPUBLIC, Aug. 24, 1987, at 7–8 (examining welfare attempts to transform the "culture of poverty" and the "culture of dependency"). *See generally* OFFICE OF POLICY PLANNING AND RESEARCH, U.S. DEP'T OF LABOR, THE NEGRO FAMILY: THE CASE FOR NATIONAL ACTION 5 (1965) ("[T]he fundamental source of the weakness of the Negro community at the present time . . . is the deterioration of the Negro family").

14. *See, e.g.*, Suzanna Sherry, *The Forgotten Victims*, 63 U. COLO. L. REV. 375, 376–80 (1993) (arguing that the race problem is largely solved, at least on a formal level).

15. *See* Richard Whitmire, *"Major Crisis" for Black Children*, DENVER POST, May 27, 1994, at 2A (quoting Marian Wright Edelman, president of the Children's Defense Fund, as saying, "We have a major black child crisis—the worst since slavery").

16. For an extensive discussion of the role of racial imagery, see Richard Delgado & Jean Stefancic, *Images of the Outsider in American Law and Culture: Can Free Expression Remedy Systemic Social Ills?*, 77 CORNELL L. REV. 1258 (1992).

17. *Cf.* Delgado, *Ever Saved?*, *supra* note 12, at 923, 928–47 (discussing Derrick Bell's "somber prognosis" of American race-remedy law).

18. *See* Bell, *Racial Realism, supra* note 4, at 373–79 (discussing racial realism, and contending that "[b]lack people will never gain full equality in this country.").

19. Girardeau A. Spann, *Pure Politics*, 88 MICH. L. REV. 1971, 1992 (1990).

20. *See* Symposium, *The Renaissance of Pragmatism in American Legal Thought*, 63 S. CAL. L. REV. 1569 (1990).

21. *See generally* RONALD M. DWORKIN, LAW'S EMPIRE (1986) (discussing conceptions of law as a stable, legitimate, and binding moral force).

22. The Professor was thinking of the Greek sophists as well as some of their more recent incarnations. *See* text immediately *infra*.

23. *See* PLATO, THE REPUBLIC, *reprinted in* 1 THE DIALOGUES OF PLATO 591, 603 (B. Jowett trans., 1937) [hereinafter DIALOGUES] (describing Thrasymachus's view that law is the will of the mighty).

24. *See* PLATO, THE APOLOGY, *reprinted in* 1 DIALOGUES, *supra*, at 418–20 (describing how Socrates rejects his friends' admonition that he flee his impending execution, on the ground that doing so would weaken the legitimacy of the Athenian state).

25. *See* David Papke, *The Black Panther Party's Narratives of Resistance*, 18 VT. L. REV. 645, 670 (1994) (noting that the Panthers harbored "no deep

respect for [the] law" and asserting that "the poor . . . and oppressed had the right to rewrite unjust laws").

26. *See* BELL, RACE, RACISM, *supra* note 4, at 26–30.

27. *See id.* at 9, 26–30.

28. *See, e.g.,* Brown v. Board of Educ., 347 U.S. 483, 495 (1954) (official segregation of schoolchildren by race violates the constitutional guarantee of equal protection of the law).

29. *See* Papke, *supra* note 25, at 662–71 (describing the Panthers' knowledge of the law while contrasting their cynical attitude toward it).

30. *See generally* Richard Delgado, *Campus Antiracism Rules: Constitutional Narratives in Collision,* 85 Nw. U. L. REV. 343 (1991) (analyzing college campus rules that prohibit racially offensive speech under the First and Fourteenth Amendments).

31. *See* DONALD L. BARLETT & JAMES B. STEELE, AMERICA: WHO REALLY PAYS THE TAXES? 39–48 (1994). Concerning the way in which deregulation and favorable tax treatment have aided the rich and disadvantaged the poor, see generally Richard Delgado, *Inequality "From the Top": Applying an Ancient Prohibition to an Emerging Problem of Distributive Justice,* 32 UCLA L. REV. 100, 129–32 (1984) (discussing legal approaches to governmental favoritism toward its friends).

32. *See* CHRONICLES, *supra* note 2, at ch. 5 (pointing out a new trend in law schools toward "abstract, vaguely aspirational teaching," which is also found in legal theory in the form of "civic republicanism").

33. Antonio Gramsci, an Italian intellectual, wrote about social critique and the relations among classes of people. *See* ANTONIO GRAMSCI, SELECTIONS FROM THE PRISON NOTEBOOKS *passim* (Quentin Hoare & Geoffrey N. Smith trans. & eds., 1971).

34. *See generally* RALPH NADER, UNSAFE AT ANY SPEED: THE DESIGNED-IN DANGERS OF THE AMERICAN AUTOMOBILE (1972) (discussing the reluctance of the automobile industry to commit resources to safety research and design).

35. For a discussion of the problem of the "indeterminate plaintiff," see Richard Delgado, *Beyond* Sindell: *Relaxation of Cause-in-Fact Rules for Indeterminate Plaintiffs,* 70 CAL. L. REV. 881 (1982).

36. On the high costs of litigation, see, for example, John E. Morris, *Cut the Going Rate,* AM. LAW., Sept. 1993, at 5; Gary Taylor, *Counsel to Firms Goes In-House: Legal Costs Are Leading Firms, Like Their Clients, to Look Inside for Advice,* NAT'L L.J., July 18, 1994, at A1.

37. *See* HENRY KISSINGER, DIPLOMACY 59–77 (1994) (attributing modern nations' pursuit of self-interest to a tradition begun by Richelieu's raison d'état, and stating that the post-Cold War challenge is to restrain nationalistic assertions of self-interest); ZBIGNIEW BRZEZINSKI, OUT OF CONTROL:

GLOBAL TURMOIL ON THE EVE OF THE TWENTY-FIRST CENTURY 87–101 (1993) (asserting that the distinction between exclusively foreign and exclusively domestic issues has blurred).

38. *See, e.g.,* DIPLOMACY, *supra* at 59–77; NICCOLO MACHIAVELLI, THE PRINCE 79–84 (Hill Thompson trans., Heritage 1954) (1513).

39. On morality as a means of manipulating the masses, see FRIEDRICH W. NIETZSCHE, BEYOND GOOD AND EVIL 103–31, 106 (Marianne Cowan trans., Gateway ed. 1955) (1907) ("What is essential and invaluable in every system of morals, is that it is a long constraint"); FRIEDRICH W. NIETZSCHE, THUS SPAKE ZARATHUSTRA 51 (A. Tille trans., J. M. Dent & Sons 1958) (1883) ("Joy in the herd is older than joy in the *I:* and while good conscience is called herd, only the bad conscience saith *I"*).

40. *See, e.g.,* Richard Delgado, *Zero-Based Racial Politics: An Evaluation of Three Best-Case Arguments on Behalf of the Nonwhite Underclass,* 78 GEO. L.J. 1929, 1940–44 (1990) (arguing that a zero-based critical analysis indicates that the nonwhite poor should consider aligning themselves with the principled Right of the Republican Party).

41. *See* CHRONICLES, *supra* note 2, at ch. 8 (discussing how society virtually equates crime and the black underclass).

42. *See* CHRONICLES, *supra* note 2, at ch. 3 (discussing how American society excludes blacks both from the economy and from networks of love).

43. *See, e.g.,* Faye Crosby et al., *Recent Unobtrusive Studies of Black and White Discrimination and Prejudice: A Literature Review,* 87 PSYCHOL. BULL. 546, 548–49 (1980) (describing the shopping bag experiment, which found that whites tend to give help to people of their own race); Stephen G. West et al., *Helping a Motorist in Distress: The Effects of Sex, Race, and Neighborhood,* 31 J. PERSONALITY & SOC. PSYCHOL. 691, 693–94 (1975) (discussing the broken-down motorist experiment, which found that black victims were helped faster in black neighborhoods and that white victims were helped faster in white neighborhoods).

44. *See, e.g.,* Anthony Appiah, *The Uncompleted Argument: Du Bois and the Illusion of Race,* 12 CRITICAL INQUIRY 21, 21–22 (1985) (noting that aside from visible differences in skin, hair, and bone, "there are few genetic characteristics to be found in the population of England that are not found in similar proportions in Zaire or in China; and few too (though more) which are found in Zaire but not in similar proportions in China or England").

45. On the social construction of race, see IAN F. HANEY LOPEZ, WHITE BY LAW (1995).

46. *See* Delgado & Stefancic, *supra* note 16, at 1260–62, 1275–76 (explaining that the use of images serves both to reassure those who disseminate them, and to legitimate their position vis-à-vis those who are demonized).

47. For a discussion of some of these conservative themes, see CHRONI-CLES, *supra* note 2, at ch. 1 (noting that conservative authors currently argue that culture need not change direction to survive, but rather must try harder at the things that were done before); Richard Delgado, *Enormous Anomaly? Left-Right Parallels in Recent Writing about Race,* 91 COLUM. L. REV. 1547, 1548 (1991) (book review) (arguing that left- and right-leaning scholars are in substantial agreement with regard to what is wrong with the liberal civil rights program).

48. *See* Delgado & Stefancic, *supra* note 16, at 1262–67, 1275–76, 1281.

49. *See id.* at 1281–82.

50. *See* Lucy K. Hayden, *The Poetry of Phillis Wheatley, in* MASTER-PIECES OF AFRICAN-AMERICAN LITERATURE 451 (Frank N. Magill ed., 1992).

51. *See* City of Richmond v. J. A. Croson Co., 488 U.S. 469, 521 (1989) (Scalia, J., concurring) ("[O]nly a social emergency rising to the level of imminent danger to life and limb . . . can justify an exception to the principle embodied in the Fourteenth Amendment that our Constitution is color-blind" (quoting Plessy v. Ferguson, 163 U.S. 537, 559 (1896) (Harlan, J., dissenting))); Lino A. Graglia, *Race-Conscious Remedies,* 9 HARV. J.L. & PUB. POL'Y 83, 83 (1986) ("It should be obvious that granting preferences to some individuals on the basis of race cannot be justified . . . as a means of remedying disadvantages suffered by other individuals").

52. For a discussion of these and other forms of turnabout, see Richard Delgado & Jean Stefancic, *Imposition,* 35 WM. & MARY L. REV. 1025 (1994).

53. 347 U.S. 483 (1954).

54. *See* BELL, RACE, RACISM, *supra* note 4, at 1–71; Bell, *Interest-Convergence, supra* note 4, *passim; see also* Richard Delgado & Jean Stefancic, Brown v. Board of Education *and the Reconstructive Paradox,* 36 WM. & MARY L. REV. 547 (1994).

55. *See* Bell, *Interest-Convergence, supra* note 4, at 518 ("today, most black children attend public schools that are both racially isolated and infe-rior"); Michael J. Klarman, Brown, *Racial Change, and the Civil Rights Movement,* 80 VA. L. REV. 7, 12 (1994) ("de facto school segregation in all large urban school districts has intensified since the late 1960s").

56. *See, e.g.,* Milliken v. Bradley, 418 U.S. 717, 745 (1974) (holding that "without an interdistrict violation and interdistrict effect, there is no consti-tutional wrong calling for an interdistrict remedy").

57. *See* San Antonio Indep. Sch. Dist. v. Rodriguez, 411 U.S. 1, 37 (1973).

58. *See id.* at 26–28; James v. Valtierra, 402 U.S. 137, 141–43 (1971).

59. *See generally* HACKER, *supra* note 12, at 170–78 (describing how schools have failed to serve black children well).

60. *See* Bell, *Interest-Convergence, supra* note 4, at 524 (stating that *Brown* gave credibility to the United States' struggle for democracy in the Third World); Mary L. Dudziak, *Desegregation as a Cold War Imperative*, 41 STAN. L. REV. 61, 63 (1988) (explaining that "efforts to promote civil rights within the United States were consistent with, and important to, the more central U.S. mission of fighting world communism").

61. *See* Bell, *Foreword, supra* note 4, at 66 (discussing both the importance of presenting a positive American racial image to the Third World after World War II and the effect of this policy); *cf.* Bell, *Racial Realism, supra* note 4, at 372 (discussing, in light of the Clarence Thomas confirmation hearings, "how frequently in American history Blacks became the involuntary pawns in defining and resolving society's serious social trends").

62. *See* Dudziak, *supra* note 60, at 98–112 (discussing the State Department's attempts at "international impression management").

63. On this phenomenon, *see generally* ROBERT J. LIFTON, THOUGHT REFORM AND THE PSYCHOLOGY OF TOTALISM 439 (1961) (discussing how a "coercive approach to changing people" could result in "'identification with the aggressor'" (quoting ANNA FREUD, THE EGO AND THE MECHANISMS OF DEFENCE 117 (Cecil Baines trans., 1946))); Bruno Bettelheim, *Individual and Mass Behavior in Extreme Situations*, 38 J. ABNORMAL & SOC. PSYCHOL. 417, 447–51 (1943) (describing the tendency of prisoners in German concentration camps during the late 1930s to adopt Gestapo values as their own); Craig Haney et al., *Interpersonal Dynamics in a Simulated Prison*, 1 INT'L J. CRIMINOLOGY & PENOLOGY 69, 95 (1973) (noting that prisoners in a simulated prison study "sided with the guards against a solitary fellow prisoner").

64. On the life and thought of the great singer-actor-athlete, *see generally* MARTIN B. DUBERMAN, PAUL ROBESON (1988).

65. On the life and thought of W. E. B. Du Bois, *see generally* W. E. B. DU BOIS, THE AUTOBIOGRAPHY OF W. E. B. DU BOIS (1968) [hereinafter DU BOIS, AUTOBIOGRAPHY]; W. E. B. DU BOIS, THE SOULS OF BLACK FOLK (1973).

66. *See* DU BOIS, AUTOBIOGRAPHY, *supra*, at 394–95 (explaining that Du Bois's status was emasculated to the point that "colored children ceased to hear his name"); MANNING MARABLE, W. E. B. DU BOIS: BLACK RADICAL DEMOCRAT 171–75 (1986) (discussing Du Bois's removal from the NAACP).

67. *See* MARABLE, *supra*, at 173 (noting that NAACP leaders felt that the organization was "vulnerable to charges that it was a 'Communist organization' "). I am grateful to Peter Jon Perla for bringing to my attention some of the sordid infighting that took place in black leadership circles during this

period. *See* Peter J. Perla, From Left to Center: The Appropriation of Anti-Communist Rhetoric by the Black Press and Leading Black Opinion-Makers, 1946 through 1948, at 95–118 (Apr. 1, 1992) (unpublished honors thesis, University of Colorado (Boulder)) (discussing the downfall of Du Bois and Robeson in the NAACP).

68. *See* MARABLE, *supra* note 66, at 201 (noting that Du Bois was invited to attend programs and hand out awards at ceremonies); Perla, *supra*, at 113–18 (describing Du Bois's expulsion and subsequent return as co-chairman of the Council on African Affairs).

Notes to Chapter 3

1. *See* RICHARD DELGADO, THE RODRIGO CHRONICLES, ch. 1 (1995).

2. For more on the "innocent white" concern, see, *e.g.*, Sheet Metal Workers Int'l Ass'n v. EEOC, 478 U.S. 421, 500 (1986) (Rehnquist, J., dissenting) (reasoning that the relief provided by § 706(g) of Title VII does not extend to victims who have not suffered discrimination because relief would come "at the expense of innocent white workers"); Regents of the Univ. of Cal. v. Bakke, 438 U.S. 265, 298 (1978) (plurality opinion) (arguing that it is unfair to compel "innocent" people to remedy past discrimination that they did not cause). *See also* Linda S. Greene, *Twenty Years of Civil Rights: How Firm a Foundation?*, 37 RUTGERS L. REV. 707, 714–31 (1985) (tracing the development of "innocent white" and similar narratives in recent jurisprudence).

3. *See* Richard Delgado & Jean Stefancic, *The Social Construction of Brown v. Board of Education: Law Reform and the Reconstructive Paradox*, 36 WM. & MARY L. REV. 547 (1995); Duncan Kennedy, *A Cultural Pluralist Case for Affirmative Action in Legal Academia*, 1990 DUKE L.J. 705 (answering various objections to the use of affirmative action in law schools and putting forward a case for affirmative action based on institutional self-interest and political fairness); Thomas Ross, *Innocence and Affirmative Action*, 43 VAND. L. REV. 297 (1990) (critiquing the argument that affirmative action is unfair to innocent whites).

4. Works questioning academia's embrace of multiculturalism include ALAN BLOOM, THE CLOSING OF THE AMERICAN MIND 347–56 (1987); DINESH D'SOUZA, ILLIBERAL EDUCATION: THE POLITICS OF RACE AND SEX ON CAMPUS 13 (1992); E. D. HIRSCH, CULTURAL LITERACY 18 (1987). *See also* ROGER KIMBALL, TENURED RADICALS 63 (1990) (arguing that support among university professors for multiculturalism is "anticultural" because it abandons traditional teaching methods in the humanities).

5. *See* D'SOUZA, *supra*, at 231–42.

6. *Id.* at 132–56.

7. *See, e.g.*, Marjorie Heins, *Banning Words: A Comment on "Words That Wound,"* 18 HARV. C.R.-C.L. L. REV. 585, 592 (1983) (prominent ACLU attorney arguing against hate speech codes); Nadine Strossen, *Regulating Racist Speech on Campus: A Modest Proposal?*, 1990 DUKE L.J. 484, 490 (presenting an argument by the current national president of the ACLU that restrictions on hate speech be narrowly drawn).

8. On Rodrigo's period in Italy, see CHRONICLES, *supra* note 1, at chs. 1, 2.

9. Henry Louis Gates, Jr., *Let Them Talk*, NEW REPUBLIC, Sept. 20, 1993, at 37 (cover story).

10. *See* Richard Delgado & Jean Stefancic, *Scorn*, 35 WM. & MARY L. REV. 1061, 1062–63, 1090–98 (1994) (arguing that powerful institutions such as the Supreme Court should reserve their use of sarcasm for the "high and mighty" and refrain from using such a tone with the weak).

11. *See, e.g.*, Richard Delgado, *Campus Antiracism Rules: Constitutional Narratives in Collision*, 85 NW. U. L. REV. 343, 387 n.354 (1991) (citing sources indicating blacks are dropping out of white-dominated schools or enrolling in all-black colleges).

12. On the "seamless web" argument, see Richard Delgado & David Yun, *The Neoconservative Case against Hate-Speech Regulation—Lively, D'Souza, Gates, Carter, and the Toughlove Crowd*, 47 VAND. L. REV. 1807 (1995).

13. With the aid of decontextualization, pairs like the following can be made to seem to stand on a similar footing: the right of a Southern legislature to fly a Confederate flag and the right of a Northern state to celebrate Martin Luther King Day; the right of a bigot to hurl a racial epithet and that of black friends to use the smiling greeting "Hi, nigger"; the right of black students to form a support organization and that of whites to form a whites-only club.

14. *See, e.g.*, Regents of the Univ. of Cal. v. Bakke, 438 U.S. 265, 284 (1978) (quoting United States v. Associated Press, 52 F. Supp. 362, 372 (S.D.N.Y. 1943) (Hand, J.)).

15. On resource attractors in the theory of distributive justice, see Michael H. Shapiro, *Who Merits Merit? Problems in Distributive Justice and Utility Posed by the New Biology*, 48 S. CAL. L. REV. 318, 344–47 (1974).

16. *See* Thomas G. Gee, *Race-Conscious Remedies*, 9 HARV. J.L. & PUB. POL'Y 63 (1986) (arguing that quotas seat unqualified people, giving rise to inefficiency); Lino A. Graglia, *Race-Conscious Remedies*, 9 HARV. J.L. & PUB. POL'Y 83, 86 (1986) (rejecting race-conscious remedies and contending that they sometimes result in qualified whites being denied admission to elite colleges).

17. On my young friend's undergraduate and law school history, see CHRONICLES, *supra* note 1, at chs. 1, 2, 5.

18. *See* Symposium, *The Critique of Normativity*, 139 U. PA. L. REV. 801 (1991) (containing articles by Pierre Schlag, Frederick Schauer, Steven Winter, Frank Michelman, Margaret Jane Radin, and the present author).

19. Richard Delgado, *Norms and Normal Science: Toward a Critique of Normativity in Legal Thought*, 139 U. PA. L. REV. 933, 956 (1991).

20. *See* Leslie G. Espinoza, *The LSAT: Narratives and Bias*, 1 AM. U. J. GENDER & L. 121, 127–38 (1993) (arguing that the LSAT is biased because the reading passages evoke emotional responses from minorities and women).

21. The chitlins test examines the test-taker's familiarity with matters that are common knowledge in black and inner-city culture.

22. CHRONICLES, *supra* note 1, at ch. 1.

23. *Id.*

24. *See* 42 U.S.C. § 2000(a), (h) (1964) (Civil Rights Act of 1964, which barred discrimination in hiring, education, housing, and other areas).

25. On the thesis that formal rules and procedures often can serve to minimize prejudice, see Richard Delgado et al., *Fairness and Formality: Minimizing the Risk of Prejudice in Alternative Dispute Resolution*, 1985 WIS. L. REV. 1359, 1400. *See also* Trina Grillo, *The Mediation Alternative: Process Dangers for Women*, 100 YALE L.J. 1545, 1586–88 (1991) (applying similar thesis to divorce mediation).

26. I am grateful to Duncan Kennedy for this example.

27. *See* Richard Delgado, *Shadowboxing: An Essay on Power*, 77 CORNELL L. REV. 813, 823–24 (1992); *see also* CATHARINE A. MACKINNON, FEMINISM UNMODIFIED: DISCOURSES ON LIFE AND LAW 50–51 (1987) (discussing the cultural power men possess vis-à-vis women); Lisa Ikemoto, *The Code of Perfect Pregnancy: At the Intersection of the Ideology of Motherhood, the Practice of Defaulting to Science, and the Interventionist Mindset of Law*, 53 OHIO ST. L.J. 1205, 1284–85 (1992).

28. *See generally* Chandler Davidson, *Affirmative Action in Undergraduate Admissions: The Experience at Rice*, 2 RECONSTRUCTION 45 (1994) (discussing the use of quotas and preferences in contemporary elite institutions of higher learning).

29. *Id.* at 47–50.

30. *See generally* Alan Grob, *Geography: The Invisible Preference*, 2 RECONSTRUCTION 55 (1994).

31. On normativity as a tool for rationalizing outright cruelty, see Delgado, *Normal Science, supra* note 19; Pierre Schlag, *Normative and Nowhere to Go*, 43 STAN. L. REV. 167, 186 (1990).

32. *See* Washington v. Davis, 426 U.S. 229, 246, 250 (1976) (holding that some relationship between object of testing and goals of police training program satisfies Constitution, despite disparate impact on black applicants).

33. *See, e.g.,* Bloom, *supra* note 4, at 336–47; D'Souza, *supra* note 4, at 59–68, 94–122, 157–67.

34. *See* Chronicles, *supra* note 1, at ch. 6.

35. *Id.*

36. On the role of these and other mainstream narratives in confining and resisting change, see Richard Delgado & Jean Stefancic, *Norms and Narratives: Can Judges Avoid Serious Moral Error?,* 69 Tex. L. Rev. 1929 (1991) (exploring the particular situation of judges); Ikemoto, *supra* (presenting the narrative of the perfect mother).

37. *See* Richard Delgado, Comment, *Beating Them at Their Own Game,* 1 Reconstruction 121, 121–22 (1992) (reviewing Stephen Carter, Reflections of an Affirmative Action Baby (1991)).

38. *See, e.g.,* City of Richmond v. J. A. Croson Co., 488 U.S. 469, 498–99 (1989) (finding no redressable discrimination evidenced in city's history of awarding construction contracts even though blacks received only 0.67% of prime construction contracts in a city approximately 50% black); McCleskey v. Kemp, 481 U.S. 279, 287, 297–99 (1987) (finding no discrimination in a state practice that resulted in a disparity of greater than four to one in racial sentencing patterns).

39. *See generally* Vicki Schultz & Stephen Petterson, *Race, Gender, Work, and Choice: An Empirical Study of the Lack of Interest Defense in Title VII Cases Challenging Job Segregation,* 59 U. Chi. L. Rev. 1073 (1992) (analyzing judicial responses to arguments that racial and sexual inequality in employment reflect a minority group's lack of interest in advancement rather than a pattern of discrimination).

40. *Why a Hispanic Heads an Organization Called U.S. English,* Hemispheres, Sept. 1994, at 42.

41. *Id.*

42. *Id.*

43. Chronicles, *supra* note 1, at ch. 1.

44. *Id.*

45. *See* Chronicles, *supra* note 1, at chs. 1, 3.

46. Shapiro, *supra* note 15, at 319–23.

47. *Id.* at 322–23.

48. *See id.* (describing the role of resource-attractors in economic and distributive theory).

49. *See generally* Stephen Jay Gould, The Mismeasure of Man (1981).

50. Stanley Fish, There's No Such Thing As Free Speech (And It's a Good Thing, Too) 63 (1994).

51. *Id.* at 63–64.

52. *Id.* at 63.

53. *Id.* at 62–64.

54. *Id.* at 64, 81, 85–86.

55. *See id.* at 4, 8–10, 85.

56. JARED TAYLOR, PAVED WITH GOOD INTENTIONS: THE FAILURE OF RACE RELATIONS IN CONTEMPORARY AMERICA (1994).

57. Charles V. Zehren, *Changing of the Species?*, NEWSDAY, July 14, 1994, at A4.

58. ARTHUR SCHLESINGER, JR., THE DISUNITING OF AMERICA: RE-FLECTIONS ON A MULTICULTURAL SOCIETY (1991).

59. *Id.* at 10–12, 71, 126–29.

60. *Id.* at 13–14.

61. MADISON GRANT, THE PASSING OF THE GREAT RACE OR THE RACIAL BASIS OF EUROPEAN HISTORY (1920); *see* FISH, *supra* note 50, at 81–86 (discussing this and other early books sounding the nativist theme).

62. FISH, *supra*, at 12–13, 81, 83–86 (analogizing current assertion that multiculturalism introduces barbarism into the educational curriculum to similar claims by those like Madison Grant); Abigail M. Thernstrom, *Bilingual Miseducation*, COMMENTARY, Feb. 1990, at 44 (discussing increased emphasis by states on bilingual education).

63. LAWRENCE AUSTER, THE PATH TO NATIONAL SUICIDE: AN ESSAY ON IMMIGRATION AND MULTICULTURALISM (1990).

64. Some of these statutes include the Immigration Reform and Control Act of 1986, P.L. 99-603, 100 Stat. 3359, Nov. 6, 1986 (offering legalized immigrant status to undocumented aliens who had arrived before January 1, 1982), and the Immigration Act of 1990, P.L. 101-649, 104 Stat. 4978, Nov. 29, 1990 (permitting an overall increase in immigration from all countries).

65. RICHARD BROOKHISER, THE WAY OF THE WASP (1991).

66. *Id.* at 29–39; *see also* RICHARD J. HERRNSTEIN & CHARLES MURRAY, THE BELL CURVE: INTELLIGENCE AND CLASS STRUCTURE IN AMERICAN LIFE (1994) (warning of split in American society along IQ-based class lines).

67. HENRY PRATT FAIRCHILD, THE MELTING POT MISTAKE (1926); *see also* HENRY PRATT FAIRCHILD, RACE AND NATIONALITY AS FACTORS IN AMERICAN LIFE (1947).

68. CARL CAMPBELL BRIGHAM, A STUDY OF AMERICAN INTELLIGENCE (1923).

69. FISH, *supra* note 50, at 85–86.

70. *See id.* at 87 (making similar point).

71. CHRONICLES, *supra* note 1, at ch. 1; *see also* Linda S. Greene, *The New NCAA Rules of the Game: Academic Integrity or Racism?*, 28 ST. LOUIS U. L.J. 101 (1984) (discussing black athletes in college sports).

72. *See generally* Frances Lee Ansley, *Stirring the Ashes: Race, Class, and the Future of Civil Rights Scholarship,* 74 CORNELL L. REV. 993 (1989) (arguing that issues of race and class are largely intertwined and must be considered together when addressing affirmative action policies); John O. Calmore, *Exploring the Significance of Race and Class in Representing the Black Poor,* 61 OR. L. REV. 201 (1982) (suggesting that plight of black poor is consequence of both race and class).

Notes to Chapter 4

1. *See* ch. 3 this volume.

2. *See, e.g.,* KENNETH KARST, LAW'S PROMISE, LAW'S EXPRESSION: VISIONS OF POWER IN THE POLITICS OF RACE, GENDER, AND RELIGION (1993).

3. *E.g.,* DINESH D'SOUZA, ILLIBERAL EDUCATION (1992) (critiquing multiculturalism and diversity on four university campuses).

4. *E.g.,* Podberesky v. Kirwan, 38 F. 3d 147 (4th Cir. 1994).

5. ILLIBERAL EDUCATION, *supra* note 3.

6. *Id.*

7. PROMISE, *supra* note 2, at 14–20, 58–65, 182–87.

8. *Id.* at 137–39.

9. *Id.* at 28, 147–48, 154, 158.

10. *Id.* at 148, 150, 154–56, 159–60. *See also* DENVER POST, Nov. 22, 1994, at 9A (full-page advertisement urging a national day of prayer).

11. PROMISE, *supra* note 2, at 31–56.

12. *Id.* at 27–28, 47–48, 69, 90–94, 103–06.

13. *See* RICHARD DELGADO, THE RODRIGO CHRONICLES, ch. 8 (1995).

14. Eric Schmitt, *GOP Would Give Pentagon Money It Didn't Request,* N.Y. TIMES, July 5, 1995, at A1; Arthur Hoppe, *Private Drab Finds the Enemy,* S.F. CHRON., July 14, 1995, at A27, col. 1.

15. On these and other manifestations of the new nativism, see THE RISE OF LATTER-DAY NATIVISM (Juan Perea, ed., forthcoming 1996).

16. *See* NEWT GINGRICH, CONTRACT WITH AMERICA (1994) (book-length treatment of Republican Party's agenda for change).

17. *See infra* this chapter.

18. PROMISE, *supra* note 2, at 139; *House Approves Deep Cuts in Cultural Funds,* DENVER POST, July 19, 1995, at 7A.

19. Laz discussed affirmative action with his two friends of color in ch. 3, this volume.

20. For discussion of utilitarian (forward-looking) and reparations-based (backward-looking) justifications for affirmative action, see Richard Delgado, *The Imperial Scholar: Reflections on a Review of Civil Rights Literature,*

132 U. Pa. L. Rev. 561, 570 (1984); Richard Wasserstrom, *Racism, Sexism, and Preferential Treatment: An Approach to the Topics*, 24 UCLA L. Rev. 581 (1982).

21. *See, e.g.*, Thomas Sowell, *Even Some Liberals Are Having Doubts*, Atlanta J. and Const., Feb. 22, 1995, at A12; Thomas Sowell, *The "Q" Word*, Forbes, Apr. 10, 1995, at 61.

22. *E.g.*, Sindell v. Abbott Laboratories, 26 Cal. 3d 588, 607 P. 2d 924, 163 Cal. Rptr. 132, *cert. denied*, 449 U.S. 912 (1980). ("D.E.S." decision); Curlender v. Bioscience Laboratories, 106 Cal. App. 3d 811, 165 Cal. Rptr. 477 (1980) ("wrongful life" decision).

23. Washington v. Davis, 426 U.S. 222 (1976); City of Memphis v. Greene, 451 U.S. 100 (1981).

24. *E.g.*, Davidson v. Cannon, 474 U.S. 344, 347–48 (1986); Daniels v. Williams, 474 U.S. 327, 332–33 (1986); *see* Mark S. Brodin, *The Standard of Causation in Mixed-Motive Title VII Actions*, 82 Colum. L. Rev. 292, 292–93, 302–10 (1982).

25. City of Richmond v. Croson, 488 U.S. 469 (1989).

26. On the role of the "bona fide occupational qualification" in antidiscrimination law, see Norman Vieira, Constitutional Civil Rights 31–33 (2d ed. 1990).

27. *E.g.*, Gleitman v. Cosgrove, 49 N.J. 22, 227 A. 2d 689 (1967).

28. *E.g.*, Curlender v. Bioscience Laboratories, 106 Cal. App. 3d 811, 165 Cal. Rptr. 477 (1980).

29. *E.g.*, Berman v. Allan, 80 N.J. 421, 404 A. 2d 8 (1979).

30. Douglas Martin, *When Holocaust Lives with Parents*, N.Y. Times, Apr. 29, 1995, A27.

31. Charles L. Black, *My World with Louis Armstrong*, 69 Yale Rev. 145 (1979); *Further Reflections on the Constitutional Justice of Livelihood*, 86 Colum. L. Rev. 1103 (1986) (hereinafter *Livelihood*).

32. Every Southern state at one time had laws prohibiting educating slaves. Richard Kluger, Simple Justice: The History of *Brown v. Board of Education* and Black Americans' Struggle for Equality 157–59 (1975).

33. On the gap in average net worth between blacks and whites, see, *e.g.*, Spencer Rich, *Gap Found in Wealth among Races*, Wash. Post, Jan. 11, 1991, at 3 (median African-American family had less than one-tenth of wealth of white ones—$4,170 versus $43,280); David Swinton, *Economic Perspectives; The Key to Black Wealth: Ownership*, Black Enterprise, July 1994, at 24.

34. On the bill (which did not pass) by which the Reconstruction Congress would have provided this minimum guarantee, see, *e.g.*, Derrick Bell, Race, Racism, and American Law 52 & n.6 (3d ed. 1992).

35. BELL, RACE, RACISM, *supra.*

36. For discussion of this argument see Richard Delgado, *Mindset and Metaphor,* 103 HARV. L. REV. 1972, 1973–79 (1990).

37. *See* Symposium, *On the Renaissance of Pragmatism in American Legal Thought,* 63 S. CAL. L. REV. 1569 (1990).

38. On racist stereotypes and beliefs, see Richard Delgado & Jean Stefancic, *Images of the Outsider in American Law and Culture: Can Free Expression Remedy Systematic Social Ills?* 77 CORNELL L. REV. 1238 (1992).

39. *Id.* at 1260–61, 1276–79, 1287–88.

40. *See* JOHN H. ELY, DEMOCRACY AND DISTRUST (1980).

41. On this step-up ("Peter Principle") argument, see THOMAS SOWELL, INSIDE EDUCATION: THE DECLINE, THE DECEPTION, THE DOGMAS (1993).

42. John D. Lamb, *The Real Affirmative Action Babies: Legacy Preferences at Harvard and Yale,* 26 COLUM. J. L. & SOC. PROBLEMS 491 (1993).

43. Chandler Davidson, *Affirmative Action in Undergraduate Admissions,* 2 RECONSTRUCTION 45 (1994).

44. Alan Grob, *Geography: The Invisible Preference,* 2 RECONSTRUCTION 55 (1994).

45. CHRONICLES, *supra* note 13, at ch. 1.

46. *See* STEPHEN L. CARTER, REFLECTIONS OF AN AFFIRMATIVE ACTION BABY (1991) (coining terms).

47. ELLIS COSE, THE RAGE OF A PRIVILEGED CLASS (1994).

48. ROY BROOKS, RETHINKING THE AMERICAN RACE PROBLEM (1992).

49. ANDREW HACKER, TWO NATIONS: BLACK AND WHITE, SEPARATE, HOSTILE, UNEQUAL 96 (1992).

50. Ruth Marcus, *The Distressing Case of Judge Hastings; '83 Acquittal, Race Issue, Nature of Evidence Complicate Senate Task,* WASH. POST, Aug. 6, 1989, at A6.

51. Martin Anderson, *The Missing Black Professors; Ph.D. Process in Need of Radical Reform,* STAR TRIB., Oct. 18, 1993, at 15A.

52. Williams, *For the Black Professional, The Obstacles Remain,* N.Y. TIMES, July 14, 1987, at A16, col. 1.

53. Emily Sachar, *Police Nab the Wrong Passenger,* NEWSDAY, May 9, 1995, at A6. *See* Diana Hunt, *Traffic Justice for All in Texas? Analysis Shows Racial Disparities,* DENVER POST, June 14, 1995, at A33, col. 3.

54. *See generally* RAGE, *supra* note 47.

55. In CHRONICLES, *supra* note 13, at ch. 4, Rodrigo and the Professor discuss the critique of normativity and the reasons why legal rules and norms often fail to achieve their intended effects.

56. *See* Jody D. Armour, *Race Ipsa Loquitur: Of Reasonable Racists, Intelligent Bayesians, and Involuntary Negrophobes,* 46 STAN. L. REV. 781 (1994).

57. *E.g.,* Black, *Livelihood, supra* note 31.

58. *See* CHARLES MURRAY & RICHARD HERRNSTEIN, THE BELL CURVE (1994).

59. Rodrigo was good enough to run off for me, later that weekend, a print-out of the sources he found during his technological *tour de force.* The reader will be interested to know that most of the information he dug up about sub-sidies for the rich and the poor can be found in standard databases, newspapers and public documents. These included the following: Maureen Harrington, *Welfare Myths Rampant,* DENVER POST, June 16, 1995, at A1, col. 2 (small part of federal budget devoted to welfare for the poor, Social Security and Medicare heavily financed); U.S. ADMINISTRATION FOR CHILDREN AND FAMILIES QUARTERLY, PUBLIC ASSISTANCE STATISTICS, ANNUAL 1992 (available on CD-ROM) (on comparative cost of AFDC); Henry Dubroff, *If America Wants Real "Welfare Reform," Let's Look at Agriculture,* DENVER POST, Jan. 15, 1995, at G-1, col. 1 (on costs of agricultural subsidies); *Sparing the Rich, Soaking the Poor,* Boulder, CO, DAILY CAMERA, June 11, 1995, at E-1, col. 2 (heating subsidies, legal services for poor, entertainment expenses, and other comparative spending subsidies); Dave Skidmore, *Tax Loophole for Rich Exaggerated?,* DENVER POST, June 3, 1995, at 2-A, col. 2 (rich people who renounce their citizenship to avoid taxes; funding of space adventures; oil dril-ling subsidies; McDonald's Chicken McNuggets); U.S. OFFICE OF MANAGE-MENT AND BUDGET, BUDGET OF U.S. GOVERNMENT, ANNUAL 1995 (avail-able on CD-ROM) (for mortgage interest deduction and similar tax loopholes). *See also* Mark Fineman, *$20 Billion Loan Helping Mexico Stabilize Markets,* DENVER POST, July 8, 1995, at 2-A, col. 1.

60. *See* Katherine S. Newman, *What Scholars Can Tell Politicians about the Poor,* CHRON. HIGHER ED., June 23, 1995, at B1 (research showed that inner city poor in Harlem and other communities desired and looked for work, but could not find it because of structural changes in job market and flight of jobs). On the debate over Head Start, see, *e.g.,* Bart Jones, *Politics Set Aside As Head Start Earns A's,* TIMES UNION, May 14, 1995, at C1.

61. On the California Civil Rights Initiative, which would prohibit most forms of official affirmative action in that state, see Charles Oliver, *Next Hot Button in California,* INVESTOR'S BUS. DAILY, May 9, 1995, at 41. On other proposals elsewhere, see Jerd Smith, *Race-Based Initiative Eyed,* 46 DENVER BUS. J. 1 (1995).

62. Miller v. Johnson, 63 USLW 4726 (June 27, 1995).

63. Missouri v. Jenkins, 63 USLW 4486 (June 13, 1995).

64. Aderand Construction, Inc., v. Secretary of Transportation, 63 USLW 4523 (June 13, 1995).

65. For these and other dreary statistics documenting blacks' misery, see HACKER, TWO NATIONS, *supra* note 49. Recently, the U.S. surpassed Great

Britain as the country with the greatest gap between rich and poor. Diana Somerville, *No, We Are Not Making This Up*, Boulder, CO, DAILY CAMERA, June 13, 1995, at 7-2, col. 1. *See also* Richard Whitmore, *Infant Mortality Rate Still Dropping: But Racial Gap Is Growing Wider*, DENVER POST, July 10, 1995, at A3, col. 5; *Top Countries for Quality of Life*, WASH. POST, Nov. 5, 1991, at B5 (U.S. ranks low in life expectancy, infant health, and similar measures of personal and economic well-being).

66. HACKER, *supra*, at 135.

67. *Id.* at 108, 116–17.

68. *Special Issue: America's Immigrant Challenge*, TIME, Fall 1993. *See also* PETER BRIMELOW, ALIEN NATION (1993). By 2000, the World Bank forecasts, white men will constitute only 45 percent of the U.S. workforce.

69. *See, e.g.*, Hugh Dellios, *Racism Reported in Wake of Prop. 187*, DENVER POST, Dec. 18, 1995, at 12A, col. 2; Richard Cohen, *Where Will This Good-Intentioned Road Lead?* DENVER POST, June 8, 1995, at 7B, col. 2 (on California initiative to end affirmative action).

70. Korematsu v. United States, 323 U.S. 214 (1944); *see* Hirabayashi v. United States, 320 U.S. 81 (1943) (also upholding wartime measures against Japanese Americans).

71. *See* DEE BROWN, BURY MY HEART AT WOUNDED KNEE 439–45 (1970); ROBERT A. WILLIAMS, JR., THE AMERICAN INDIAN IN WESTERN LEGAL THOUGHT: THE DISCOURSES OF CONQUEST (1990) (on broad pattern of treachery and broken promises in U.S.-Indian dealings).

72. IAN HANEY LOPEZ, WHITE BY LAW (1995).

73. *Id.*

74. Frank Rich, *Smoking G.O.P. Guns*, N.Y. TIMES, June 29, 1995, at A21.

75. On the rise of the private militias, see *Patriot Games*, TIME, Dec. 19, 1994, at 48.

76. Gustav Niebuhr, *A Vision of an Apocalypse: The Religion of the Far Right*, N.Y. TIMES, May 22, 1995, at A6, col. 1.

77. "The Civil War" (PBS, Sept. 1990).

78. SHELBY FOOTE, STARS IN THEIR COURSES: THE GETTYSBURG CAMPAIGN June–July 1863 (1994); CHICKAMAUGA, AND OTHER CIVIL WAR STORIES (Shelby Foote ed., 1993).

79. JACK GREENBERG, CRUSADERS IN THE COURTS: HOW A DEDICATED BAND OF LAWYERS FOUGHT FOR CIVIL RIGHTS REVOLUTION (1994).

80. *Patriot, supra* note 75.

81. PETER IRONS, JUSTICE AT WAR (1983).

82. David Johnston & Stephen Labaton, *FBI Shaken by Inquiry into Idaho Siege*, N.Y. TIMES, Nov. 25, 1993, at A1. *See also* Steve Higgins,

Former Director of ATF Explains "Why We Had to Act in Waco," Denver Post, July 15, 1995, at 7B, col. 1.

83. *E.g.,* Richard Delgado et al., Words That Wound: Critical Race Theory, Assaultive Speech, and the First Amendment (1993); Isabel Wilkerson, *Racial Harassment Altering Blacks' Choices on Colleges,* N.Y. Times, May 9, 1990, at A1.

84. Susan Sward et al., *Pardee Dies after Melee with Police; Witnesses Describe It As Brutal Beating,* S.F. Chron., June 6, 1995, at A1.

85. Carl Rowan, *Law Enforcement Needs to Clean Up Its Act,* Denver Post, July 18, 1995, at 7B, col. 2.

86. *See* Juan Perea, *Demography and Distrust: An Essay on American Language, Cultural Pluralism, and Official English,* 77 Minn. L. Rev. 269 (1992); Abigail M. Thernstrom, *Bilingual Miseducation,* Commentary, Feb. 1990, at 44.

87. Sam Howe Verhovek, *Stop Benefits for Aliens? It Wouldn't Be That Easy,* N.Y. Times, June 8, 1994, at A1, col. 1. *See also* ch. 6 this volume.

88. California Assembly Joint Res. #49, Aug. 23, 1993, urging Congress to amend Fourteenth Amendment to limit citizenship to persons "born in the United States to mothers who are citizens."

89. *See* Ben Wattenberg, The Birth Dearth (1987); Bell Curve, *supra* note 58. For a critique of this movement, see Stephen Jay Gould, The Mismeasure of Man (1981). For brief recent surveys of the movement, see Richard Lacayo, *For Whom the Bell Curves: A New Book Raises a Ruckus by Linking Intelligence to Genetics and Race,* Time, Oct. 24, 1994, at 66; *Is It Destiny?* Newsweek, Oct. 24, 1994 (cover story).

90. Richard Delgado et al., *Can Science Be Inopportune? Constitutional Validity of Governmental Restrictions on Race-IQ Research,* 31 UCLA L. Rev. 128, 137–44 (1983).

91. Memo from John Tanton to Witan IV Attendees (Oct. 10, 1986, on file with author).

92. Jean Raspail, Camp of the Saints (1973).

93. *Id. See also* Ruth Coniff, *The War on Aliens: The Right Calls the Shots,* The progressive, Oct. 1993, at 22.

Notes to Chapter 5

1. The dark tale to which Rodrigo refers is his friend Laz's race-war scenario, which he laid out in ch. 4, *supra* this volume.

2. *See id.;* Elizabeth Shogren, *Immigrants Denied Welfare under Plan,* Denver Post, July 26, 1995, at 9-A, col. 1. *See also* ch. 6, *infra* this volume.

3. Every law school must undergo periodic inspection by a committee of outside lawyers and law professors in order to remain accredited. Teams of

about six visitors spend two or three days at the school conducting interviews, reviewing documents, and examining the physical facilities, following which they issue a report and note any significant deficiencies.

4. Martha Nussbaum, *Patriotism and Cosmopolitanism*, BOSTON REV., Oct./Nov. 1994, at 3.

5. Todd Gitlin, *The Rise of Identity Politics: An Examination and Critique*, DISSENT, SPRING 1993, at 172.

6. The professor is referring to Jeremy Waldron, *Minority Cultures and the Cosmopolitan Alternative*, 25 U. MICH. L.J. REF. 751 (1992).

7. For an elaboration of Rodrigo's views and novel, self-interest-based argument for affirmative action, see RICHARD DELGADO, THE RODRIGO CHRONICLES, ch. 1 (1995).

8. *See* CHRIS BROWN, INTERNATIONAL RELATIONS THEORY: NEW NORMATIVE APPROACHES (1992); UNIVERSALISM VERSUS COMMUNITARIANISM (David M. Rassmussen ed., 1990); David Hollinger, *Postethnic America*, 2 CONTENTION 79 (1992).

9. Waldron, *supra* note 6, at 754.

10. *Id.* at 751, 793.

11. *Id.* at 762–63.

12. *Id.* at 762.

13. *Id.* at 763.

14. *Id.* at 762.

15. *See* Gary Peller, *Race Consciousness*, 1990 DUKE L.J. 755.

16. Waldron, *supra* note 6, at 762–63.

17. *Id.* at 771 (quoting Karl Marx).

18. *Id.* at 761–63, 776.

19. *Id.* at 754, 756, 769–74.

20. *Id.* at 763.

21. *Id.*

22. Ch. 4, *supra* this volume.

23. Robert Williams, *Encounters on the Frontiers of International Human Rights Law: Redefining the Terms of Indigenous Peoples' Survival in the World*, 1990 DUKE L.J. 660.

24. *See* Theresa Simpson, *Claims of Indigenous People to Cultural Property in Canada, Australia, and New Zealand*, 18 HASTINGS INT'L & COMP. L. REV. 195 (1994).

25. *See supra* notes 23–24.

26. *See* Derrick Bell, Brown v. Board of Education *and the Interest-Convergence Dilemma*, 93 HARV. L. REV. 518 (1980); Richard Delgado & Jean Stefancic, Brown v. Board of Education: *Law Reform and the Reconstructive Paradox*, 36 WM. & MARY L. REV. 547 (1995).

27. Waldron, *supra* note 6, at 751–52, 775.

28. SALMAN RUSHDIE, SATANIC VERSES (1992).

29. John H. Merryman, *Two Ways of Thinking about Cultural Property*, 80 AM. J. INT'L L. (1986); *Thinking about the Elgin Marbles*, 83 MICH. L. REV. 1881 (1985).

30. Simpson, *supra* note 24, at 197.

31. *Id.* at 196–99, 218–20; Robin A. Morris, *Legal and Ethical Issues in the Trade of Cultural Property*, 1990 N. Z. L.J. 40.

32. Simpson, *supra* note 24 (analyzing four countries' laws).

33. *Id.* at 197 n.7, 199–204 (discussing treaties and U.N. conventions).

34. Merryman, *Two Ways; Elgin Marbles,* both *supra* note 29.

35. *Elgin Marbles, supra.*

36. Waldron, *supra* note 6, at 763–64.

37. *Id.* at 793.

38. RODRIGO CHRONICLES, *supra* note 7, at ch. 1.

39. *Id.*

40. BOSTON REV., *supra* note 4 (comment by George Fletcher).

41. *See* RODRIGO CHRONICLES, *supra* note 7, at ch. 5.

42. *Id.*

43. *Id.*

44. BOSTON REV., *supra* note 4, at 29 (comment by Michael Walzer).

45. For an earlier version of this argument, see Richard Delgado & Jean Stefancic, *Cosmopolitanism Inside Out,* 26 CONN. L. REV. (1995).

46. Waldron, *supra* note 6, at 26 (quoting Rushdie—"a love song to our mongrel selves . . . I was already a mongrel self ").

47. *See Inside Out, supra* note 45, at 2, 13–15.

Notes to Chapter 6

1. *See* RICHARD DELGADO, THE RODRIGO CHRONICLES, ch. 2 (1995).

2. *Id.*

3. For a description of the California resolution urging Congress to begin the process of amending the Constitution to delete the Fourteenth Amendment's grant to citizenship to persons born in the United States—that is, citizenship by birth—see ch. 4, *supra* this volume. *See also* 1994 H.J. Res. 396 (103d Cong., 2d Sess., Aug. 3, 1994) (congressional version of California resolution proposing amendment to deny citizenship on account of birth alone; a parent must be a U.S. citizen). For a description of other similar measures limiting immigration or making things difficult for immigrants once they are here, see ch. 4, *supra;* THE NEW NATIVISM (Juan Perea ed., forthcoming 1996); Dogan, *Affirmative Action Foes Multiply: Sparked by California Initiative Legislation Bids Spread Like Wildfire,* DENVER POST,

Aug. 6, 1995, at 23A, col. 1; Elizabeth Shogren, *Immigrants Denied Welfare under Plan,* DENVER POST, July 26, 1995, at 9-A, col. 1.

4. *See* sources cited *supra* note 3.

5. For a description of these sorry chapters in U.S. history, see Richard Delgado & Jean Stefancic, *Images of the Outsider in American Law and Culture,* 77 CORNELL L. REV. 1258 (1992); IAN HANEY LOPEZ, WHITE BY LAW (1995); ROBERT WILLIAMS, THE AMERICAN INDIAN IN WESTERN LEGAL THOUGHT (1990); HELEN JACKSON, A CENTURY OF DISHONOR: A SKETCH OF THE UNITED STATES GOVERNMENT'S DEALINGS WITH SOME OF THE INDIAN TRIBES (1880); sources cited *supra* note 3, *infra* note 17; Curtis Robinson, *Calif. Governor: Welfare Breeds Thugs,* DENVER POST, Aug. 9, 1995, at 4B, col. 2 (on today's versions).

6. *See* Gerald Neuman, *Rhetorical Slavery, Rhetorical Citizenship,* 90 MICH. L. REV. 1276 (1992) (reviewing JUDITH N. SHKLAR, AMERICAN CITIZENSHIP: THE QUEST FOR INCLUSION (1991)); Immig. & Nat. Act § 347, 8 U.S.C. § 1481 (1992) (loss of nationality); T. ALEXANDER ALEINIKOFF & DAVID MARTIN, IMMIGRATION: PROCESS AND POLICY 854–931 (1985).

7. Rodrigo is concerned that the professor's actions could constitute evidence of intent sufficient to support a denaturalization proceeding, *see supra* note 6.

8. That is to say, initiated by the professor's father while the professor was still a minor.

9. The professor is referring, of course, to the current wave of anti-immigrant and anti-foreigner nativism, *see supra* notes 3–5; and the right-wing assault on minority hiring and affirmative action, *id.;* Donna St. George, *Preferences Targeted,* DENVER POST, July 28, 1995, at 2A, col. 3.

10. *See Letter from Birmingham Jail, in* WHAT COUNTRY HAVE I? POLITICAL WRITINGS BY BLACK AMERICANS 117 (Herbert J. Storing ed., 1970).

11. *Compare* PLATO, *Socrates' Apology, in* THE DIALOGUES OF PLATO (B. Jowett ed., 1937).

12. Missouri v. Jenkins, 63 U.S.L.W. 4486 (June 13, 1995).

13. Miller v. Johnson, 63 U.S.L.W. 4726 (June 27, 1995).

14. Aderand Construction, Inc., v. Secretary of Transportation, 13 U.S.L.W. 4523 (June 13, 1995).

15. 60 U.S. 393 (1856).

16. *See* Richard Delgado & Jean Stefancic, *Norms and Narratives: Can Judges Avoid Serious Moral Error?* 69 TEX. L. REV. 1929 (1991).

17. *E.g.,* DINESH D'SOUZA, ILLIBERAL EDUCATION (1992); Patrick Healy, *Budget Cuts Threaten Programs in English as a Second Language,* CHRON. HIGHER ED., June 16, 1995, at A-26. *See also* note 3 *supra.*

18. *See* LAURENCE TRIBE, AMERICAN CONSTITUTIONAL LAW 629–63 (2d ed. 1988).

19. *See* Symposium, *The Referendum Process*, 65 COLO. L. REV. 709 (1994) (on direct democracy).

20. *Id.*

21. *E.g.*, Reitman v. Mulkey, 405 U.S. 625 (1972).

22. Peter Schuck, *The Transformation of Immigration Law*, 84 COLUM. L. REV. 1 (1984); PETER SCHUCK & ROGERS SMITH, CITIZENSHIP WITHOUT CONSENT: ILLEGAL ALIENS IN THE AMERICAN POLITY (1986).

23. *See* sources cited notes 3–5, 9.

24. *E.g.*, CHARLES MURRAY & RICHARD HERRNSTEIN, THE BELL CURVE: INTELLIGENCE AND CLASS STRUCTURE IN AMERICAN LIFE (1994).

25. *See Images, supra* note 5.

26. *Id.*

27. EUGENE D. GENOVESE, ROLL, JORDAN, ROLL: THE WORLD THE SLAVES MADE 561–66 (First Vintage ed., 1976). FRANCIS L. BRODERICK, RECONSTRUCTION AND THE AMERICAN NEGRO 1865–1900, at 77 (1969).

28. PETER BRIMELOW, ALIEN NATION: COMMON SENSE ABOUT AMERICA'S IMMIGRATION DISASTER (1995) (anti-immigration tract).

29. LAWRENCE AUSTER, THE PATH TO NATIONAL SUICIDE: AN ESSAY ON IMMIGRATION AND MULTICULTURALISM (1990).

30. *See* THE RODRIGO CHRONICLES, *supra* note 1, at ch. 1.